Krasovskaĭa, Vera
Mikhaĭlovna

Nijinsky

DATE DUE

NIJINSKY

Vera Krasovskaya

NIJINSKY

Translated from the Russian by John E. Bowlt

A Dance Horizons Book

Schirmer Books

A Division of Macmillan Publishing Co., Inc., New York

Frontispiece   Vaslav Nijinsky, St. Petersburg, c. 1908.

First published in Russian (Leningrad, 1974)

English translation copyright © 1979 by Dance Horizons

SCHIRMER BOOKS
A Division of Macmillan Publishing Co., Inc.
866 Third Avenue, New York, N.Y.   10022

Collier Macmillan Canada, Ltd.

Library of Congress Catalog Card Number: 79-7368

PRINTED IN THE UNITED STATES OF AMERICA

printing number

1   2   3   4   5   6   7   8   9   10

Library of Congress Cataloging in Publication Data

Krasovskaia, Vera Mikhailovna.
Nijinsky.

Translation of Nizhinskii.
"A Dance Horizons Book."
Includes index.
1. Nijinsky, Waslaw, 1890–1950. 2. Dancers—
Russia—Biography. 3. Choreographers—Russia—
Biography.
GV1785.N6K7213   792.8'092'4 [B]   79-7368
ISBN 0-02-871870-4

PHOTO CREDITS

The photograph on page 281 (top) is copyrighted by
Sotheby Parke Bernet, Inc., New York, and is reprinted
here by their permission. Photographs on pages 3, 38
(left), 39 (left), 218, 289, 295 (bottom), 322, 335, and
339 are from the archives of Dance Horizons, Brooklyn,
New York. All other illustrations were selected and supplied by E. Norkute, research assistant at the Leningrad
State Theater Museum, from museum holdings.

Preface

THIS IS A LITERARY BIOGRAPHY of Vaslav Nijinsky, the famous dancer and choreographer; it is not a piece of scientific research. My four volumes on the Russian ballet have preceded *Nijinsky,* and these were written on the basis of careful historical investigation: *Russkii baletnyi teatr ot vozniknoveniia do serediny XIX veka* [The Russian Ballet from Its Origin to the Mid-nineteenth Century] (Leningrad and Moscow, 1958), *Russkii baletnyi teatr vtoroi poloviny XIX veka* [The Russian Ballet in the Second Half of the Nineteenth Century] (Leningrad and Moscow, 1963), *Russkii baletnyi teatr nachala XX veka* [The Russian Ballet in the Early Twentieth Century] (Vol. 1: *Khoreografy* [Choreographers], Leningrad, 1971; Vol. 2: *Tantsovshchiki* [Dancers], Leningrad, 1972). *Khoreografy* contains a chapter on Nijinsky and this, of course, relies exclusively on factual data and documentation.

In my literary account of Nijinsky's life I have pursued aims rather different from those in the above volumes, and I have here ventured to present my material in a less academic manner. One aim was to tell the story of the tragic fate of an artist who expressed the abrupt disjunctions of his age and who, in many ways, anticipated the later paths of development in twentieth-century ballet. A second aim was to apprehend—within Nijinsky's fateful life—certain general characteristics of the psychology of artistic creativity, links between the artist and his time, and ways in which a historical period conditions artistic personality. Consequently, I wrote so that I could incorporate what I presumed to be probable statements and conversations attributable to the characters of my book. There are only a few such passages, and I compiled them only after a very careful study of actual events and personal destinies. I felt obliged to include them so as to give a sense of historical background, to depict the everyday life and theatrical ambience of those days, and to elucidate the interrelationships of my *dramatis personae*. Of course, these passages have not been footnoted.

Finally, I wish to express my gratitude to John E. Bowlt for his faithful and conscientious translation of my original Russian text.

December 1976   V. M. Krasovskaya

Translator's Note

MADAME KRASOVSKAYA'S BOOK is the first Russian biography of Vaslav Nijinsky ever published, and this fact alone constitutes a historic event. Moreover, the book was written by the foremost authority on the Russian and Soviet ballet, a scholar who possesses not only an extensive and detailed knowledge of published and unpublished materials on the subject but also considerable practical experience in the dancing and teaching professions.

Inasmuch as Nijinsky, both as dancer and, increasingly, as choreographer, is attracting ever greater attention, the appearance of this new appreciation is particularly opportune. For the Western reader, the value of the book lies not only in the author's own idiosyncratic interpretation of the man and artist but also in the many relevant descriptions and comments adduced from the Russian press. For us, therefore, the many unfamiliar statements in periodicals and newspapers such as *Teatr i iskusstvo* [The Theater and Art] and *Birzhevye vedomosti* [Stock Exchange Gazette] by familiar critics such as Anatolii Lunacharsky and Valerian Svetlov provide us with a new and often unexpected perspective on Nijinsky and the Ballets Russes. These extracts indicate, in turn, the wealth of material on the Diaghilev enterprise still to be culled from St. Petersburg and Moscow sources. In view of the importance of these references, documentary and explanatory notes, absent in the Russian edition, have been included here, at the end of the text.

Because there is not always a direct correspondence between the letters of the Cyrillic alphabet and those of the Latin alphabet, rendering Russian pronunciation into English can present problems of spelling. Matters are complicated by the fact that there exist several transliteration systems and that some names and titles have received traditional English renderings that depart from established scholarly conventions. However, for the sake of consistency, a single transliteration system has been adopted here, namely a modified version of the U.S. Library of Congress system. Apart from the rendition of the Russian soft and hard signs, which have been omitted, the Library of Congress system has been followed throughout, although well-established variant spellings (for example, Benois, not Benua; Nijinsky, not Nizhinsky; Preobrajenska, not Preobrazhenskaia) have been maintained.

Translating the Russian text was an exacting but rewarding task, and I consider it an honor to introduce Madame Krasovskaya's book to the English-speaking public. I should add that, without the patience, advice, and unfailing cooperation of the author, this translation would scarcely have been possible.

John E. Bowlt
The Institute of Modern Russian Culture
at Blue Lagoon, Texas

NIJINSKY

1

In the 1880s a troupe of Polish dancers wandered the length and breadth of the Russian Empire. Among its members were a certain husband and wife—Thomas and Eleonora Nijinsky. Although neither could boast of theatrical ancestors, they were destined to become the parents of the most famous dancer in the world.

Thomas's father had lost his small estate after fighting with the armies of the Polish patriots in 1863. But the slanting eyes and high cheekbones of Thomas made one suppose that Tartar as well as Polish blood coursed through his veins. As a provincial dancer he took various roles and was distinguished by his gift for mime and by his remarkable jump. As a man he was venturesome and was fond of merrymaking, although he sometimes had attacks of rage that bordered on insanity.

Eleonora was the daughter of a Warsaw cabinetmaker, one Nikolai Bereda. As a child she had been enrolled in the Ballet School at the Warsaw Opera Theater. She had then gone on stage, where she had met Thomas. When he left Warsaw, so did she, and for his sake she consented to endure the vagrant life of a touring player. She was a meek, affectionate woman whose love was absolute and constant. She would have liked to have had an intimate family life and a permanent home, but Thomas was a wanderer and had soon tired of his wife, becoming cruel and unfaithful.

Eleonora, a devoted mother, found solace in her children. Two boys and a girl—Stanislav, Vaslav, and Bronislava—had been born in different towns. From their cradles on they were accustomed to rooms at cheap boarding houses or to tenement rooms rented from land-lords. They also grew accustomed to the hustle and bustle of the wings, to the confusion of rehearsals, and to the wonders of the evening performances. Even before the Nijinsky children knew how to read, they understood what theatrical playbills held in store.

The repertoire of the Lukovich troupe was not very strong in ballet. Alexander Lukovich, an experienced entrepreneur, also presented operetta, vaudeville, and farce, selecting titles that he hoped were attractive: *The Naval Garrison, A Sensitive String, The Soldier of the Queen of Madagascar*. The ballet productions always included a divertissement of various kinds of dances. The leading couple in the mazurka was always danced by Thomas and Eleonora Nijinsky, and the round of mazurkas, cracoviennes, and comic polkas always featured a pas de trois or a grand pas de deux (designated by the French terms) "with the participation of prima ballerina Mme. Falieri and first dancer M. Nijinsky." Apart from these top numbers, Thomas Nijinsky also played parts in genuine ballets, the same ones that were performed on the stages of the Imperial Theaters. For the Lukovich troupe, however, these ballets were considerably shortened.

For example, the ballet *Catarina, the Robber's Daughter* (music by Pugni, production by Jules Perrot) had been playing in St. Petersburg, Moscow, and Warsaw for over thirty years. The five acts told the story of an artist, one Salvator Rosa, who had been captured by a band of robbers, and of Catarina, daughter of the ataman, who had fallen in love with him. Jules Perrot, the choreographer, was rather short, was not very handsome, and did not lay claim to any heroic roles. But he did possess the rare gift of the true actor; and his well-developed leg muscles enabled him to achieve leaps beyond the dreams of other dancers and, in his flight, to rival even the lightest of

2

Eleonora and Thomas Nijinsky, Moscow, 1882.

ballerinas Marie Taglioni In *Catarina* he had created for himself the role of the robber Diavolino, who was hopelessly in love with the beautiful daughter of the ataman—Fanny Elssler (another of his partners).

In the Lukovich troupe this ballet, called *Ekaterina, the Bandit's Daughter,* was cut to one act to avoid the expense of multiple sets and a large cast. Still, even though the action was now much accelerated, the basic conflict of the plot was preserved and Diavolino was the most active part. The role of Diavolino, with its touch of deviltry, seemed tailor-made for Thomas Nijinsky. The romantic villain made love, was jealous, suffered, hated, rescued the heroine, and perished from the saber of her lover Salvator Rosa, played by Stanislav Lenchevsky, the principal actor and ballet master (that is, the choreographer) of the troupe. And the famous leap of Diavolino across a wrecked bridge above a waterfall suited the dashing Thomas to a tee.

Thomas Nijinsky's leap was, indeed, long remembered in his family and was regarded as a tradition, as part of a heritage.

Legend had it that, in the late winter of 1889, the Lukovich troupe had stopped off in Kiev after traveling in south Russia. The town was celebrating Shrovetide. The theaters were organizing lottery-masquerades, dances, performances by actors. Thomas, an inveterate participant in masquerades, was not particularly eager to hasten back to his pregnant wife, who had stayed at home with their two-year-old son Stanislav. On 28 February he stayed until the party broke up, at which point the organizers—on stage—started to throw to the audience anything that had not been claimed in the lottery. A silver chalice flew through the air. Thomas leaped up and caught it in midair. When he got home, he learned of the birth of a second son. The boy was named Vaslav, and his father presented him with the chalice "for luck." [1] It was preserved in the family as a sacred relic. Even so, the most enduring and most valuable thing that Thomas Nijinsky left behind (he soon abandoned his family) was his leap. It was inherited by Vaslav and Bronislava (born two years later) and by a third generation consisting of their daughters.

Anyway, the Nijinsky parents knew that they would never amass much of a legacy. A nomadic life did not allow for that. And so, Kiev was exchanged for Odessa, then Kharkov, then Minsk. July found them in Moscow, as artists at the summer theater of the Zoological Gardens. Then they moved on to Rostov. They reached Warsaw only two years later, and at last Vaslav was christened—after the priest had given them a good scolding for such long procrastination. [2]

The children were sometimes left unattended. Stanislav paid dearly for this. Once, as a little boy of six, hearing a barrel organ strike up, he leaned out of the window, lost his balance, and fell to the road below. Physically he did not suffer any harm. But opinion had it that from that day on his mental development stopped. Gradually growing worse, he would end his days in a mental asylum, where he would die while yet a young man.

Still, the children were happy. When their mother could get away from the theater, she gave them all her time. She even managed to give their lodgings, always arranged in haste, an atmosphere of permanence and homeyness. She often took the children to the theater—at first because she was forced to, but subsequently to amuse them. And there was also a long-range aim in this: Eleonora Nijinsky hoped that her children could look forward to careers in dancing, and she was no doubt relying on the wisdom of the saying "Habit becomes second nature,"

The theater and the dance were in the very blood of Vaslav and Bronislava Nijinsky. They had assimilated them through the customs of a wandering troupe of players—provincial to be sure, but not totally unprofessional. Despite the wide diversity of the repertoire, the ballet productions were of high quality. Apart from *Catarina*, there were the Pugni–Oge comic ballet *Robert and Bertram, or the Two Thieves*, and the authentic Polish ballet *A Peasant Wedding* by Jan Stefani and Maurice Pione, both well known to the theater of St. Petersburg.[3] To take part in these ballets required solid preparation, which Thomas and Eleonora had received at the Warsaw Ballet School. Despite rehearsals and performances, they rarely neglected their daily training sessions. That is why the rules of ballet exercise were familiar to the Nijinsky brother and sister from their early days.

Years later, in 1912, an interviewer from the Paris magazine *Je sais tout* asked the famous Vaslav Nijinsky when he had first begun to dance. Nijinsky, the taciturn "miracle des saisons russes," answered in unusual detail: "My parents considered it as natural to teach me to dance as to walk and talk. Even my mother, who, of course, could recall my first tooth, couldn't say just exactly when my first lesson was." [4] No less natural had been Nijinsky's desire to learn to dance: not even a desire, rather a need, like the need to breathe. This persistent need compelled, enabled, Nijinsky to exercise anywhere and everywhere. (Nijinsky did his exercises on the deck of an ocean liner with the same ease, the same precision, as he did anywhere else. When the members of the Diaghilev troupe were en route for South America and tried to follow the example of the premier danseur, they soon found out that a rolling deck is not so stable as a studio floor.)

Nijinsky's need to dance became a torment if it could not be satisfied, but it also softened the blows of fate. When Thomas Nijinsky moved in with his mistress, Eleonora left the Lukovich troupe and took her children to St. Petersburg, the citadel of ballet. There, as fate would have it, the young Vaslav would exchange his carefree, nomadic life for the strict routine of the Imperial Theater School.

The image of southern towns—green, sunny, noisy, and warm-hearted—faded and was enveloped by the mist of St. Petersburg. Rows of brick red houses stretched along the streets. In order to get to Mokhovaya Street, you had to go down the stairs, stinking of cabbage soup and cats, and into the courtyard; you'd then go along Mokhovaya and turn off by the circus, and so you'd come to Theater Street. But you could also turn off toward Panteleimon Street and come out into an extraordinary, vacant expanse.

This is where another St. Petersburg began: majestic, unapproachable. Here were the avenues of the Summer Garden where, in autumn, yellow, brown, and red leaves swirled around the many statues, stretching off in the distance in long rows. As if in an enchanted dance, their poses entered at regular intervals. The dance quickened to the music of the falling leaves and of the first snow. Swaying to the measured rhythm, the statues seemed to disperse, then come together, then circle. On the other side of the River Moika two huge statues guarded the stairway of the Mikhailovsky Castle. It was the color of congealed blood. Crowned by a spire, it looked out over the dusty Field of Mars. At the end of the Field, beyond the monument so tiny for this grand scale, heaved and flowed the River Neva. And beyond the Neva was

(*right*) Theater Street, St. Petersburg, early 1900s. At the end is the back of the Alexandrinsky Theater. The Imperial Theater School is on the right.

(*left*) A music lesson in one of the ballet studios at the Imperial School.

another spire, only this time not of a castle, but of the Peter and Paul Fortress.

Whether the St. Petersburg of every day or the St. Petersburg of grand ceremony, it was an unfriendly city. Theater Street concealed a humdrum routine behind its façade of ceremony. The future alumni of the Imperial Theater School approached through duplicate colonnades and rows of arched windows. This mirrorlike effect inspired some with an unrelenting respect. It made others tremble.

An artistic nature presupposes a certain nervousness. Vaslav Nijinsky had been artistic since early childhood. But he concealed his alarm, made an effort to concentrate, withdrew into himself, and grew silent. His examiners did not notice his alarm, but neither did they discover his artistry. On the contrary, they found the boy rather stupid. His Mongol eyes glazed, his mouth half-open, Nijinsky fought shy of the other boys and showed none of their childish spontaneity.

The little recruits were led into the hall a few at a time. There, standing along the entire length of a huge mirror, were tables covered in green cloth. The generals of the St. Petersburg ballet sat at these tables, their necks reflected in the mirror. The recruits could see themselves in the same mirror, although quite reduced in size because of the distance. But they turned their gaze to the two old men sitting in the middle. One had an almost military bearing; he looked important and very stern. People talked to him in a subdued voice, addressing him as Marius Ivanovich. His neighbor was a lean man who kept fidgeting and arguing in a piercing voice. But all the dignified ladies and gentlemen, looking at him from behind each other, also concurred with him most respectfully. Among them Vaslav recognized a man who, an hour before, at the medical examination in the clinic, had felt his legs very carefully, had then taken his chin in his hands, and with a gentle laugh had looked into his eyes. He was a wiry man of medium height, and although he was obviously young he was already balding. Vaslav was surprised to learn that this was the premier danseur of the Mariinsky Theater—Nicolas Gustavovich Legat.

Nijinsky became even more surprised when Legat suddenly approached him. George Rosai, a lively lad with shining Italian eyes, the handsome Anatole Bourman, and five other boys were told to move to the right. The others, evidently disapproved of, were sent over to the tall, tiled stove. Vaslav stood alone in the middle of the hall. Cringing beneath the stares of all, he was absolutely convinced that he had failed.

He realized with some difficulty that Legat was ordering him to move on a bit farther, to take a run and jump, and he noticed that the fussy old man was shrugging his shoulders in annoyance. Moving back automatically, the boy saw Legat raise his hand, give the sign— and, already running, he obeyed the sweep of the arm: he leaped.

The first witnesses of Vaslav Nijinsky's leap were connoisseurs of the first order. But even they were astonished by the metamorphosis of consciousness that later perplexed so many. As he ran, the boy cast off his apathy. His body, which only a moment ago had been so clumsy, became resilient, elastic, as if it were the body of a tiger cub obedient to instinct. With a perfect coordination of physical forces, with an absolute comprehension of the rhythm indicated by Legat, Nijinsky took off from the floor and for a second seemed to be suspended in air. He hung in a pose not yet in accord with the canon of classical ballet, but it was a pose that thrilled the high priests of this canon by its natural beauty.

Nature often levies a tax in lieu of her gifts. She gave Nijinsky a magical, natural aptitude for dance, but she deprived him of naturalness in everyday life. Even as a little boy, Nijinsky was scarcely able to be himself. Later on, thousands delighted in Nijinsky the dancer, but hardly anyone knew Nijinsky the man.

And so it was here. The boy dancer landed smoothly. For a moment he retained the memory of his flight. Then he returned to dull indifference. Or so it seemed to most of the judges. However, Legat quickly asked the angry old man something, addressing him as Christian Petrovich. This was Johanssen, who had taught practically all those who were sitting at the table. He nodded, and Legat departed, waving the last boy toward the group of successful candidates.

Eleonora Nijinsky was told on 20 August 1900 that her son had been accepted as a day student. On the one hand, this was joyful news because mother and son did not wish to be separated. On the other hand, it was distressing because they were very low in funds and their hopes for state aid were disappointed.

When classes began in September, this arrangement turned out to be better. At home Vaslav was able to recover from the loneliness that hung over him at school. After two years he was put into boarding school. By then he had grown used to solitude, and it was a condition that endured throughout his school years. His classmates didn't take long to christen this lad with the slanting eyes and high cheekbones "the little Jap." It was a nickname that stayed with him until graduation, and it became particularly insulting when Russia entered into war with Japan. Nijinsky's shy and unsociable nature, his way of speaking Russian with incorrect, Polish accents, prompted the cruel behavior that children have toward things they don't understand. But then there appeared a rather more valid reason for this: Nijinsky's dancing was above competition.

9

The dance was the criterion for all relationships. Any sin could be nullified by achievement in dance. And sins there were aplenty. True, Nijinsky was not a mischief maker, but he had a hard time with academic subjects even within the modest confines of the school curriculum. Sitting at his desk, he was always lost in thought. Many of his teachers felt that he had no thoughts at all, judging by the apathetic—although sometimes intense—gaze of their pupil. But they did not try to go to the root of this eccentricity. They set assignments, but usually Nijinsky got bad marks. Still, his teachers knew that Nijinsky would get on well because he had been blessed with physical talent. In any case, how could the teachers of arithmetic, geography, and penmanship understand the nature of their strange pupil—a nature undivined even by those masters of ballet who knew Nijinsky later on, at the height of his fame?

Tamara Karsavina, a dancer whose intellect was appreciated by all the snobs of Europe, alluded delicately to the mental limitations of her partner. Alexandre Benois, an artist enraptured by the art of bygone eras, declared that Nijinsky was the perfect embodiment of his designs—but was amazed at this since he knew how "dull-witted" Nijinsky was. Only Diaghilev—not an artist himself, but a creator of artists—immediately comprehended Nijinsky. He divined the rare gift of his artistic intuition, the real nature of Nijinsky's individuality. But for many artists who also possessed this gift, the genius of Nijinsky remained an unknown quantity.

At school his talent for self-transformation went long unrecognized. Rosai, Nijinsky's principal rival in class, begrudged the preference that teachers showed the "little Jap" on exclusively professional grounds. Rosai also had an exceptional leap, which he practiced persistently and zealously. He cut through the air with malicious delight and did the most audacious combinations of movements in the air. He was well on the way to achieving virtuosity. His teachers noted with approval Rosai's penchant for the grotesque. But their praise concealed a note of annoyance, for it was academic discipline above all that was appreciated at the ballet school. And the criteria for this were clarity of line, strictness of proportion, fluency of transition. For generations, dancers had observed the perfect harmony, the crystal-clear tradition of the dance.

(*above*) Nicolas Legat
(*right*) Sergei Legat

The first teachers that the class had were the Legat brothers. Their artistic family could trace its lineage back to the 1840s. The grandfather, Johann Legat, used to be in charge of the Shrovetide *balagany* on the Field of Mars.[5] The father, Gustav Legat, became a soloist of the Imperial Ballet in St. Petersburg and Moscow. He ruthlessly instilled in his sons a respect for the rules of the classical dance. In the late 1880s the eldest and youngest sons—Nicolas and then Sergei—were given premier roles in the ballets of the Mariinsky Theater. People used to refer to them as the inseparable twins; and, indeed, they shared each other's work and leisure. Both had a perfect mastery of their art. Both were musical and could paint very well. The company liked them for their sociableness and good humor, and their caricatures of colleagues did not offend; in some cases they exposed the excesses of the classical style, and in other cases they

11

exposed its tendency to deaden talent. Whether on stage or in class, the Legats were the staunch supporters of style in its unadulterated forms.

That is why Sergei Gustavovich and later Nicolas Gustavovich singled out Nijinsky for his total allegiance to the classical style. The boy went through the ritual of daily classes with exceptional attentiveness. But the main thing was that he would perform each exercise to near perfection. He would immediately comprehend the assignment and delineate every detail as if to prove the expediency and meaning of the whole. He didn't cut corners, he didn't pass over anything, and even the auxiliary movements such as a préparation or a glissade he brought out with precision and completeness. Whenever he did an exercise in class, it resembled some exercise being played by a skillful musician when every note is polished and it seems that beyond this abstract perfection nothing else exists. And that's essentially how it was. Still, unconsciously, Nijinsky was deceiving his teachers, because for the moment the image of the perfect schoolboy was, for him, the only reality of art. Later, on stage, he would throw off that cocoon and reveal characterizations that would astonish his audiences. However, for some academics the image of Nijinsky in class remained the height of his mastery. This was partly true in the case of Nicolas Legat (Sergei died in 1905 and never saw Nijinsky on stage). Nicolas did put on productions for Nijinsky, but he never really understood the basis of his talent.

Technical perfection was also the goal of the premier danseur of the Mariinsky, Samuil Andrianov, who had entered the school five years before Nijinsky. Boris Shavrov, the Leningrad dancer and pupil of Andrianov, recalled how Andrianov, during class, would leap and make every effort to reach the "Nijinsky mark" that was preserved in one of the school halls. Shavrov was overjoyed to see Andrianov getting near the mark, but then he realized that it wasn't simply a question of the height of the leap, but of its quality, the ability to subordinate the leap to the emotions.

Nijinsky understood this by intuition, through some inner part of his being, while he sought and found freedom in his roles as various characters. Whenever he changed his makeup and put on a different costume, he saw in the mirror a reflection that was his own and yet

12

not his own. Inwardly he submitted to the force of music, and music always assisted in the rebirth of his spiritual double. This was a psychological phenomenon of Nijinsky's art. His debut on stage—in the children's number from a ballet divertissement—had already brought him close to the secrets of artistic reincarnation. By a strange coincidence this debut invoked both the joy and sadness of the past; and Nijinsky, unlike his colleagues, already had a past.

It was his second autumn at school. After holidays spent in the country by a crystal lake as round as a bowl (Eleonora had taken her children there for the summer), it was a painful autumn, indeed. As in the previous year, Nijinsky found it difficult to get used to the school routine. Seated at his desk, he couldn't follow the lesson, but tried to resurrect that feeling of spaciousness, of nature, that he had experienced lying flat out on the sand: his head in his hands, he had gazed unthinking at the water rippling in the sun.

One day the teacher's monotonous drone was interrupted by the order to go downstairs to the girls' section, which was usually out of bounds. The season had just opened at the Mariinsky and the selection of participants for future performances was already underway. The pupils stood in rows downstairs in the hall, juniors in front, seniors at the back. Alexander Viktorovich Shiriaev, assistant to ballet master Petipa, was walking up and down, inspecting them. A famous performer of character and grotesque dances, Shiriaev walked with a spring to his gait, and his whole manner displayed great adroitness. But he was so short that his twinkling eyes were on a level with the faces in the first row.

Shiriaev loved children. He realized that in a moment some of them would suffer a loss of face, an undeserved insult, and might lose faith in themselves unnecessarily. He also knew that others would rejoice, still others would turn up their noses, perhaps also unnecessarily. That is why he pondered, he contemplated, and waited a while before leading the chosen ones from the ranks.

Nijinsky was one of the lucky ones.

When the selection was over, a few boys remained behind in the hall. Then class assistants brought in the girl students, also in their second year.

Shiriaev said that they would learn the mazurka.

(*above*) The Mariinsky Theater, early 1900s. (*below*) The foyer.

(*above*) The artists' foyer (greenroom).   (*below*) The auditorium.

The mazurka! The word evoked the past. Nijinsky remembered the very person whom he was trying to forget. Spurs clinking, one arm akimbo, leaning slightly away from his lady so as to present her to the onlookers, the image of his father flashed through his mind. And this seemed to usher in the musical phrase that leaped to life beneath the fingers of the pianist.

Nijinsky came to himself when he was told to shut his mouth and to take up his place in line so as to learn the movements of the dance. He had learned them a long time ago. Toward the close of the rehearsal, Shiriaev paired off the children and put Nijinsky in the first couple.

The mazurka was part of the divertissement in *Paquita* and crowned the happy-ever-after ending of this ballet-cum-drama. The children were taken to the theater early, but they were not allowed out of the dressing rooms until the final bell of the last intermission. They went downstairs to the stage—tin soldiers in blue and gold uniforms, in *konfederatki* [6] slanted at a rakish angle and with dabs of rouge that the teacher on duty had applied, not very assiduously, to their cheeks.

Bathed in light, the stage, with its floor sloping down toward the inside of the drop-curtain, was teeming with people in ballet costume and in everyday clothes. They walked up and down, twirled about, jumped around, went over the difficult parts of their roles, or simply "warmed up" their legs with exercises while holding onto the bannister of the fire escape in the wings. Some of them examined the audience through the "eye" cut in the curtain. Suddenly a bow-legged man—a prop man—began to dash about in the midst of this hubbub and to scatter yellow rosin powder over the stage. The assistant stage manager worriedly clapped his hands and, above the noise of countless voices, declared that the conductor had entered the pit and wanted the stage cleared. It emptied at once.

The act started with the ceremonial procession of guests at a wedding ball. Advancing in procession up to the footlights, they dispersed to the sides of the stage and formed into a background of standing and seated groups against which the dances were to be performed. One of the first numbers, like an hors d'oeuvre before the more substantial dishes, was a touching bagatelle—a children's mazurka.

16

In a minute the balletomanes would be called upon to consider and to evaluate the artistry of the ballerina, the merits of her technique, and that of her rival soloists. But for the moment they could sit back and watch the entertaining diligence of the children.

The cavalier of the first couple threw out his leg at every step with swiftness and precision; he led his lady now kneeling before her, now turning her with true gallantry—a match for Felix Kshessinski himself. The contrasting tempos of the mazurka both urged and restrained the dancers. Its musical progression, at once glissando and staccato, seemed to be in the very blood of this little boy. But the seriousness with which he danced was not in keeping with his age or with the visage of a toy soldier.

The dance appealed to the audience. The producer allowed the children to take several bows. With smiling faces and in much embarrassment, they ran out on stage in a flock, attempted to pass one another, collided, and hastened backstage again. It was at this juncture that one of the artists laughingly referred to Nijinsky as "the young monkey." The words hurt deeply and penetrated to the recesses of his consciousness, even though he seemed to have forgotten them by the time of the next performance of *Paquita*. Nijinsky remembered the episode much later, as an experience long past and hence as something impersonal. Amid many other impressions, this episode helped Nijinsky to see the abyss separating the internal and the external, dream and reality, on the evening of the première of *Petrouchka:* his cheeks painted with the uneven dabs of rouge, it was then that the dancer Nijinsky looked into his mirror and saw the tragic eyes of a man turned dull.

That fate, along a path that would lead to spiritual tragedy, that would advance impetuously between the consciousness of life's fatality and the impossibility of escaping it, was still far ahead. All that could be discerned at the moment was the end of childhood.

It had been a rather uneventful childhood. The significant and the insignificant had sometimes strangely come together, and this was because the shadows thrown by the impressions and feelings from certain events, rather than the events themselves, had fused and interlaced. The idea of violence, for example, for some reason brought together two rather distant and unequal memories.

The first one was of the fall when the student Nijinsky had enrolled in boarding school. After the freedom of summer, he had been forced to submit to a regime of early rising with the bell and of promenades in twos under the tutor's supervision. He had experienced the melancholy of long evenings, the morose melancholy of an adolescent who could not enjoy a free and easy communication with his comrades. And he had had to put on the official jacket, in essence a uniform, with lyres embroidered as insignia on its stand-up collar. Other boys were proud to wear this uniform. But it had inhibited Nijinsky, depriving him of the sense of freedom alive within him and controlling his sensitive and resilient body.

His second recollection, as distinct from the first, was connected not with a period of long duration, but with a chance encounter.

Vaslav was then entering his sixteenth year. He was in the senior classes and enjoyed relative independence. Once in midwinter he was given permission to visit his mother, who had lived alone since Bronislava had also entered ballet school and Stanislav was being kept in an asylum.

Obtaining leave of absence, Nijinsky hastened downstairs to the cloakroom where the porter gave him his coat, with lyres on the buttons. Clad in this coat, he looked like a student. He went out into the school yard by the side door, crossed the square in the direction of the Alexandrinsky Theater, skirted Ekaterinsky Square, and came out on Nevsky Prospect. From there he would have turned right, toward the River Fontanka, but he fell in with a crowd of people. They weren't moving as people generally do, in different directions, but were advancing in one direction, and they weren't at all like the gentlefolk whom one normally saw on Nevsky Prospect; they were dressed simply and all seemed preoccupied with the same thing.

Nijinsky was forced to go along with the crowd in the direction of the Admiralty. Gradually he was carried into the center of the strange procession, but he hoped that by making his way through to the other side of Nevsky Prospect he would be able to turn on to Sadovaya Street.

He almost managed to do that. But just as he got to Sadovaya a ripple ran through the human mass and it exploded into fragments. Horses' hooves suddenly sounded on the wooden sidewalk, and almost

Nijinsky in schoolboy's uniform, 1902.

immediately a riding crop was slashing about Nijinsky's head. Behind it he could see someone's face red from the frost and twisted
in a savage grin.

The scar of the Cossack whip remained on Nijinsky's forehead
until his dying day.[7]

Nijinsky moved on to the class of Mikhail Konstantinovich Obukhov, a young teacher of seniors. The aspiring student was well known

in the school, for people spoke of his extraordinary leap. But Nijinsky was rather short, and although he had mastered the academic system of dance in all its purity of form, his future was still uncertain.

In general, male dancers at the Mariinsky had long ago conceded first place to the ballerinas. Occasionally the names of Gaetan and Auguste Vestris—the idols of the Paris public in the time of powdered wigs, gavottes, and passacaglias—would surface amid the oral traditions of the ballet world. Once one of the teachers, remembering the *Letters of a Russian Traveler,* was talking about Auguste (Gaetan's son) and made the boys laugh when he quoted the words "Vestris pranced like a frisky goat," with which Karamzin had characterized the French "god of the dance." [8] Then there was Louis Duport. Legend had it that when he was touring Russia he was the undoing of his beautiful partner, Marie Danilova, because she contracted consumption from unrequited love. Even earlier than the Vestrises and Duport was Timofei Bublikov, who, during the reign of old mother Catherine the Great, had traveled to Vienna to dance Zephyr. He had the reputation of a dancer of unique talent, but nothing else was known about him.

Male dancers then began to shy from their art, or so it seemed, and to turn into pantomime actors. That was almost the situation in the time of the ballet master Charles Didelot, whose name was still honored in the Mariinsky a hundred years later. And no wonder—it

Mikhail Obukhov

was Didelot who established the worldwide renown of the Russian ballet. Still, it's strange that even though he taught many ballerinas and gave them the principal roles in his productions, Didelot instituted a scholarship fund and bequeathed it not to the girl students but to the boys. Nijinsky was now receiving this scholarship—for his dancing, not for his good looks as a potential premier danseur. On the contrary, there was much in Nijinsky that contradicted the normal appearance of the premier danseur. And it wasn't just his short stature. Constant exercise in dance (since his childhood he had been used to trying out and checking a bodily movement, a dance phrase, or a whole variation) had overdeveloped his muscles. As strong and elastic as steel springs, they protruded on the calves of his legs and on his thighs, reducing the proportions of his legs. In any case, Nijinsky was rather stocky and, as they say, well knit. He had the shoulders of an athlete and large hands. His face retained the sallow complexion, slanting eyes, and rather full lips of a "little Jap." Actually, his eyes were rather lovely. Depending on the light, they might appear impenetrably dark or gray-green and transparent.

In a word, young Nijinsky's appearance ensured his future as a dancer, but hardly as a premier danseur. For that, one had to have a commanding presence, the more so since dance technique was no longer so essential for leading male roles as was pantomime. And that required aristocratic poise, a broad, imposing gesture, and a somewhat exaggerated facial mime. Old theatergoers could still remember such giants as Johanssen and Petipa in this kind of role: Johanssen had taken lyrical parts, the best of which was the rather dry but gallant Count Albrecht in *Giselle*, and Petipa had excelled in dramatic parts—his rendition of Conrad in *Le Corsaire* had amazed both dancers and spectators by its vigor.

Pavel Andreevich Gerdt combined the talents of both. A handsome figure, blue-eyed, blond, and with finely molded features, Gerdt had begun his career over fifty years before, and few could remember his dancing now. Still, old-timers used to say, "You young ones aren't the same!" alluding to Gerdt's knightly robbers, his elegant princes, and his shepherds as handsome as Adonis. True, during his last years Gerdt seemed rather corpulent in the role of suitor, and to those who were unable to "correct" his plastic expressions by earlier experiences

(*left*) Sergei Legat

(*above*) Nicolas Legat

(*near right, above*) Mikhail Obukhov

(*near right, below*) Samuil Andrianov

(*far right*) Michel Fokine

24

М. М. Фокинъ.

25

than his brother. Many people had simply shrugged their shoulders when, while still a youth, he became the lover and the partner of the much experienced Marie Mariusovna Petipa. He acted like a desperate gambler playing by instinct one moment on the red, the next on the black. And, like a gambler, he placed everything on the ballet revolt of 1905. When the revolt fell through, he cut his throat with a razor.[9]

George Kiaksht was not very imposing, but he was good-looking. Nimble and skillful, he had the reputation of an excellent partner. But his repertoire was basically a comic one, including Colin in *La Fille Mal Gardée,* Franz in *Coppélia,* Harlequin in *Harlequinade.*

As for Obukhov, he ended up taking secondary roles simply because he was useful as an artist (although he danced well) and never merited any more than that.

Fokine, on the other hand, could look forward to a primary position in the company. He possessed all the attributes of a premier danseur: he was well built, had long legs, was very masculine, and had eyes as deep and dark as velvet. The authorities had already begun to promote him. They did it little by little, according to etiquette, but each time they placed him a bit higher. Like all novices, Fokine had to dance with the shepherds in the interlude in *The Queen of Spades;* he had to take part in the character and classical dances of the corps de ballet that adorned every spectacle at the Mariinsky. But he was very soon entrusted with leading roles. Even so, his promotion up the ballet ladder didn't seem to meet with much enthusiasm, and Fokine, in spite of all his very difficult work, seemed to be seeking outlets for his energies in other occupations, one moment in painting, the next in music making.

The work was hard because, contrary to Gerdt's experience, it was not limited to pantomime. All young actors were obliged to dance, and they could and did. As far back as the late 1880s the dancer Enrico Cecchetti, representing the Milan school, had appeared on the Mariinsky stage. Thanks to him, interest in the male dance and in its new capacity for virtuosity had been renewed. So what had been hidden in the inmost recesses of the school—and male virtuosity was still being taught there in the proper, old-fashioned manner—had suddenly gained its rights to the stage again. Dancing, which had long been relegated to casual interludes and entrusted to performers who never managed to get as far as primary roles, was once more expected of the principal heroes of ballets. And this despite the fact that Cecchetti himself never took heroic roles.

There were various reasons for this. First of all, although Cecchetti did possess an attractive and rather funny appearance, he was too thickset to cut a very good figure. Furthermore, he wasn't so young anymore; he was approaching fifty. Second, he had an exceptional gift for mime, not in grand heroics but in comedy and character parts. Third, his manner of execution was very different from the academic method of the dancers and, in general, from the whole St. Petersburg school. But the clever Italian certainly had no intention of disdaining the Russian academic system. On the contrary, he had a deep respect for it, and, advanced in age as he was, he even managed to refurbish his own still brilliant but rather frayed style of dancing. Certain entrechats that bordered on acrobatics he rejected altogether; certain leaps and turns he subordinated to the narrative action of the staging (one of the Russians' strong points). His pupils repaid him a hundredfold when, after retiring from the stage, he became the tutor of some of the finest dancers, male and female. Among them he singled out Vaslav Nijinsky, of whom he became very fond.

But in the early days nothing suggested such an encounter. Up until 1902 Cecchetti was teaching in the girls' section at the St. Petersburg school. He was then transferred to Warsaw and, on his return, worked neither at the ballet school nor at the Mariinsky, but instead gave private lessons. The fate of this ardent Italian lover of the dance and the fate of the Russian ballet were joined later under very different circumstances and on very different grounds.

For the moment, Cecchetti was responsible for the renaissance of the male dance on the academic stage. True, the virtuosity that he had restored to the arsenal of the premier danseur now occupied a rather isolated position. It neither fused with pantomime nor derived from it. It was displayed only in individual numbers.

The young dancers did everything they were supposed to; indeed, discipline was inculcated in them from the beginning. Only Fokine used to gripe and make snide remarks about the absurdity of the roles they were made to take. Not in vain did one of the pillars of tradition once say of Fokine that he had got everything but that he still imagined he had a millstone around his neck. Eventually, Fokine did cast a stone at the moribund traditions, but that came later. By the spring of 1905 everything had returned to normal after the political assemblies and agitation among the younger members of the ballet company. Things went on in their own sweet way. Even a premier danseur presented himself who obviously appealed to Gerdt as a worthy successor: Samuil Andrianov, "Samosha" as he was soon called in the company, had just finished his schooling. He was tall, of noble appearance, and good-looking. But, alas, he had a depressing lack of artistic intuition. He lacked it so badly that as soon as he walked out on stage his picturesque appearance melted into thin air.

A rather extraordinary incident occurred at the school in the spring of 1905. Nobody paid particular attention to it since it fell within the school routine. In February of that year the school authorities discussed the program for the annual students' production. They themselves didn't give it much thought, but relied on the opinion of the teachers, who saw better how to exhibit the pupils in the best light. As far as they could, the teachers composed ballets that best corresponded to their opinions of choreographic principles in general and of the art of performance in particular.

Klavdia Mikhailovna Kulichevskaya, who had retired from the stage in 1901, and Gerdt took the old format of the one-act ballet as their model. Such a format, with its Anacreontic, fairy-tale plot, ensured a minimum of content but a maximum number of occasions for dancing. Cecchetti preferred genre themes, but his objective remained the same: to present an eye-catching, classical dance for the principal personages within the round of the various character dances.

In 1899 Alexander Gorsky had composed the ballet *Clorinda, Queen of the Mountain Fairies* based on Andersen's fairy story *The Ice Maiden* (music by Keller, a flautist in the Mariinsky orchestra). The young teacher from the ballet school had deviated from the rules of ballet by preserving the tragic finale of the fairy tale; such finales were not encouraged on the professional stage, let alone in school theatricals. But Gorsky's audaciousness had won out because the basic conflict in the tale was dissipated by the many conventional dances. The whole school, from top to bottom, had been involved. The performers of the principal roles did not go down in history, even though Liubov

28

Petipa, second wife of Marius, was among them, but those in secondary parts had included future talents. Tamara Karsavina, one of two butterflies, the emissaries of Clorinda, queen of the mountain fairies, would graduate in three years' time. Fedor Lopukhov, playing the monster in the queen's suite, had another six years of study before him. As for Vaslav Nijinsky, a participant in the children's dance at the village festival, he had still to cover practically the whole of his studies. This dance had represented a game with arbalests. At rehearsals Gorsky, with his thin goatee and extraordinarily kind eyes, had grown excited as he gave the commands.

"Slope arms, kneel, place arbalests upright on the floor, cock them, take out a bullet, put it in the muzzle—and fffffire! Now, present arms, right wheel, take your lady by the waist, take up your arbalests. . . ." [10]

The dance really had seemed like a game. The little "marksmen" and their "ladies" had done their movements with enthusiasm.

But Gorsky had soon gone off to Moscow.

Six years later, in the spring of 1905, the pupils of two new teachers were about to graduate: Mikhail Obukhov's male class and Michel Fokine's female class. Both men had the right to put on their own productions, but Obukhov was not tempted. Fokine, on the other hand, was keen on the idea, and the authorities thought it reasonable to let him choose a ballet, choreograph the dances, and direct the production. They reasoned like this: Fokine was a troublemaker and conspirator (during the recent disturbances he had shouted loudest about certain privileges and liberties for ballet dancers); better to put his energies to some use.

Fokine set to work with great fervor, although he was forced to cool his ardor a bit. At first everything went well. The new-found ballet master dug around in the music library and came up with music by Kadlets for the ballet *Acis and Galatea*. This ballet, which Lev Ivanov had once produced, had long been removed from the repertoire. But it was at this juncture, or so Ivan Manuilovich Mysovsky, the school inspector, thought, that Fokine began to entertain rather nonsensical ideas.

The previous December the American dancer Isadora Duncan had given several recitals on the stage of the Noble Assembly and, to tell the truth, had created a sensation. Her style had been a very open one, if the word "open" may be taken as a synonym for a state of undress. Her very feminine figure had scarcely been concealed by her transparent tunic à la grecque, and she had danced barefoot. The decadents were everywhere. Certain adolescent poets and artists had been publishing the journal *The World of Art* [11] for the past five years. Apparently supposing that everyone else was involved not with art but with the devil knows what, they ranted and raved, screamed with delight, and filled the newspapers with their idiotic raptures. And now we see the result: an instructor from an official institution intends to dress up young girls in the antique style, having hung around the Public Library for days on end examining ancient artifacts, and he intends to compose antique dances. Nobody in the theater had thought of that before, thank God.

Still, it wasn't worth getting worked up about. Fokine renounced his intentions as soon as he saw how inappropriate they were. It was useless to argue. He simply arranged a totally academic work for his students, demonstrating his good taste and knowledge of convention. Yet, he did manage to introduce one gesture of comparative liberty, the more so since it was not the final-year students who carried it out.

The theme of *Acis and Galatea* had a substantial ballet tradition. It had been brought to Russia by foreign ballet masters, but they would have been hard put to say who had first found this poetic episode in Ovid. In those distant times the theme had been changed to conform with the rules of a light genre that permitted no unhappy endings. The nymph Galatea and her lover, the shepherd Acis, overcame the intrigues of Cyclops by the grace of the gods and celebrated their happy union in divertissements. The dancer and ballet master Ivan Valberkh recalled that at the end of the eighteenth century he had represented Acis in a powdered wig with curls and in shoes with buckles and red heels. If Fokine had become involved in this ballet two years later, after he had met the artist Alexandre Benois, he would probably have stylized the mythological subject as a Rococo bagatelle—which would have encountered no objections from the authorities. But Fokine was as yet unfamiliar with such subtleties, and he produced *Acis and Galatea* just as Lev Ivanov had, using the forms of the classical dance he despised so much.

He gave the roles of Galatea and Acis to final-year students—to his own student Marie Gorshkova and to Obukhov's student Fedor Lopukhov. Fokine immediately began rehearsals with the principals' main pas de deux. There wasn't much time left to the première, and the dancers had little experience. However, the project made some progress.

The teacher knew the strong and weak points of his pretty student and the nature of her style, at once flirtatious and shy. As he began to choreograph, Fokine devised effective positions for her in the smooth adagio and in the gliding movements of her variation. Unexpectedly, he resolved her variation with a series of brilliant entrechats, which the young Galatea performed almost to perfection, repeating them as if they were a prayer.

Fokine had to take rather more trouble with Acis. There was much that was outstanding in the student Lopukhov—outstanding, that is, in his personality, not in his ability as a dancer. His eyes, so penetrating, so clear, so challenging, expressed intelligence. He was quick on the uptake and, in fact, mastered his part quickly, the more so since he was exceptionally musical. But his body, not yet that of a man, did not obey him readily. His arrogance emphasized the angularity of his body, a condition peculiar to adolescence, which in Lopukhov's case had gone on too long. When Fokine, in the middle of rehearsals, began to introduce the ensemble, Lopukhov's pride received a great blow.

In the dances for the ensemble Fokine permitted himself one liberty that no one really noticed. Perhaps even Fokine himself did not realize that it was a liberty. Much later, when he was settling accounts with his rival, Nijinsky—or, rather, with the shadow of his rival, who had already escaped into insanity—Fokine did claim it to be a liberty. In his memoirs he hinted that his idea of having a dance of fauns in *Acis and Galatea* had been an innovation. This is dubious, even though he did make many innovations later on. For Fokine it was simply important to "prove," by making false implications, that *L'Après-Midi d'un Faune*, Nijinsky's first experiment as choreographer, had derived from Fokine's own undertakings.

In any case, Petipa and Lev Ivanov had long ago started to use fauns as personages in their ballets. Fauns danced in *The Awakening of Flora* and in *The Seasons* as well as in *Acis and Galatea*. They were used as a kind of contrast, as a kind of paint that diluted the pink-white and blue-white clouds of nymphs, naiads, and wood fairies of ballet mythology. The fauns, playing tricks on the inhabitants of the forests and the rivers or frightening them, always appeared on stage in the same guise. According to wardrobe lists this was "brown tights and vest, a brown pelt (put on across the shoulders), a brown wig with curly horns"—and, from the props, a reed pipe. Fokine's fauns had all these items; his nymphs wore long skirts of decent thickness and bodices with puffed sleeves, because new costumes were never made for graduation performances.

The movements of the fauns were also traditional: the stealthy creep, the soft jumps on bent knees, poses in which the limbs were turned inward despite the outward positions of the classical canon. These movements were part of the genre of the grotesque and gave a certain dissonance to the monotonous harmony of ballet pastorales. Fokine remembered only one of the novelties that he devised: in the finale the fauns turned somersaults. But although everyone took note of the fauns' dance at the performance, it was not the somersaults that aroused their interest. Fokine did remember that.

Recalling the first rehearsal, he remembered the young boys who had crowded together by the window waiting their turn. He remembered that he decided to let them on as a group, and he showed them how they were to move. After taking a run (in the theater a run had to begin a long way back in the depths of the upper wings), everyone had to leap at the same time so as to appear in the middle of the hall. In its own way this idea was already a threat to the conventions of traditional staging. The new ballet master calculated that each boy would leap according to his own limitations and so the many-headed flock of fauns would end up scattered all over the stage. And that's how it was. There was just one boy who jumped, suddenly broke loose from the center, seemed to suspend himself above everyone else, and then landed on the floor far in front of the rest.

Obukhov, who had dropped by to take a look at his pupils, was standing next to Fokine. He shouted at "that little devil," telling him to watch the others; it was not him that the orchestra had to keep up with. Fokine pushed Obukhov aside and went up to the wrongdoer. The latter stood to attention, as was the rule, but fixed his eyes on the

32

A scene from *Acis and Galatea,* produced at the end of the school year, 1905, with students of the Imperial School. Nijinsky is the faun in the center, on the floor.

toes of his shoes. Fokine looked at him closely and, full of curiosity, showed him unexpectedly not a leap but an intricate pose. His slanted eyes shining, the boy sat down firmly on one leg, curled his other one around it, and an invisible pipe seemed to appear in his hands; deep in blissful thought, he raised it to his lips.

Fokine always remembered this transformation of a gangling schoolboy into a half-man–half-beast rejoicing unconsciously in his nature. He remembered how he quickly asked Obukhov the boy's name and then ordered Nijinsky to step aside for the moment. He did this so that he could devise a dance for a solo faun after he had marked out steps for the corps de ballet.

This dance, unplanned, soon occupied an important place in the ballet. Long before the graduation performance everyone at the school was talking about this new-found talent. Teachers and dancers began to drop by the hall. Many of them came on the pretext of observing Nijinsky, although they wished also to find out what Fokine was up to. The pretext was not in vain. Throughout his long life Lopukhov (Acis) was jealous not of Fokine (although later on as a choreographer he did dispute his testament) but of Nijinsky, whose success wounded the ambition of this danseur manqué.

Among those who dropped by the hall was Kulichevskaya. Like most people, she valued first and foremost not the artistry of Nijinsky, which had so taken Fokine, but his dance technique. Although Nijinsky still had two years of study to go, his technique was perfect. And it was perfect not because of the impulsive force of his flight and the noiseless precision of his landing, the brilliance of his pirouettes accelerating and decelerating according to the will of the music, the absolute coordination and interconnection of each movement, but because of that natural freedom that comes to a performer only after considerable experience on the stage. Nijinsky's dance technique dissolved in the natural force of the music and was saturated with its rhythm. But, while subject to the rhythm, while exposing the slightest nuances of the music, his technique enriched the simple scheme of the ballet accompaniment with flashes of virtuosity.

For her students Kulichevskaya resurrected Petipa's *Le Marché des Innocents*, a ballet of fifty years' vintage. This innocuous divertissement allowed for all kinds of additions and insertions. The kindhearted Obukhov, surprised at the sudden and universal recognition that his recent student was enjoying, agreed to assign his pupil to Kulichevskaya. He even polished up the variation that dear Klavdia Mikhailovna had hastily composed.

Obukhov did not worry about the reasons for this recognition, nor did anyone else. In any case, this recognition was linked to the psychological enigma of the personality of his strange pupil. Fokine's timid search for new forms and Kulichevskaya's experience delineated, albeit faintly, the two camps that were soon to engage in battles between the academicians and the innovators of the Russian ballet. Nijinsky satisfied both camps. He did so thanks to his remarkable ability to embody opposite artistic goals, to elevate them to the ideal to which all aspired. Fokine gasped inwardly when the obedient boy demonstrated to him in reality his dream of the dance in antiquity. Kulichev-skaya granted the youth the rights of premier danseur long before he graduated.

It was not only artists who perceived Nijinsky's ability to submit to another's will and to please. The most ordinary people also made use of it. But either they did not understand Nijinsky's complex nature or they did not wish to. Many used him to their own egoistic and (for Nijinsky) pernicious ends.

What made Nijinsky's nature complex was its duality. Along with his passivity, his ability to submit to another's will as if entirely dissolving in it, there existed his creative independence, the boundless intuition of a genuine and sincere artist. These two divisions of his soul were in constant discord, condemning its bearer to tragic paradoxes. Nijinsky himself feared independence even though, inwardly, he aspired to it. And this fear doomed to utter failure all his desperate attempts to become the master of his own fate.

On the night of that graduation production, both Fokine and Kulichevskaya calmly took this pliant material in their hands. They ascribed the results to themselves and did not question the assumption that Nijinsky was dull-witted. But for the first time Nijinsky disturbed tradition: he demonstrated that the male dance could compete with the female dance and could even eclipse it. He became the subject of numerous reviews in which the name of the male dancer Nijinsky was mentioned more often than the names of female dancers. But success did not change Nijinsky. He only became more bottled up, more unsociable, and fenced himself off from the often hostile probes of curious outsiders.

Rosai was openly hostile. The more evident the superiority of the "little Jap," the more persistent the maliciousness of his ambitious rival. Sometimes Rosai, with an ardor worthy of his Italian forebears, would start a fight—so intense that the instructors had to separate the two rivals locked in combat. The other pupils reconciled themselves, and some of them even tried to be friends, anticipating that one day this might be useful. But it was easier to pick a fight with the "little Jap" than it was to win his trust. Anatole Bourman had to act against his conscience when he described in his book his friendly relations with Nijinsky and his family.[12]

35

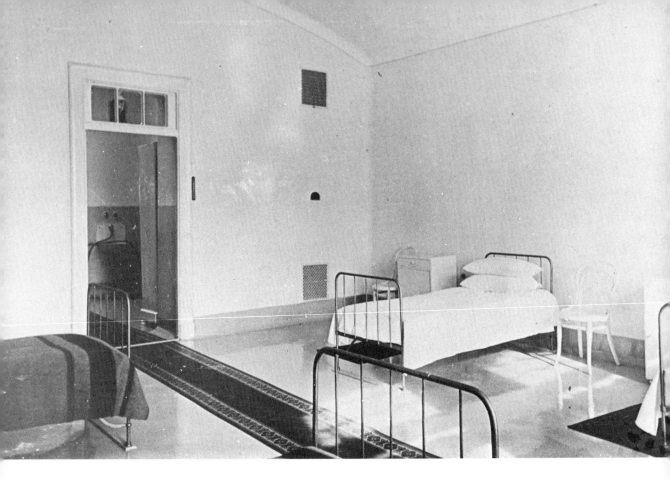

Dormitory at the Imperial School.

The Nijinsky family was an amicable one, although it did not allow strangers into the fold. Primarily it was Vaslav who would not let them in. He never grew accustomed to his colleagues at school, even though everything favored this: the beds close to each other in the dormitory, the tables in the dining room at which the students sat on long benches, the classrooms and the cloakrooms where each desk, each closet was meant for two persons. On the contrary, this enforced proximity only intensified his loneliness.

As a child, as a teenager, and as a young man, Nijinsky became increasingly aware that he could not get on with other people. During the critical period of his adolescence these differences of thought and feeling began to produce a sharp reaction.

The period of his stay at the school was especially difficult because any communication between girls and boys was forbidden. Living on different floors, meeting only at the lessons in ballroom dancing, in partnering classes, and at rehearsals (under the supervision of the instructors and governesses) stimulated early romances. During the dances crumpled love notes were passed from hand to hand, and the pupils used a special code of smiles, looks, and signs. Anybody caught doing this was punished. These unnatural taboos only inspired the imagination. In the evenings the boy students would whisper together in corners, revealing "indecent" things to each other. Nijinsky was afraid of such conversations. He did not venture to adopt an "object of attentions" in the girls' section; he was shy and avoided them. But he did conjure up a vague although ideal image of love. He was therefore terrified and revolted to hear the other boys, who were aware of his idealization of love and showed off their vulgarities in his presence.

Nijinsky escaped even deeper into himself. He transferred his ability to love completely to his mother and his sister. Both of them took his misfortunes to heart and delighted in his successes. And both knew how he could laugh. Nobody ever saw him cry.

Later on, during one of the climaxes of his illness but before he cut himself off forever from the world behind his eternal, lunatic smile, Nijinsky wrote in his diary: "I wept in my soul, but tears would not appear. . . . I often cried alone and I was glad to have my separate room. I thought that I was grown up, because I had a room to myself. In a separate room I could cry a lot."

What is the meaning of these words? In his dimmed consciousness, did Nijinsky see the classroom as his own room—the classroom where, in the evening, lessons over, he could cry his heart out? Did his mother give him a room in their poor apartment? Were his tears caused by people who did not understand his solitude, his anguish, his inability to be like others?

By 1906 Nijinsky had reached manhood. He had changed from an adolescent into a young man. A new feature appeared in his personality—a thoughtfulness and feeling of responsibility for the fate of his family. With this came further justification for him to feel himself grown up.

Quite rightly, Nicolas Legat ascribed to himself the honor of discovering Nijinsky, and he followed his progress intently, even though he went to the school only rarely now. Legat occupied the place that Petipa had before he was fired, and business connected with the company took up a lot of his time. In January, for example, Legat was obliged to compose the dances for the opera *Don Giovanni* for a gala performance in honor of the 150th anniversary of Mozart's birth. Legat had no wish to resurrect the theatrical epoch of Mozart, and so he devised a ballet number called *Roses and Butterflies* based on the formulas of the classical dance so close to his heart. He chose four female dancers. Of the four, Olga Preobrajenska was a ballerina, but the others —Agrippina Vaganova, Liubov Egorova, and Anna Pavlova—were not yet called ballerinas, although they did dance leading roles. For their

(*far left*) Agrippina Vaganova

(*near left*) Anna Pavlova

(*above*) Liubov Egorova

(*right*) Olga Preobrajenska

39

partners he appointed three soloists—Samuil Andrianov, Adolf Bolm, and Leonid Leontiev. The student Nijinsky was summoned to be the fourth.

A closed gallery connected the ballet school with the rehearsal hall. At the general rehearsals of the company and the school the hall was often full of the artists. It seemed cramped when the children were let in in pairs, so they were kept back in the corner by the entrance. But now Nijinsky turned up there alone. Not a soul was in sight. The space seemed immense, as if in a nightmare. He was so timid that he almost turned back. But a door opened at the other end and Preobrajenska and Vaganova came in.

Preobrajenska, a slightly reddish blonde with very fine features, adjusted her tight bodice above her pink tutu and, from habit, straightened her stooping shoulders. Vaganova, with her dark hair and green eyes, seemed bigger than her colleague, but this was only because of her sweeping gestures and the precise movements of her feet, turned outward at a pronounced angle. She was wearing a bluish-gray tutu covered in sequins that had certainly seen better days.

Nijinsky gave a start, pulled himself together, clicked his heels, and bowed, in accordance with the rules of ballet etiquette. The ladies responded graciously. Vaganova quickly whispered something that made Preobrajenska laugh, and then both of them took hold of the barre and began to do pliés, bending their knees and changing smoothly from first to second and then to fifth position.

The handsome Andrianov threw open the door and ushered in Egorova. On her neat figure everything was immaculate, from the ribbons on her ballet shoes (with the points skillfully darned so that they wouldn't slip) to her new, light blue tutu. Even so, she went up to the mirror and, inspecting herself critically, began to adjust the intricate bow on her bodice.

Bolm and Leontiev came in chuckling loudly. This was their third year in the theater and they were classmates, but in appearance they were very different. Bolm had curly hair, was well formed, and in a boyish sort of way was rather pretty. Leontiev on the other hand, short by nature, seemed even shorter because he had a big, round head with a round nose and protruding eyes. Still, his eyes shone with vitality and his thickset body moved resiliently and with skill. Leontiev controlled it extraordinarily well when he was dancing, although his real (and still latent) talent lay in his uncommon gift for mime.

Looking over at the downcast Nijinsky, Leontiev raised his eyebrows, walked across the hall with an intricate and deliberate gait, and, ending up beside Nijinsky, asked him whether they still filled everyone with *kasha* in the mornings at school. Nijinsky raised his eyes. He did not smile at Leontiev's conspiratorial grimace, but answered quietly and cordially. Leontiev also became suddenly serious and murmured that there was no point in being a coward and skulking in a corner. But a loud clap interrupted his attempt to give courage to the future creator of Petrouchka, a role that only Leontiev would perform on the Russian stage in the same tragic key.

The clap came from Legat, who was sitting with his back to the mirror—as if he'd appeared from nowhere. He clapped once again like a gun going off and, irritated, asked the newly arrived assistant régisseur where Pavlova was.

The man hadn't finished answering when Pavlova herself appeared in the doorway. She was all in white. Her black hair, not piled up like the other dancers', lay flat on the opaque declivity of her cheeks like thick, smooth wings. Nervously, Pavlova distended her nostrils. She went up to Legat. An argument arose between them.

Nijinsky made out that Pavlova was being sent to Moscow on Gorsky's request in order to dance the role of some "Bint-Anta." Legat seemed to be most annoyed by this name. He said that Marius Ivanovich had called the role in *The Daughter of Pharaoh* Aspicia, but that Gorsky, of course, would give it an absurd name like Bint-Anta, and ho put the stress on the *Bint*.[13] At last he waved his hand, mentioning to Pavlova that, just for today, she would go on with Nijinsky, and he ordered the régisseur to summon Trefilova for the next day.

He then turned to the pianist, who was taking his seat and massaging his frozen fingers, and asked him to begin. The pianist began to play something clear and sweet, but he was interrupted after a few bars. Legat arranged the ballerinas in the four corners and, once more giving the sign to the pianist, demonstrated how the entrance was to be made: pas de bourrée en diagonale, the hands to be gradually raised and then, like branches, to circle one above the other. Meeting in the center, the "roses" were to maintain their wavering steps and to

41

continue their motif of flowering in the choral dance; they were to change places and to bend so as to slip through the archways made by their own arms, then they were to freeze in their low arabesques for the briefest second and then to continue circling.

The music was unlike anything that Nijinsky had heard before, and the successful pattern of the movement enchanted him. He stood on demi-point, soussus (his legs so firm that they looked like solid stalks), bent slightly, and entwined his head with his arms so that his rather rough fingers with their thick joints suddenly turned into half-open petals.

He quickly came to himself, and nobody noticed this sketch for the future *Spectre de la Rose,* which came and went so swiftly.

After this, Legat got back into the old routine. The artist in him was overcome by his complacency, and the female dancers ruined his design, which had almost reached fruition. After her entrance, each was supposed to do a solo number, and each of them showed Legat what she deemed the most effective. Preobrajenska, a quick run and dainty hops on point; Vaganova, broad leaps; Egorova, pirouettes. Only Pavlova preserved the essential purpose, not so much in her choice of movements as in her feeling for the nature of a flower.

The male dancers did not attempt to assert their independence. At this point Legat did not manage to find anything original for the "butterflies" (it would have been better to call them moths). Their dancing, in any case, was really quite remote from such an analogy. The men were supposed to support the women during the adagio, and in their own solo parts to compete as virtuosi with each other. Not without a smile did Petipa seem to observe all this from his portrait on the wall, watching as Legat demonstrated for the second or third time a copy of the variation of the four cavaliers from *Raymonda.*[14]

There was no need for any artistry. Legat had reason enough for passing over Fokine when he was selecting dancers for the butterflies. Fokine spoke more and more often of his abhorrence of orthodox dancers who knew only how to form up in front of the audience in a straight line. And they were now being lined up at regular intervals and were being asked to do tours en l'air, now in unison, now one after the other. Nijinsky realized that all that was wanted of him was

Nijinsky in *Roses and Butterflies,* the pas de huit danced at the Mozart gala, 1906.

Vera Trefilova

what he did every day in class, so he easily outstripped the other
dancers in lightness and agility.

On 18 January, the day of the performance (Pavlova had been
replaced by Trefilova, who was as pretty as a porcelain figurine), it
was not the dancing itself that scored the success as much as the
dancers, Nijinsky above all. The audience, none of them ballet connoisseurs, applauded everyone immediately and uniformly. But on
stage, after the curtain had been lowered, Legat patted Nijinsky on
the shoulder, Obukhov kissed him generously, and Gerdt himself, with
royal magnanimity, complimented him.

Any schoolboy would have been proud. But Nijinsky remained
unchanged. Only his absent-mindedness and alienation became more
noticeable against the background of the encouraging smiles from

the administration and the attitudes of his colleagues, now divided into antagonists and proponents. Nijinsky didn't seem to care whether they mocked him or praised him. Enjoying comparative freedom, he now found isolation with greater ease. In the evenings the teachers on duty, who were supposed to know how their pupils were spending their time, anxiously searched for him all over the school.

One evening one of the duty teachers heard some music being played and set off toward the sound. Passing through a number of unlit halls, he found Nijinsky in the last one, a small hall, also unlit. At the piano sat Nijinsky, playing the overture to *Tannhäuser,* although where and when he had heard it is not known. As soon as the teacher lit a lamp, Nijinsky jumped up, rushed into a corner, and stood with his face to the wall until he was alone again. The next day the music teacher couldn't believe the duty teacher, since Nijinsky had been cutting his lessons and couldn't analyze the simplest piece of music. Nijinsky was silent to all questions. Eventually, the duty teacher himself thought that he had imagined the *Tannhäuser* music and everything that had happened the day before.

Nijinsky was often seen with a book. The classics stood on the shelves in the small school library. The shy young man discovered life in them and immersed himself in a world of new feelings, of ideas that he could not always fathom. No doubt he was disturbed by the figure of Lermontov's Mtsyri [15] and understood the novice's aspiration to freedom at all costs, at any price. He copied pages of Pushkin and Gogol in the naïve belief that he would learn to write as they did. "I copied a lot, but then felt that this was nonsense and gave it up," he confessed as he reviewed his past, so recent and yet so terribly remote. He mentioned the title of only one book: "I read Dostoevsky's *The Idiot,* at the age of eighteen, and I understood its meaning." [16]

Perhaps not entirely. But he loved its hero and regarded him as an ideal that he strove to attain, or at least to approximate. Nijinsky never reached that level, but he saw their affinities and was stunned by what he saw.

First and foremost, for him it was a book about a certain illness. From time to time Eleonora Nijinsky took her children to see their elder brother. Vaslav never admitted to his mother how terrified he was by Stanislav's gaze, a gaze that seemed to be cut off from the world by a transparent wall. Vaslav was further terrified by the smile that never left Stanislav's lips and by his fingers, fidgeting aimlessly. What was there to admit anyway? He was not afraid of Stanislav. On the contrary, he experienced melancholy and pity whenever he saw this compliant and silent man who had long since passed the violent stage of his illness. He was afraid to imagine what was going on in that head, behind that prominent brow, like his, that emphasized his haircut. Fearful of mysterious analogies and premonitions, he concealed them from his mother, and from himself.

Still, there was something else in the book that was of most importance for Nijinsky. After finishing the novel, he once more returned to the words of the hero: "I really don't like to be with adults, with grown-up people. I noticed this a long time ago. I don't like to be because I don't know how to react to them. Whatever they say to me, however kind they might be to me, I still find it burdensome to be with them for some reason." [17] Nijinsky found a reflection of his own soul in these words, and he tried to comprehend how Myshkin found his frankness and simplicity in dealing with people. He searched for these qualities but could not find them. Perhaps for the first and only time Nijinsky envied a man his ability to remain natural in the midst of vain, fussy people even though he did not like to be with them. Nijinsky did not know that he also possessed that rare gift. He never realized that he could give this gift only from the stage, only across the footlights and in his many guises—diverse, yet free, open-hearted, natural.

At that time, as an eighteen-year-old in his final year, Nijinsky was fortunate in one immediate coincidence. "It was for some reason or other always burdensome for me to be with them, and I am awfully glad whenever I can escape to my friends—and my friends have always been children. This is not because I myself am a child, but because I am simply drawn toward children," [18] explains Dostoevsky's hero of himself (but who never meets any children in the course of the novel). Nijinsky was also drawn toward children and likewise hardly ever met them. His life and his unexpected fame held him in their grasp too tightly. Only on rare occasions were the shackles of his conventional reality loosened.

It was at this time, in 1906, that Nijinsky savored the joys of just such a moment of rest. A twenty-two-year-old pianist by the name of Asafiev turned up at the Mariinsky. A modest man, he did not flaunt his brilliant mind and erudition, either then or later in life. As often happens, Asafiev was attracted by something that did not come easily to him, in his case composing. His choice was definitely the art of the theater, but he was still undecided as to which sphere of the theatrical arts he should lay claim to as a musician. Although ballet attracted him the most, he began with an opera called *Cinderella*, which was intended to be performed by children. Nevertheless, Asafiev's interest in the ballet showed itself in the many dances he composed for the ball in the second act.

At the performance of *Don Giovanni*, Asafiev's observant eye had singled out the young Nijinsky, who had carried out Legat's exercises for the Mozart motifs with a remarkable sense of musicianship. Asafiev had made inquiries, but he hadn't really learned anything instructive. So he sought out this interesting young man during one of the school breaks. Unexpectedly, Nijinsky agreed immediately to compose and rehearse the dances for *Cinderella*, which was to be presented at Christmas to a family that Asafiev assured him was hospitable and had lots of children.

Nijinsky was received cordially, but his cold silence remained unbroken. Asafiev began to regret his hasty invitation to Nijinsky, but nothing could be done now, and so he started off the rehearsal. In the drawing room the furniture was moved to the walls and the carpet was rolled up. Asafiev played a waltz on the piano: it was to be sung by a choir as accompaniment to the dances. Nijinsky listened to the music standing by the window and looking into the street. Then he asked where all the participants were.

They were being kept in readiness in an adjacent room. And then, embarrassed but still happily impatient, they came in, boys and girls of different ages and different looks, from those who still retained a touching childishness to awkward teenagers. The door was just closing when there was a noise of argument and suddenly a low, unhappy howl. This aroused Nijinsky from his apathy. Silently he ran to the door, flung it open, and saw a small boy awash with tears.

"Won't they let you in?" Nijinsky asked, for some reason, in a whisper. The boy, choking with sobs, shook his head. "Let's ask together," and Nijinsky turned to a lady standing in the doorway: "Why don't you let him dance? He's not a little boy. He'll understand everything perfectly."

No sooner said than done. Nijinsky was understood by everyone. A simple and natural relationship was established between the "ballet master" and the "artists," even those who were a bit dumb and unmusical. "His ability to rehearse with children was amazing," recalled Asafiev. "Like no one else, he knew how to arouse enthusiasm, to arouse interest in his projects, to attain conscious mastery of the subject. Like no one else, he inspired the child's imagination, devising what seemed to be complex dance-games, and it was astounding how he could discipline a child's attention without raising his voice or flaunting his grown-up experience. The members of the choir and the dancers ranged from eight to thirteen years old. The one exception was the little six-year-old Petka, Nijinsky's friend." [19]

When Asafiev recorded this memoir, in November 1918, Nijinsky, struck down by illness in the Swiss town of St. Moritz—it had also been a Swiss town in Prince Myshkin's case—was then dreaming of returning to Russia and of founding his dance school there. Perhaps, in his disturbed consciousness, there echoed the sounds of the children's choir, fragments of the dances that he composed, the image of the serious and trusting Petka. Hastily he jotted down the points of his aesthetic program, crossed them out, repeated them.

"The primary concern in *The Dance School* must be for the spiritual and physical well-being. . . . For a pupil (a child) to be spiritually healthy, it is not enough to explain things to him and to read him good books; examples from his own life and from his teachers' lives are also necessary." To the word *teachers'* he added parenthetically *adult*, but then crossed it out and put *grown-up*. He went on: "Art can exist only where there are healthy feelings; via these we transmit our thoughts." [20]

But in 1906 Nijinsky still enjoyed spiritual health and, above all, he was independent because he revealed the essence of his soul only to children. First-graders at the Theater School knew that in Nijinsky they could always find protection from the gibes and clips on the ear distributed so generously by pimply and arrogant youths. He was especially popular because he did not use the familiar *ty* pronoun for

(*right*) Nijinsky as the Blackamoor in *Le Roi Candaule*, 1906.

(*below*) Nijinsky as Aquilon in *The Awakening of Flora*, 1906.

(*left*) Nijinsky as the Mulatto in *Le Roi Candaule*, 1906.

(*left, below*) Nijinsky in costume for *Paquita*, 1907.

(*below*) Nijinsky as the Youth in *Eunice*, 1907.

those in a lower form, as was the custom, but addressed everyone without exception by *vy*.[21] But his own years at school were coming to an end. Final exams were not far off.

The authorities at the school were glad to be rid of their strange pupil who had performed so brilliantly at the graduation spectacle. Nijinsky got through the examinations somehow, thanks to the promptings of his classmates and of the teachers themselves, who maintained that a dancer did not really need scholarship. Of course, Nijinsky shone in this year's production too, although conditions were less advantageous for him than in the previous year's piece.

The year before, Fokine had obviously been carrying on polemics with Legat's *Roses and Butterflies,* because he had put on a number called *The Flight of the Butterflies* to Chopin's music for Nijinsky and his own pupil Elena Smirnova, who was graduating that year. Fokine conducted his polemics on the basis of the classical dance. But in this he selected only those elements that could transmit the idea of flitting to and fro, of ceaseless flight within a composition of vertical, parallel, suffusing, and intersecting lines. Tantalizing in her gypsy beauty, Smirnova seemed to be a real butterfly, wild and exotic. Nijinsky appeared as a marvelous and mysterious creature, a butterfly–phoenix that, in patches of light and shade, by trees or by water, constantly changed its color. Without touching each other, they advanced and retreated in flight; in coming together, they wove circles, only to part once again and to delineate more clearly their aerial lines in every direction of the stage.

In 1907 Obukhov himself decided to put on a demonstration of his student, thinking that no one knew Nijinsky's talent better than he. He judged from the position of an academic dancer and, consequently, selected what he deemed the apogee and boundary of this kind of dancing.

The end-of-school production took place on 15 April 1907.

According to the reviews, Nijinsky "danced with everyone throughout the entire spectacle,"[22] including his part in the ballet *Salanga,* a monotonous production by Kulichevskaya to Schenck's monotonous music. The praise he received was of a very general kind. Critics wrote that he was distinguished by his "extraordinary elevation" and his "great ballon" and that his "entrechats and pirouettes are bold and pure: he does them with ease." [23] Critics even hinted that here at last was a replacement for the "awfully heavy cavaliers in the present ballet company." [24] Nothing more definite could be said of the Lightning variation from *The Magic Mirror* or of the pas de trois from *Paquita* and other numbers. It was the teacher, not the pupil, who earned most of the praise. The reviewers declared the end-of-school production to be an "absolute triumph for Mr. Obukhov, teacher of the male section in the Theater School." [25]

Anyway, even if Nijinsky did dance "with everyone," he certainly did not dance in everything. This time Obukhov did not let him join Fokine. Not because Obukhov was jealous, but because, like other adherents of academism, he observed Fokine's latest experiments with some misgivings. Fokine was leaving tradition dangerously far behind. In February, for example, he had presented Shcherbachev's ballet *Eunice* for a charity production. In this he had implemented his beloved theme of antiquity by using "antique" (à la Semiradsky and Alma-Tadema) dance movements and dress. So Obukhov was afraid that Fokine might make Nijinsky, the pride and joy of his classical method, dance barefoot or do grotesque tricks. For this he let Fokine have Rosai.

At that time Fokine had been digging around in various scenarios that the administration had shelved, and he had come up with something the artist Benois had once proposed and with music already prepared by the young composer Nicolas Tcherepnin. The scenario was called *Le Pavillon d'Armide*, but Fokine extracted from it only one episode, calling it *Le Gobelin Animé*. An antique tapestry, on which are "embroidered" the figures of Armida and Rinaldo surrounded by their suite, comes to life and then, after a parade of dances, returns to its former immobility. This plot contained nothing unusual. Since time immemorial, paintings and statues had been coming to life on the ballet stage. But the dances themselves, even the classical ones, were rather disturbing, thanks especially to the erosion of conventional forms and the exceptional character of their introductions and finales.

As for the dance of the buffoons led by Rosai—well, Obukhov, when he saw it, was very glad that he had not given Nijinsky to Fokine. The buffoons made such patterns on stage with their dances in squatting position, they made such jumps, bending their knees

52

Graduates of the Imperial Theater School, 1907. Left to right:
A. Erler, V. Nijinsky, L. Goncharov, A. Khristapson, G. Rosai, V. Bocharov.

and hitting the floor with them straight on, they coiled themselves
up like snakes and made such somersaults through the air, that the
result could only be detrimental to a classical dancer. Rosai, in particular, did the most incredible stunts.

The dance of the buffoons eclipsed the dances of Armida (Elizabeta Gerdt, a rather delicate girl, blond like her father) as well as those
of Nijinsky in the remaining part of the spectacle. At the end of the
dance, the hall echoed with shouts of "Encore!" Rosai lost his head,

forgot to take a bow, and, stupidly, got stuck on stage in the midst of other, even less experienced buffoons. When he recovered from his state of shock, Rosai swaggered in front of Nijinsky. Inwardly, he was very angry: Nijinsky seemed to be as indifferent to another's success as he was to his own.

Nijinsky was not troubled by the trivial business of rivalry, and it never occurred to him to be envious of anyone, but he was worried by the responsibility of his new position. His student days were over. They had ended on that day in May when, to the voice of one of the clerks emphasizing each capital letter, he had written: "Having completed the entire course in the Imperial St. Petersburg Theater School (Ballet Department), I have the honor to submit a most humble petition that the Office of the Imperial Theaters appoint me to active service as a dancer in the ballet troupe. *Vaslav Nijinsky.*" [26]

2

NIJINSKY WAS "APPOINTED" TO THE IMPERIAL THEATERS at 780 rubles a year, and it was made clear that he was being allocated such a generous salary "because of outstanding talents for dancing." [1] He left it to his mother to work out how the two of them could live on this salary. After paying the landlord of their tenement house and the local storekeepers, nothing was left of the 65 rubles at the beginning of each month. Moreover, since he had given in his official uniform, he had to dress so as not to degrade his rank as an artist of the Imperial Theaters. And next year, 1908, Bronislava would also be graduating and would also need a complete wardrobe. But while his sister promised to be an excellent dancer, she would receive a niggardly salary. Come autumn, one might secure a few private pupils—the aristocrats and rich bourgeois families of St. Petersburg regarded foreign languages, music, and dancing as essential attributes of a good upbringing. But autumn was still a long way off.

The Nijinskys spent the summer in the city. Their apartment, which gave out on a back courtyard, was rather dark. But it remained cool when the days were oppressive and dusty. In the evenings the walls of the houses gave off the heat that had accumulated over the day, and one could take a breath of fresh air and throw off the sticky limpness only by going to the Neva. Vaslav used to go down to the water, sit on the granite steps, and look long at the tugboats pulling along whole caravans of barges or at the seagulls that had flown inland. The sun would set downstream, in the harbor, and the white night would descend. Then everything seemed to lose its color, but could be seen distinctly in every detail. Sounds took on a clarity and fullness—the whistle of a tugboat, voices on the barges, the footsteps of an occasional passerby. A wind might spring up and then subside, bringing the fragrance of the lilac that bloomed behind the iron fence of the Marble Palace. Perched on the steps, this young man in his cheap suit looking like a sack of potatoes could have been a small-time

Julia Sedova

civil servant or a shop assistant. Shivering, he would get up and disappear in the direction of the Lebiazhy Canal.[2]

In the mornings Nijinsky went off to practice, repeating in solitude the lessons he had learned from Obukhov. Later in the day the dancers would appear in the rehearsal hall. After doing warm-up exercises, they would study certain numbers under Kulichevskaya's supervision. Nijinsky used to install himself at the back so as to finish his exercises to the music of their dances. He tried to get away quickly since he sensed his alienation and awkwardness among people who were on such close terms with each other, even though some of them looked at him in an affable manner.

Once, when he was still doing his battements tendus while holding onto the barre, a dancer came in. She had a long, ugly face, and her proportions were not exactly elegant. With a smile and a quick nod of her head, she also took hold of the barre. Nijinsky immediately appreciated her serious style of work. This was Julia Sedova, one-time student of Cecchetti, who, as rumor would have it, had learned the secrets of his virtuosity. At this very moment she was doing everything in fast tempi: she stretched and bent her legs accurately and forcefully, pirouetting, moving skillfully from one pose to another, checking her movements with great enthusiasm in the mirror.

Nijinsky caught the rhythm of her exercises. He did not notice that he was already repeating several unfamiliar motions in flight after her. And he found it quite in order when, without stopping, she shouted at him in the mirror to "hold his back." Sedova made a preliminary demonstration of the next combination (a short adagio in the center of the hall) with her hands, accompanying this with a patter of French terms. At the end of the class, both of them were covered in sweat, having finished with sixteen quick, vigorous jumps. She went to the windowsill, where earlier she had thrown a spare pair of shoes. She then proposed that they try partnered adagio.

While she was changing shoes, Kulichevskaya and the pianist came over. Nijinsky took his towel from the barre, rubbed himself down, threw the towel over his shoulders, and started to go. But he was stopped.

A few minutes later Kulichevskaya was demonstrating to the new partners their future dance. She was not striving for originality.

57

The Krasnoselsky Theater. (*right, above*) The foyer. (*right, below*) The auditorium.

Nijinsky and Sedova, to the music of a waltz by Waldteufel, were now supposed to represent . . . butterflies. This number was something of a pastiche of the Legat and Fokine dances—less restrained than the Legat but less stylized than the Fokine.

This was exactly what the audience of the Krasnoselsky Theater wanted. The ballet program of this theater included a piece called "game between two butterflies," designated in French as *Jeux des Papillons.* In the summer months troops on maneuvers were billeted in Krasnoe Selo. The most diverse uniforms decorated the stalls, from lieutenants to generals; and the theater garden had witnessed the start of many romantic intrigues—the most historic of which was the affair between Mathilde Kschessinska and the emperor, which had begun when he was still the heir to the throne. Kschessinska no longer danced there, but other stars from the Mariinsky often appeared. The Sedova–Nijinsky number was so successful that the unenvious Legat included this "poetic picture" (to quote one reviewer) in his later production of the ballet *La Source.*

58

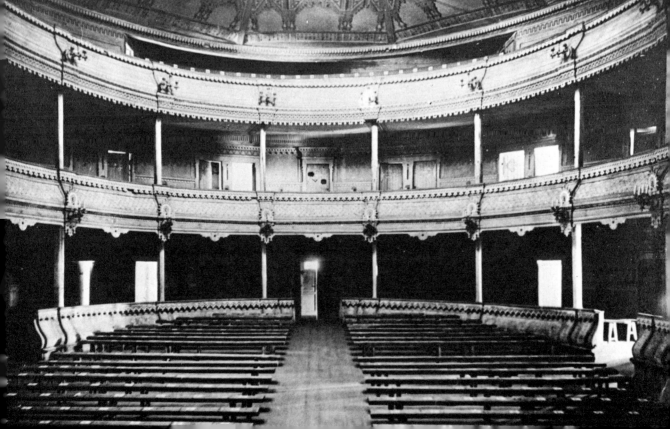

Nijinsky, in Krasnoe Selo, 1907.

The concerts in the Krasnoselsky Theater helped the Nijinsky finances. In the fall Vaslav procured a few private pupils. He was as busy as he had been at school, although he was now free of the tedious routine there. In the mornings, after a hurried breakfast, the young artist of the Imperial Theaters would set off on foot for Theater Street. After his class with Legat came rehearsals. Their schedule was put up at the entrance to the rehearsal hall, and practically every day Nijinsky found his name alongside the title of some new number and the name of a new partner. Danseuses vied with one another to dance with this much desired cavalier, even though they knew beforehand that the lion's share of any success would fall to him. And the cavalier, for his part, did not object to any of his assignments, unlike others who said this partner was too big for them, that one was too heavy, or a third one was just lazy and regarded her partner as a mere prop. Nijinsky did not express any particular feelings regarding the roles themselves. He would look through the schedule, turn on his heel, and go off alone, ignoring anybody who wished to fall in with him.

On 17 September, at the beginning of the season, Nijinsky appeared with the younger sister of George Kiaksht—the mischievous Lydia, blessed with golden hair and a peaches-and-cream complexion. They danced in the last act of *Paquita*, performing a pas de deux that had been inserted. The next day one of the leading critics of the St. Petersburg ballet, Valerian Svetlov, declared Nijinsky to be a dancer "without equal on our stage," implying, of course, that this stage was also without equal.[3] A week later Nijinsky danced another pas de deux, this time in *La Fille Mal Gardée*, with Smirnova, his partner from the previous year. And again the critics gave him first place.

October came and Nijinsky saw his name in the rehearsal list alongside the names of the ballerina Mathilde Kschessinska and the young soloist Tamara Karsavina.

The same age as Lydia Kiaksht, Karsavina was appearing in her sixth season on stage. Nijinsky remembered how two or three years earlier Karsavina had come into his class at the end of the Obukhov lesson. Obukhov had been demonstrating an intricate combination of leaps and tours, but the boys, as if by command, had fixed their gaze on the girl in the doorway. Dark-complexioned, although pale, with fine features and velvety hazel eyes, Karsavina was pinning up a thick lock of her dark chestnut hair that had come loose. As it turned out, Karsavina differed from the neat, fashion-conscious women such as Egorova in that she was always pinning something up or adjusting something (perhaps the straps of her bodice had come loose or her headdress had been badly pinned on), and sometimes she almost didn't finish a dance because a ribbon had broken on one of her shoes. But her carelessness in her toilette did not detract from her languid beauty; on the contrary, it accentuated it.

Nijinsky could also remember how Obukhov had said something not very flattering about the mental ability of his pupils, and quickly regained their attention. The boys diligently recommenced their leaps. Karsavina had gone up to Obukhov and, resting her gaze on Nijinsky, suddenly exclaimed something under her breath. Probably, she had asked something about him because Obukhov asked everyone to move to the side; he then made Nijinsky do leaps and pirouettes. No doubt, she thought him a fool when, with eyes downcast, he muttered something incoherent in response to her words of praise.[4]

He was silent now, too, as he and Karsavina rehearsed the "peasant pas de deux" from the first act of *Giselle*. But she was engrossed in the difficulty of her part. She did not take easily to the polished,

bravura phrases of the duet, and when she had to grasp Nijinsky's arm so as to preserve her pose on point after the pirouettes, she kept missing. Nor could they come to a proper standstill, because she either fell on to her partner or collapsed to the side of him, no matter how much he tried to catch her and to maintain her balance in the required pose. Even when they made their entrance on stage, they were not sure that everything would be all right.

They were greeted with applause. Karsavina had many admirers, especially among students; and the more the critics scolded her for her soft, "marmaladelike" points and her slovenly dancing, the more zealous her admirers became. The adagio passed off tolerably well and without breaks; and then, after they had taken their bows and Nijinsky had carried Karsavina off stage, he ran out from the upper wing for his variation. Unexpectedly, the audience began to applaud again and continued to do so for a long time. After a series of leaps, now sparkling in their virtuosity, now smooth and fluent, the dancer spun to a frenzied tempo in a pirouette and then, gradually slowing down, stopped. He flung open his arms and smiled to the people on the other side of the footlights, people who were now brought close to him by the power of his art.

The pas de deux came to an end. Nijinsky bore Karsavina away into the wings, bowed to her, and installed himself behind the assistant régisseur in order to see the first act through to the end.

Giselle was danced by Pavlova. Her Albrecht (Legat) seemed very prosaic. But, in love with a dream, this Giselle mourned not his betrayal but the destruction of a dream. Biting his fingernails, Nijinsky saw how Giselle sank to her knees and how, enveloped in the mist of her tutu, she lost consciousness and dropped the imaginary flowers. He looked and knew already that, just like this, she would bend her head absent-mindedly, would take up the sword by its blade, would draw a strange pattern in the earth with its hilt and then flee from its convolutions, taking herself deeper and deeper into the recesses of insanity. Nijinsky sensed that beyond the threshold of death the tragic fate of this Giselle would prove to be a new-found freedom. He divined correctly: in the second act the young Pavlova was a radiant spirit, and Albrecht's sorrow was for her only the echo of something long forgotten.

63

Tamara Karsavina

But Nijinsky had to forgo the second act. He had to go home and go to bed early. Tomorrow would be the rehearsal with Kschessinska. The prima ballerina had been back from abroad only five days, but she had immediately announced her intention of dancing with Nijinsky and was annoyed that he was delayed by his rehearsals with Karsavina. She flashed her pearl-white teeth, shrugged her shoulders, stamped her elegantly clad foot, and said that actually it was all the same to her—she was in excellent form and could dance right now, but Nijinsky needed two weeks to learn such a large number of dances.

And there were indeed a lot of dances. Billboards for the 28 October performance advertised, in addition to the well-worn *Fille Mal Gardée*, the première of the ballet *The Prince Gardener* (production by Kulichevskaya). Nijinsky was listed as Kschessinska's partner in both ballets.

The régisseur warned Nijinsky that Mathilde Felixovna always appeared on time.

The mistress of the St. Petersburg ballet observed this "courtesy of kings" and set in motion her exceptional charm in order to subjugate her partner, this shy young boy.

She had just turned thirty-five, but her carefully tended femininity showed no sign of fading. She loved to test out her charms and included in her list of "victims" two grand dukes and many momentary whims and infatuations. Theretofore she had encountered inattention only once. A few years earlier the theater had been graced by a new official for special commissions—Sergei Pavlovich Diaghilev. He was just her age, and he attracted her with his noble elegance, the ironic twinkle in his eye, and the gray lock in his brilliantined hair. Her interest was immediately noticed in the ballet company; and, as always, people tried to intensify it either by flattery or by provocation. However, "Chinchilla," as the dancers called Diaghilev because of the gray strand in his dark hair, did not venture beyond the boundaries of an elegant but cold amiability during the short time that he worked in the theater office.

It was no good expecting affability from Nijinsky either. He was awkward and timid with everyone, even with the energetic Smirnova, whom he knew from school. The reputation, the savoir-vivre of the omnipotent Mathilde Felixovna seemed to mean nothing to him.

Needless to say, this young man simply aroused her sporting instinct. For the main reason for her successes in life was not her beauty (many women were more beautiful than she) and not even her charm, but her inexhaustible energy. She had more than enough for her adventures as a fashionable socialite and for her high professional demands as a dancer. Nobody could reproach Kschessinska for using her connections dishonorably on stage. As a "ballerina assoluta"—that is, "beyond conventions"—she was the first to merit this title. She had dislodged all the Italian ballerinas who had imported the term and had mastered all the secrets of their dance. And now she imagined that this sensational young dancer would lend support to her own brilliance and virtuosity.

Nijinsky disappointed her by his lack of apparent artistry, just as he had disappointed others. But Kschessinska was bold and could afford to take risks. It was thanks to her that Nijinsky moved from being the kind of dancer whose dancing is instrumental, like a violin solo, and became a ballet actor. Instead of performing like these dancers who always did variations of the same combinations of leaps and gyrations, he now had to embody a character, however simple it might be.

To Nijinsky, Kschessinska danced her first scene in *La Fille Mal Gardée*, not merely "marking" the movements at half strength but doing them "full out," in complete earnestness. She enjoyed rediscovering the traditional but beloved details of her character Lise, "sly rogue Lise," as one reviewer said. She watered her flowers from an imaginary watering can, she scattered grain for invisible chickens, she pretended to caress her mother. Kschessinska's Lise seemed to be improvising all this right on the spot. She was aroused by youth, by an abundance of vigor and strength, by her impatient expectation of her sweetheart.

Nijinsky watched attentively. But the more excited Kschessinska became in her role, the more entertaining her pranks, the sadder his expression became. Controlling her vexation, she suddenly declared that, evidently, either he didn't understand what was going on or he didn't like it. Hanging his head, he quietly responded that, on the contrary, he understood everything and liked it. Kschessinska raised her eyebrows and suddenly burst out laughing, a natural, ringing

66

laugh—as if Kschessinska, who could desire and attain her goals with such ease, could understand that reverse reaction was one of the properties of the character of her strange partner.

Charlie Chaplin also possessed this quality and he discovered it when he made the acquaintance of Nijinsky. Both men tacitly understood each other. But this occurred later on. It was not for Kschessinska to comprehend this, for her art was the consummation of the sorrowless perfection of nineteenth-century ballet. And there was no reason why she should have. Everything went off quite well as soon as the awkward youth assumed his duties as partner. Immediately he changed into Colin, Lise's heartfelt friend who had been rejected by her mother because he was poor. His Colin was less enterprising than Kschessinska's sprightly heroine, which is as it should have been, but in the actual performance his spontaneity delighted the audience.

Balletomanes smiled complacently when Lise, in the scene they knew so well, discovered her sweetheart among the sheaves of grain scattered on stage. The duet came off very nicely and retained its harmony both in the moment of alarm, in the embarrassed estrangement between the two pastoral lovers, and in the passage introducing the declarations of love, the timid embraces, and the dreams of a future family. As far as the dances were concerned, Kschessinska's new partner responded to the rhythm of her energetic, audacious, and forthright movements. He responded to her and at the same time surpassed her in some way, managing a precise combination of dancing and acting. At least, the next day the critics vied with each other in declaring him to be a "gifted mimic"; they admired his "ballon and the brilliance of his extraordinary entrechat huit" in *The Prince Gardener* where there was really nothing that had to be acted.[5] One critic summed it all up. He called Nijinsky the hero of the spectacle and observed (diplomatically in the plural) that "ballerinas might be vexed with him—with the fact that he secures our exclusive attention through his own success."[6]

But Kschessinska was not annoyed. With a roguish smile, she flaunted a long Polish sentence, and her words of praise uttered in the language of his childhood caused Nijinsky to start. There and then the prima ballerina proposed a trip to Moscow.

They danced in the Bolshoi Theater on 2 December 1907. Danc-

(*left*) Sergei Diaghilev

(*below, left*) Leon Bakst

(*below, right*) Alexandre Benois. Drawing by Konstantin Somov.

ing a piece set to a Chopin nocturne by Kulichevskaya, they appeared at a benefit performance for the Bolshoi corps de ballet. Thanks to Duncan, Chopin had become popular in the ballet world. Fokine and Gorsky had already used his music a number of times. Kschessinska also wanted to show herself as a Romantic dancer, an image that Pavlova had recently revived in Fokine's *Chopiniana.*

Kschessinska cherished other dreams. On 29 November, the day of their departure, the *St. Petersburg Gazette* advertised their Moscow tour and, in addition, announced that "the young dancer will, in all probability, go with the ballerina to Paris in February." But Kschessinska was forced to go to Paris with Legat because of a division that occurred in the ballet company and, as a result, she and her young partner became members of opposing factions. This is how it happened:

Since the beginning of the season the company had been working on rehearsals for *Le Pavillon d'Armide.* After the success of *Le Gobelin Animé* the administration had recollected Benois' forgotten scenario. It had been forgotten on purpose. The dispute of 1901, when the then director, Prince Volkonsky, had allowed his *miriskusniki* friends to work on the production of *Sylvia,* was still vividly remembered.[7] At the time they had so infiltrated everywhere that the official routine had begun to disintegrate. Apart from Benois, who had wanted to revive the Delibes ballet, a whole crowd of his artist friends had also been involved in *Sylvia:* Bakst, Lancéray, Korovin, Serov. And, of course, Benois' closest adviser was Diaghilev. According to the other officials, Diaghilev had become quite conceited after his clever escapade with *The Annual of the Imperial Theaters.* Until he came along, this official organ had published lists of companies, repertoires, information concerning anniversaries, and obituaries. Diaghilev, assisted by his same allies, had turned this functional publication into a luxuriously illustrated journal, inviting high-brow writers to contribute. He had become renowned the length and breadth of St. Petersburg. But when he interfered in the *Sylvia* production, even the good-natured Prince Volkonsky had suspected that this intriguer was aspiring to usurp his position. He had requested that Diaghilev leave *Sylvia* alone, and Diaghilev had responded by threatening to resign from *The Annual.* The affair had been discussed in the highest places and, unexpectedly, had ended with the order for Diaghilev's dismissal. Moreover, in accordance with the Third Clause, he had been divested of the right to apply for government service.

Since then, Diaghilev had been fantastically busy. Essentially, he was an upstart, some kind of "noblette" from Perm, to use the words of Baron Fredericks, minister with responsibility for the Imperial Court and for affairs of Russian art. But Diaghilev had arranged vernissages of antique portraits one day and of Finnish artists the next; he had. taken a huge exhibition to Paris and had immediately gained recognition among its urbane elite; and then, in 1907, he had turned into an impresario and had established, again in Paris, his concerts of Russian music. The venerable baron could perceive in all this a sort of general displacement, but exactly what kind of displacement he would have been hard put to explain.

However, Diaghilev, on the other hand, really didn't care much about the state theaters any more. After Petipa had been fired, the ballet in the Mariinsky had really become the victim of stereotype. Since the production of *Die Puppenfee,* which Nicolas Legat and his late brother had put on, Legat had been composing ballets that were becoming more and more tedious. So Krupensky, who was in charge of the St. Petersburg Office of the State Theaters, proposed that Fokine should choreograph *Le Pavillon d'Armide* seeing that he (Fokine) had done such a good job with the principal class at the ballet school.

Everything got off to a good start. The administration made no objections to the Benois designs, even though to all intents and purposes these would require a substantial outlay. Fokine presented his list of performers: the principal roles were to go to Kschessinska and Gerdt. From the very first rehearsal the company manifested unprecedented enthusiasm.

But this made the officials take heed. Any enthusiasm that transcends the boundaries of official propriety always threatens to disturb the given routine. But the main trouble was that in the wake of Benois all his friends started to infiltrate the theater; and, when work on the ballet was transferred from the rehearsal hall to the stage, lo and behold, there, sitting in an orchestra seat, was Diaghilev.

There was almost a repeat of the *Sylvia* episode. The chief of theater police, acting on Krupensky's orders, demanded that Diaghilev leave the rehearsal at once, which caused Benois to make a scene. What happened to his intelligence and diplomacy! Not very tall, already rather portly, he pulled off his pince-nez (for some strange reason) and, blinking short-sightedly, white with rage, he blurted out something very indecent about the toadies in the state theaters. Krupensky listened, smirking into his magnificent Assyrian beard. Although he was unable to cancel the imminent première, he began gradually to create all kinds of hindrances. Not in vain did people in the theater say of him that he had a knack for intrigue. It seemed that everything was destined to go wrong right up to the disaster at the dress rehearsal.

Gerdt started to be capricious. Either he was really convinced that he was too old for the part of the young Vicomte or he sensed a change in the air. In any case, he had not quarreled with the Office of the State Theaters for many a day. Fokine only just managed to persuade him to appear at least in the première. But one week before the première Kschessinska renounced her part and renounced it categorically. She had long been displeased that Armida did not have a single variation and that even her entrance was not particularly effective. And now everyone was whispering about it.

Benois and Fokine were in the director's box when Kschessinska dropped in rather casually and, like a bolt from the blue, told them she was resigning. Perhaps on her way out she heard Fokine calling her a she-devil. And she probably flaunted her boldness. Like a fuse burning toward a barrel of gunpowder, people began to talk about imminent cancellation of the spectacle.

But Benois and Fokine had scarcely collected their thoughts when into their box came, or rather, flew, Pavlova. Squinting at the two sorrowful figures, she went round them, moved aside the chairs with an impatient and ardent gesture and sat down on the guardrail. Against the background of the dark theater shrouded in dust covers, she appeared as a lithe and lissom silhouette. Neither asking outright nor offering advice, she implied to "Misha" (Fokine) that the part of Armida should be hers. Within moments the news flashed through the theater that "Annushka" had stolen a march on Mathilde Felixovna.

Thereafter, rehearsals proceeded without hindrance. But the authorities were becoming more and more stingy with regard to the costumers. Benois had actually managed to spend more on a one-act ballet than the usual four-act production cost. Krupensky moaned about this and forbade the dancers to don their costumes until the dress rehearsal for fear they might get frayed. Consequently, at the dress rehearsal the dancers couldn't recognize their partners in their intricate wigs and headdresses; they confused everything and distorted the patterns of the staging and of the dances. The administration agreed to postpone the première for one week, from 18 to 25 November, only after Benois, in an interview with the *St. Petersburg Gazette,* had angrily explained that "a certain person in government uniform" had done everything in his power to ruin the ballet.[8] Then the administration had the last laugh by billing *Le Pavillon d'Armide* as a makeweight for *Swan Lake*. So only at midnight did the curtain finally rise on the new ballet.

In the semidarkness of a mysterious pavilion in which everything was in Louis XIV style, flashes of lightning outside the windows and the candelabra being carried by a footman illuminated a tapestry. Beneath this tapestry stood a clock adorned with the figures of Cupid and Saturn. The master, an old Marquis, appeared behind his servant. With a grand and exquisite gesture he bade the Vicomte René, caught unawares by the storm, to come in. The traveler eventually settled down to sleep.

Hardly had he closed his eyes when the gilded Cupid (Love) and Saturn (Time) began to move, and after a momentary duel Time yielded his scythe to Love. To the melodic music of the chimes the tiny spirits of the clock advanced forth from the little door. In white tunics and carrying little lanterns, they covered the stage with the regular pattern of their "tick-tock" dance and bathed it in a brilliant light. They conducted the hero into a dream of a courtly festival in some bygone age.

Ladies, cavaliers, captive knights (looking like Louis XIV in *Le Ballet de la Nuit*) descended from the tapestry and surrounded the beautiful Marquise dressed in the costume of the fateful enchantress Armida. The old Marquis, escorting her, was now transformed into a personage resembling a grand seigneur from the court of the Sun King or perhaps Armida's father, the magician Hidraot in Tasso's poem. Just behind them appeared a being who seemed to embody a fairy-tale dream from the masquerades of the seventeenth century: a young man whose cheeks were still touched with the bloom of childhood, whose sweet smile countered the perplexing languor of his eyes, whose movements were made with cunning grace. To judge by appearances, he was the page of the Marquise, pampered and beloved by her. The mother-of-pearl hues of his costume echoed the colors of her own attire; he wore a turban decorated with feathers and a velvet ribbon about his neck, tied, perhaps, by his mistress.

In the Benois box the artist's wife recognized Gerdt as the Vicomte René de Beaugency and was lost in admiration of Pavlova (Armida). When she saw the young page, she asked her husband who he was.

Costume design for Armida's Page, by Alexandre Benois.

(*left*) Anna Pavlova as Armida in *Le Pavillon d'Armide*.

(*below*) Nijinsky as the White Slave in *Le Pavillon d'Armide*. The role is also known as the Favorite Slave and as Armida's Page.

Alexandre Nicolaevich did not answer Anna Karlovna at once.

He was recalling how the atmosphere of the rehearsal hall had so delighted him at that first rehearsal that Fokine had shown him. He remembered how the daylight, falling from the double windows, made the tarletan of the girls' skirts transparent and frothy, how the unpainted faces of the dancers had seemed so fresh, so innocent. He remembered being introduced to the company, talking with Kschessinska and Gerdt and making the acquaintance of the young Nicolas Soliannikov to whom Fokine had given the part of the Marquis. He also recalled how Fokine from afar had pointed out a young graduate from the school, the "miracle dancer" Nijinsky, who was standing not with the dancers but with the pupils practicing "clocks" and "little nigger boys." He had then seemed very ordinary and uninteresting. Later on, in the wake of the confusion just before the première and the problems caused by the administration, he had quite forgotten about Nijinsky, to whom Fokine insisted on giving the part of Armida's White Slave. And now Benois could not believe his eyes. He saw Nijinsky, the "choreographic essence of the Rococo period." Such was his belated response to his wife's question.

Meanwhile the action of the ballet was developing with elegance and ease. Crowds of little black boys teemed out of the traps on the sides on the stage. With their white costumes, white turbans, and huge fans of white feathers, they scattered "like a blizzard of hailstones" [9] into Armida's dazzling suite. And now Armida herself began her dance, devised as an aria from Gluck's opera. In Pavlova's rendering, "Armida's Lament" for her lost love Rinaldo became a noble passion.

Then came the entrance of the masked witches, the demons, and the almehs from whom the fat sultan chased off his lustful slaves with his stick. Rosai, protagonist of the buffoons, brought forth applause. The audience had already immersed themselves in this whimsical and illusory Orient of a bygone France when the young page, dressed in the costume of Armida's Slave, invited two entrancing ladies to dance.

Bold but timid, naïve and yet the possessor of some secret knowledge, this Cherubino of the seventeenth century was indifferently attentive to both ladies, for he danced to entertain his mistress. And then, tired of the two beauties, he left them, smiled at his mistress, and prepared to dance alone.

75

Fokine, who had deciphered the character of this "miracle," knew how to prepare the audience for him. Nijinsky, bending his fingers affectedly and spreading his hands just slightly above the festoons on the skirt of his hip-length coat, raised one hand above his head and with the other made a circular gesture on his breast. And then, suddenly stretching his legs as taut as a bow, he detached himself from the floor and flew from one side of the stage to the other. And back again. Playfully he executed a few varied pirouettes, which gradually dissolved into a series of courtly bows, and ended, as it were, by placing this madrigal-dance at the feet of Armida.

He was unreal. He was the embodiment of Benois' dream of the art of Versailles and Fontainebleau. It was a subtle and refined dream sprinkled with the golden dust of legends.

At the coda, the personages in masks crowded together. They executed a number of intricate figures and then formed a gigantic heart that beat rhythmically. Against this background Armida tied her scarf over the shoulder of her newly found Rinaldo, the Vicomte René.

The traveler awoke, startled by his dream. He prepared himself for the road, but on the threshold of the pavilion the old Marquis handed him the enchanted scarf that had been left by the fireplace, while Armida enigmatically smiled down at him from the tapestry.

It was one o'clock in the morning, but the audience was in no hurry to leave the Mariinsky hall, brilliant in its blue, gold, and crystal. Vladimir Arkadievich Teliakovsky, director of the Imperial Theaters, still stood to attention in his box as if on military parade. With two fingers of his right hand he clapped the palm of his left.

The artists took their bow in front of the curtain. Nijinsky let Pavlova and Gerdt go ahead of him and stood back so as to let them leave first. Each time Gerdt gave him a gracious smile, but Pavlova virtually ignored him. Unlike Kschessinska, she was no diplomat, and she was annoyed that this youth had had the greatest success. She would have been more justified in addressing her complaint to Fokine. He had been so afraid of breaking the action that after "Armida's Lament" he had ensured that the events ran without any interruption. But it was not the cause, but the effect, that hurt Pavlova's pride, and she didn't trouble herself with the details. So she exchanged kisses with the happy Fokine and, to his declaration that he would replace her partner Obukhov by Nijinsky in *Chopiniana,* she silently shrugged her shoulders.

Nijinsky received praise from other quarters. People kissed him, thumped him on the shoulders, shook his hand. But he had already assumed his pose of awkward absent-mindedness and remained silent to all the compliments. He didn't even notice that someone had shoved him a note. It said: "I would like to make your acquaintance. Would you agree to celebrate your success in a restaurant? My friends and I will be waiting for you at the stage door. *Prince Lvov.*"

Nijinsky's first thought was to run away. But as soon as he had stepped through the stage door (on the right wing of the theater building) into the square, a certain man moved away from the brilliant black sheen of his motor car and, barring the way, introduced himself: Prince Pavel Dmitrievich Lvov.

Nijinsky was wearing a short and modest overcoat with a velvet collar; confronted by the tall prince whose expensive fur coat was flung open to reveal an elegant dress-coat, he cut a very unprepossessing figure. Nijinsky began to stammer out that he was expected home and that he was not dressed for the occasion. But the prince, measuring him with his beautiful, but slightly goggling eyes, and speaking assuredly, slurring over his *r*'s, rejected all arguments. He would send word home right away. As for the proper attire—well, he had foreseen this difficulty and had therefore ordered a separate room.

And Nijinsky, who had just attained his first important success along the upward path of his breathtaking career, now took his first step toward the abyss—by submitting to the evil will of a man he did not know.

Prince Lvov belonged to the set of "gilded youth" who regarded not just St. Petersburg but the whole of Europe as a place for having fun and good times. This seducer of souls and bodies knew no limits to his aristocratic caprices. At the moment he passionately desired to patronize a new and flourishing talent, and so he initiated his new-found friend, the dancer Nijinsky, into the intoxicating delights of night clubs and restaurants. He bewitched him with the songs of gypsies; he introduced him to bored and idle ne'er-do-wells hungry for new pleasures; he showered him with gifts. He thus initiated him —and then declared arrogantly that he regarded him as just another of his toys. The cruel disdain of the prince—like that of the conjuror who nonchalantly drags the disemboweled Petrouchka along behind him, leaving his melting footprints in the snow of the Petersburg fairground—was a theme destined to take root in Nijinsky's biography.[10]

Nijinsky now arrived for his morning class in a smart cab and flung his fur coat into the hands of the waiting doorman. Nijinsky was now rarely at home, although he did move his mother into a comfortable apartment. And now, no longer so shy as restrained and silent, he avoided children.

Life in the theater went its normal course. Nijinsky danced in all the ballets although, as before, only in the interpolated numbers. And as before, the critics described him in the same words, whether he danced the Bluebird in *The Sleeping Beauty* (with Kiaksht or Egorova as Princess Florine), the pas de deux (with Karsavina) added to *The Little Humpbacked Horse*, the pas d'action in *La Bayadère*, in which he "excelled" himself in the variation, or the pas de trois in *Paquita*, in which he "flew like a bird" and "repeated the variation to the thunder of applause." [11]

His "safety valve" was his work with Fokine, who was now thinking of doing the ballet *Les Nuits d'Egypte* and a new version of *Chopiniana* for a charity performance. Two roles were set aside for Nijinsky. For the second one he was indebted to Pavlova, although at rehearsals she treated him with nervous detachment.

The previous year Fokine had produced *Eunice* and also a ballet set to music by Chopin. Fokine had introduced all his ideas about the era of the Romantic ballet into this twenty-minute spectacle. At the beginning the partners at a splendid Polish ball marched past to the sounds of a polonaise. The next episode recalled the ballet scenes in Meyerbeer's *Robert le Diable:* the black shadows of monks arose from their coffins and surrounded Chopin immersed in his music making, but the Muse protected him by summoning a crowd of radiant visions, the female dancers in their white, transparent tulle. The third scene was dedicated to the characteristic genre of the Polish wedding. In the fifth scene, a tarantella was danced against the background of Vesuvius. The fourth and shortest scene had the greatest success. Pavlova and Obukhov, dressed in designs by Bakst, had danced Chopin's waltz in C sharp minor. Pavlova had worn a long tutu with bodice and wings, the type seen in engravings of the 1830s that convey the aerial grace of Taglioni. Obukhov had on tights, a jacket of black velvet, and a white shirt with a dashing bow beneath the turn-down collar, just as Taglioni's aerial partner, Jules Perrot, used to wear. This dance now gave rise to the second *Chopiniana*.

Pavlova's hostility toward her new partner soon evaporated, thanks to Fokine's inspired enthusiasm and to the artistic sympathy that soon developed between her and Nijinsky. Everyone involved in the new *Chopiniana* obeyed Fokine without question. They did their best to fathom, to evoke, the mood of an engraving that reincarnated the Romantic ballet. Both Pavlova and Nijinsky were very sensitive to this mood. In some way they transcended the limits of what was required, but they did this in such a way that to Fokine, so meticulous in his needs, they seemed to carry out his wishes to perfection.

The administration granted the use of the Mariinsky for the charity performance for 8 March 1908. One could detect a certain ulterior motive in this. The season was coming to an end. Apart from *The Little Red Flower* (*Beauty and the Beast*), which no matter how much it was cut still turned out to be long and tedious, Legat had not offered the Theater Office any new projects. Fokine on the other hand, even though he was not regarded officially as a ballet master, had many schemes in reserve. But Teliakovsky did not trust this protégé of Benois. A charity performance did not commit the administration to anything, although at the same time any of its components could always be put into the repertoire later on.

Anyway, the spectacle brought together the cream of society. This was not just because the playbills advertised the names of Pavlova, Preobrajenska, Karsavina, Nijinsky, and Fokine himself, but because Fokine as ballet master was attracting a good deal of attention. True, the attitude toward him was not always one of delight. The supporters of the classical dance, the fans of Kschessinska, Trefilova, and Vaganova, spoke of his tendency to substitute an amorphous plastic art of pantomime for the priceless treasures of the dance. But Fokine's supporters rushed to his defense, proclaiming his innovations to be new insights into the Dionysia of antiquity.

At the première the atmosphere was the same as always. Those in the boxes displayed their indispensable and customary elegance. Ladies drifted in and, affecting a languid grace, sank into the chairs proferred by their escorts. They started up their trivial conversations. Down below on the orchestra level officers discussed the latest promotions and the results of the recent races. Civilians exchanged opinions on current politics or the outcome of a sensational trial connected with the misappropriation of millions of rubles. From the royal box the Grand Duke Andrei Vladimirovich inspected Kschessinska, covered in diamonds, sitting in the dress circle.

In contrast, people in the upper circle were arguing about modern art. Many condemned it, regarding the Fokine ballets simply as the latest affectation. But there were also defenders of the liberated dance, who recognized its democratic spirit in its clashes with the court ballet.

At last the lights went down. Riccardo Drigo took his place at the conductor's stand, tapped his baton, flourished it, and the orchestra started the polonaise.

The polonaise promised something picturesque and even pompous. But, as it turned out, this was merely a way of ingratiating the audience. If someone had accidentally switched on the light in that dim and darkened hall, surely only shadows would have been present.

The curtain went up to the sounds of a slow, pensive melody and revealed a youth surrounded by sylphs. Obedient to the music, aerial beings floated on the tips of their toes. Bathing in the reflections of the setting sun that gilded the romantic forest, they wove roundelays of fairy lightness; they arranged themselves like garlands of blossoms. The youth now vanished, now reappeared, smiling distractedly at their tender but persistent touches. At times he stretched one hand in pursuit of the ephemeral music and with the other brushed aside a lock of his long, shoulder-length hair that had fallen onto his forehead. The haze of his noiseless flight gleamed with the trills of his batterie; lightly he touched the earth and once again soared above the clusters of silent sylphs. In the midst of their immaterial games he himself seemed incorporeal. And at the most translucent, most ephemeral sounds of the music, he began his duet with the most ethereal sylph of all. She lured him and he listened to the whisper of her movements, and hesitated to respond to the mysterious call. And then, as if by chance, he was whirled away, pursuing her into

80

Karsavina and Nijinsky in *Chopiniana*.

Красавина и Фрикени

the reminiscences of an almost forgotten dream—only to return again and restore the weary sylphs to their original pose, as in an antique engraving.

As the curtain slowly fell, the audience was silent, wondering whether they might have imagined this phantom of Romantic dreams. And then, when the lights came on, they stirred and came to life.

In the smoking room, the balletomanes differed in their opinions. Some proclaimed that what they had seen was a symbol of their age and that, in fact, it was a terrifying one; unlike the Romantics, they said, we are no longer fighting for an ideal; we are simply escaping into illusions that do not belong to us. But not many people took heed.

The audience liked *Chopiniana*. Most people spoke of its brilliant design, of its clever composition with its authentic and exquisite groupings, of its smooth passages, and of the good taste with which Fokine had resurrected the image of the Romantic ballerina. They spoke of the danseuses who had sensed and conveyed a forgotten style with such delicacy. And, of course, they spoke of Nijinsky and his "divine dancing," of his "remarkable, truly remarkable artistic intuition!"

Only a few skeptics objected, saying that the Youth in *Chopiniana* was really a variation of the White Slave in *Armide*, little more than that. He had the same refinement, the same femininity in his appearance and general manner. Nijinsky was not really capable of doing much more than that.

But when the second ballet began, Nijinsky demonstrated his ability to undergo the most varied and unexpected transformations.

On stage was the decor of the Egyptian temple and palm trees from *Aïda*. But this didn't trouble anyone—any old thing did for charity performances. And although the overture did not contain anything that sounded particularly "Egyptian," the program did promise *Les Nuits d'Egypte* to music of Arensky. Neither did it seem to be nighttime. In the light of electric suns appeared Pavlova and Fokine, not at all reminiscent of personages normally thought of as "Egyptian" in the balletic meaning of the word. The straight lines of their eyebrows, their elongated, painted eyes, their thick hair carelessly done up with headbands, their bodies dark and sallow, enveloped in striped fabrics—all this promised something exotic.

And, indeed, this soon became apparent in the idyll of two children of nature on the verge of falling in love. Their dance was unrestrained yet stylized in accordance with the profile movements of "Egyptian" paintings. The ballet's theme evolved outside the canons of the concert format to which Petipa had accustomed his audiences. The temple priest blessed the idyll of Véronique and Amoun (as Pavlova and Fokine were billed), but the arrival of Cleopatra undid this. Captured by the queen's beauty, Amoun shot an arrow above the heads of her suite to her couch and, at the price of death, he was granted her favor.

The audience watched the ballet with great interest. It was all so exotic, just like the cinema. Moreover, the plot was so simple that no explanatory program notes were needed. At the height of the dances, which were really more like divertissements, Amoun ascended to the couch of the young and beautiful Cleopatra. In the program she was listed as Elizabeta Timé, a student from the drama classes. The slave girls provocatively drew the curtains across the couch. Meanwhile the divertissement continued.

Apart from the slave girls dancing with zithers and the Jewish girls with their tambourines, the divertissement also contained the dance of the veil by Cleopatra's favorite slaves—Preobrajenska and Nijinsky. Thitherto they had guarded every step of their queen, had attended to her toilette, and had lain on the cushions spread around the couch. Preobrajenska had graduated from ballet school the year of Nijinsky's birth and so she performed her part with unwarranted affectation. She probably didn't feel quite herself after exchanging her academic tutu for the tunic and sandals of a slave girl. Nijinsky, divested of his Romantic hero's costume, had now turned into a strange creature. The Slave of Cleopatra, like the Slave of Armida, seemed to be the caprice of his mistress, but he did not raise his eyes to his queen just as he would not have raised them to the statue of Isis. Affectionate but indifferent, he simply dwelled at the feet of his goddess like a pampered kitten sure of its master's favors. In graceful idleness a kitten will claw a paper dangled on a string, gradually entering the spirit of this hunting game. Similarly, this dark-skinned slave began to dance reluctantly, seizing the ends of the veil billowing from the slave girl's hands. And then, vexed at the twisting and turning of the light fabric, he himself began to leap and catch the veil. The dance ended and, like an animal bored of a game, he fondly stretched himself and lay down in his usual place.

The story progressed. Picturesquely, Amoun drank the poison from the cup and fell lifeless. A triumphal car harnessed with white horses from the Cavalry Barracks entered the stage. Gerdt, in the guise of Antony, presided over them. Cleopatra advanced carefully, putting her feet toe to heel and turning her left profile toward the footlights. She crowned Antony with laurels. Then, when the crowd of dancers and supers had parted in triumphal procession, Véronique appeared on the empty stage, bewailing the dead body of Amoun. But he came to life: the clever priest had substituted a sleeping potion for the poison.

Les Nuits d'Egypte provoked more arguments than *Chopiniana* did, and heated ones, too. Those who championed freedom in dance and movement were delighted, but the connoisseurs of strict classical ballet were indignant. Two such connoisseurs were Akim Lvovich Volynsky and Andrei Yakovlevich Levinson. They met often in the Mariinsky and impressed each other with their erudition and the closeness of their views on ballet. Both men respected the art of the classical dance, the poetry and music of its metaphorical images, and the severe beauty of its forms.

They now bumped into each other in the cloakroom. Volynsky had just been handed his coat, hat, and cane by the usher and, exasperated, was trying to sort it all out, not noticing that he was in the way. The dry, "Anglicized" Levinson (so very different from the rather careless and absent-minded author of the sensational books on Leonardo da Vinci and Dostoevsky) moved him to the side. They exchanged a couple of words about *Chopiniana*, a masterpiece from all viewpoints. But they condemned *Les Nuits d'Egypte* as so much trash, rubbish fit for a masquerade. They predicted that, once this fashion had passed, people would no longer go to see Fokine, and they said that, in any case, he had already begun to repeat himself. They both agreed that among the fossils of this "nightmare of two-dimensional dancing" (to quote Volynsky's angry exclamation)[12] the only natural dancers were Pavlova and Nijinsky.

At that time, neither Levinson nor Volynsky was writing about ballet. They began to do so four years later, in 1911, after the St. Petersburg theater had lost Nijinsky. But no doubt Levinson recalled Cleopatra's Slave later when he meditated on the "primordial" condition in certain of Nijinsky's characters and the extraordinary intuition with which the dancer expressed his conception of the primitive, beastlike serenity in man.[13] Volynsky, who preferred Nijinsky to the dancers who had replaced him, wrote, remembering his long-ago impressions of *Chopiniana* and *Les Nuits d'Egypte:* "Nijinsky's dances fuse with colors, reminiscent of the colors of the Umbrian Primitives. Their most delicate harmonies sound as an enigma."[14] Later on Volynsky was to write of the "quiver," the "confusion of forms," and the "intriguing chaos" that Nijinsky's body created as "it moved and flew."[15]

Time was marching on. Nijinsky became enmeshed ever deeper in his new, double life. No longer did the routine of his daily work erase the murk of sleepless nights. Gradually Nijinsky began to master his most difficult role—the role of a spoiled and fashionable actor. This morose adolescent, his mouth always half-open, his stare always vacant, donned the mask of a dandy. In a suit from the best tailor, with an impeccable haircut, Nijinsky became an interesting enigma. His silent lips pressed together suddenly revealed the serious expression of his mouth; they emphasized the exquisite modeling of his cheeks with their rather high cheekbones. Beneath the dark lines of his eyebrows delineating the purity and smoothness of his brow, his eyes gazed forth mysteriously, rarely admitting an intruder into their fathomless grief. His constraint gave way to an aristocratic reserve, although it never finally left him. He concealed it deep down, but it often showed forth in the convulsive tensions of his will. As it was, Nijinsky discovered his freedom only on stage.

The first season was coming to an end when, suddenly, Nijinsky received a letter from his father. As always, his father had been wandering from city to city, but after hearing about his son's success he suggested, unexpectedly, that they meet.

At the beginning of May 1908 Vaslav Nijinsky set off on his first and last journey by himself. He reached Nizhnii Novgorod by train, embarked on a Volga steamer, and, after a few hours, walked down the gangway onto the Kazan pier.

At home nobody ever mentioned Thomas Nijinsky, the man who had deserted his family, but Vaslav knew that he was not the only one who was thinking of him. Nijinsky's thoughts were complex. His grudge against his father had not passed with time. On the contrary, he had suppressed it and had driven it deep into his heart. At the same time, his father appeared to him in many different guises, all of them exotic and in the vortex of some fantastic dance. More and more his father had assumed the appearance of a fairy-tale hero.

A cheap hotel room. A middle-aged, weary man rose to meet his son. In his thickset, well-built figure, in the high cheekbones of his face the young Nijinsky could perceive the prototype of his own visage. But this man, his double, had been crushed by life.

Both men were embarrassed. With the father this expressed itself in a kind of patronizing familiarity; with the son, in an even greater reserve than usual. But then Vaslav experienced feelings quite unlike those that he had previously had when he thought about his father. These new feelings were also complex and contradictory. Beneath the affected tone and manner of Thomas Nijinsky, Vaslav could detect the fate of a provincial dancer, maybe a talented dancer, but one who knew well that everything was over and that none of his one-time hopes had come to fruition. Moreover, Vaslav suddenly realized that his father was jealous of him, jealous of this nineteen-year-old boy who had already attained heights of which he, the father, had long dreamed, but in vain.

Vaslav felt sorry for him and, for the first and last time in his life, he felt stronger than somebody else, felt a responsibility toward him. He did not lose his timidity, but his constraint left him. As he wandered about the town with his father, eating with him in a tavern, he faltered and blushed when he recalled the events of early childhood. Memories came thick and fast, and in the chaotic stream the figure of the dancer Thomas Nijinsky appeared unreal, apocryphal in his total perfection. But this was what Thomas Nijinsky needed—a man who could remember nothing but failure in life.

By the time their conversation touched on the silver chalice, the talisman that Thomas had given his son the day he was born, father and son were already friends. That evening, in the narrow passage between their two beds, Vaslav demonstrated the entrance and variation of Armida's Slave, while Thomas Nijinsky, expansive from the wine drunk in honor of the reunion, indicated his approval of both dance and dancer.

Vaslav Nijinsky left Kazan carrying a gift of cuff links decorated with Ukrainian gems—stones with a golden sparkle known by the name of "assembly of love." Vaslav also took away with him mixed feelings of attachment, perhaps even a sorrowful attachment, to his father. He had lost a hero whose image had remained with him during childhood and youth, but the wounds of old grievances had now healed. This all seemed irrelevant to the figure of the sad old man waving goodbye on the pier to the departing steamer.

Nijinsky never saw his father again, but in 1919, on the pages of his diary among a maelstrom of frenetic thoughts and images, the following fragment appeared: "My father died ten years ago." (In fact Thomas Nijinsky died in 1912.)

Fokine's ballets became part of the official repertoire. Besides these, Nijinsky also appeared in the same old roles of the traditional ballets. Toward the end of 1908 a rumor began to circulate among the ballet company about some kind of trip to Paris, and once again the names of Benois and Diaghilev were mentioned.

Diaghilev had become a notable figure among the Paris elite. In the summer of 1908 he had contrived to take to the capital of the world nothing more nor less than *Boris Godunov* with Chaliapin and the best forces of Russian opera. It had received rave reviews. Benois had then prompted Diaghilev to dilute opera with some ballet and, with this in mind, took him to see the Fokine productions one evening.

At thirty-five Diaghilev had put on some weight. His complexion had assumed a yellow-gray color and he had bags under his eyes, indicating a kidney disease. However, his whole bearing was even more impressive than before. Like a suzerain visiting a rather luckless vassal, Diaghilev entered the Mariinsky auditorium, whence he had twice been thrown out. His monocle flashing, he nonchalantly surveyed the audience.

Obviously, *Eunice* bored him stiff. But *Le Pavillon d'Armide* drew his attention. Diaghilev at once bestirred himself when Nijinsky, the White Slave, entered for his variation, circled his hands above the festoons on his coat, and smiled sweetly at his beautiful mistress.

After the performance the friends (Benois and Diaghilev) went to a cabaret. Seated at one of the tables, they drew up their program for the next season. Diaghilev proposed repeating *Boris Godunov* and acquainting Paris with *Ruslan and Ludmilla, Judith, Prince Igor,* and *Pskovitianka* (changing its name to *Ivan the Terrible*). He rejected *Eunice* absolutely, and a lot of things in the other ballets troubled him—first and foremost, the music. He repeated that, of course, Tcherepnin was a professional, but no more than that. Still, *Le Pavillon d'Armide* did have one positive property: it would be amusing to show the French their Versailles "as you see it, Shura."

But as it stands now (so their conversation went on), *Les Nuits d'Egypte* is not much better than *Eunice,* although the Paris Opéra doesn't even have that; its ballet is amazingly provincial. Whereas there are any number of historical plays and period pieces at other theaters. Well, why don't we shorten poor Arensky as much as we can, select some real music, and let Bakst invent his own version of Egypt, such an Egypt that people would realize what Russian painting can offer. In addition, we must throw out all this sham nonsense about Antony, the horses, and all the supers and make the finale a truly tragic one. We could interpolate a few more dances, for example— well, even Glazunov's bacchanal from *The Seasons.* And we might try out that banker's daughter for the role of Cleopatra. Levushka Bakst is always raving about her: you know her—Ida Rubinstein. We can leave *Chopiniana* as it is, but let's call it *Les Sylphides.*

The conversation dragged on until well after midnight. Blue cigar smoke wafted through the hall; the crystal chandeliers, reflected endlessly in the mirrors, seemed to push back the walls. The celebrities of St. Petersburg night life came and went on stage. An ugly singer suddenly began "A Merchant So Dashing Was Leaving the Fair" in a high-pitched, peasant woman's voice. A crowd of merrymakers passed the two friends. As Diaghilev quickly looked them over, his eye rested on a rather short young man who stepped with a soft, resilient gait but who seemed to keep himself aloof from the others. In the fantastic plans for his ballet tours Diaghilev, cool, calm, and collected, mentally set aside a place for this strange lad.

Diaghilev soon put his plans into action. He overcame what seemed to be insuperable barriers with a titanic persistence. This was one of the conditions of play, of an exciting game, which was his real vocation, even though he had not understood that before.

He smiled somewhat fastidiously as he remembered himself almost twenty years ago, the eighteen-year-old lad who had come up to St. Petersburg from Perm, from the provinces. He frowned and grew somber as he recalled the friendly indulgence that his relatives in the capital had shown toward him. That's how his cousin Dima Filosofov had met him, and Dima's friends, Shura Benois and Valechka Nouvel. It had never occurred to them that they were hurting his pride so much when they made what they considered to be innocuous jokes about his blissful state of backwardness or when they made subtle efforts to guide his immature taste. At that moment Diaghilev had set himself the aim of "showing" them—what, exactly, he really had no idea. But he had set to work with determination.

Life had tossed him about. He had taken singing lessons, but his voice, thank heavens, would have been suited only to salon romances (although by nature his voice was a free and unrestrained one). Then had come the composition class at the Conservatory of Music. What a good thing it was that Rimsky-Korsakov had declared that he would never make a good composer! Good because these blows of fate kindled, stimulated his ambition; they forged his determination into an iron will that, thitherto, he did not know he possessed.

But Diaghilev had been lucky in trivial things. He had decided to change his appearance, realizing that a striking appearance was a great incentive of his time. At first he wished to distinguish himself simply by this. There were no dandies in his circle of friends. On the contrary, in fact. Descendants from intellectual families of long standing, they respected modesty. It was really only Benois who loved fame, but he flaunted his scholarship and his artistic talent, not his outward appearance. So among themselves they now regarded Diaghilev as something of an upstart. He had seized on the idea of shocking people, like any "upstart" would. The gray lock in his hair, carefully brushed and darkened from brilliantine, the neatly trimmed moustache, the monocle and its chain that issued from a pocket in his impeccable tuxedo, the arrogant importance of his bearing so very different from the impetuous and open manner of the recent Sergei Diaghilev—all these things arrested attention.

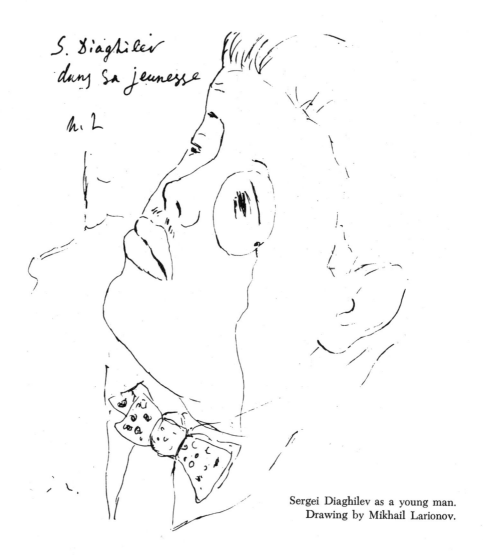

S. Diaghilev
dans Sa jeunesse

N. 2

Sergei Diaghilev as a young man.
Drawing by Mikhail Larionov.

Undoubtedly, he had become the antihero of the day, and he considered this his first real success. It was then that he had realized that if he himself had no real artistic talent, then he should become the patron of other talents. Only he would become a distinctive patron surpassing in grandeur all others, no matter whether they hailed from the nobility (which had discovered and ruined so many men of genius among its own serfs) or from the millionaire merchant-class. Both types operated only within the boundaries of their own country. He, Diaghilev, would destroy these boundaries. Not in vain did the family chronicle speak of the legend that the Diaghilevs were the illegitimate offspring of Peter the Great. Not without reason did Diaghilev himself bear some resemblance to Tsar Peter. Was he not destined, therefore, to open a new "window on Europe"? And through this window there would pour forth a stream of new artistic ideas, of new creative strength—but from Russia into Europe, not vice versa. In this lay Diaghilev's talent. A great talent that caused the destiny of art to suddenly change course.

As time went on Diaghilev's prospects had become ever more ambitious. As far back as 1897, after the success of his first painting exhibition, he had made a frank admission to Benois: "All my life [and, of course he was only just beginning life] I have done everything in defiance of everyone else. . . . Remember how you used to think me such a braggart? Then society began to attack me for my outward appearance, for my pomposity, for my being a dandy. And now it's reached the stage where everyone is regarding me as some kind of creep, as a profligate or businessman and God knows what else. I know this all too well. Even so, I play the dandy and continue to frequent the Noble Assembly. You'll say this is all bravado. Not so. There are two feelings at work here. First, a very human feeling of hostility (and no small measure of scorn) toward this world of ill-wishers; and second, a definite conviction that this stage will pass, providing success will enter my life. It is success and only success, my friend, that saves and redeem all. . . . My success will be that of a champion of these or those ideas. My party will convene—and, there you are, success, and I'm the best man in the whole world. . . . I do have a rather vulgar insolence and I am accustomed to telling people to go to hell. Which is not easy to do, but it's almost always beneficial. And that's as far as I go. There is a very, very small group of people before whom I cast off my boldness, before whom I bow my head in expectation of their judgment. Meaning Dima, you, and Valechka. It even seems to me that whatever I do, I do precisely for you or, rather, because of you. However you judge, so shall it be." [16]

A long and cruel confession. One is free to criticize one's own human qualities, but essentially, the frankness of this "confession" is illusory. Diaghilev renounced what he had written; inwardly he freed himself from the "judgment" of his friends and set out to conquer the "contemptible world." To this end he favored the image of the strong and solitary individual. He began to cultivate this fashionable image, but also clothed it in an unusual form. It was not a matter of external appearance. This was simply a means to an end. He saw power as his real aim and, quite correctly, saw art as the instrument of this power. In those days art, for many people, was seen to be an anchor of salvation, the only real value to which people could cling as they tried to escape the unstable and inconstant realities of life. He resolved to test the limits of his strength and to attain the height of art in its various principles. And then on high, rejoicing in his proud solitude, he would create; he would change the course of art; he would guide talent and nurture taste.

Thenceforth he saw that he had not been mistaken and that he had not overestimated himself or his audacious schemes.

For his jump forward he had to take a step back. Diaghilev's apartment on the Fontanka Quay (no. 11, opposite the Sheremetiev Palace) once again witnessed the rebirth of his group of accomplices. They all acknowledged his leadership. Diaghilev began his enterprise in grand style; he was intrepid, had no interest in getting rich, and grudged neither his own nor other people's money. He knew how to secure money by infecting the most uninspired people with his fantastic schemes, and sometimes he used sources quite unrelated to art. So it was right now. He embarked on a grandiose "negotiation," as Diaghilev himself said jokingly, alluding to Chichikov, the hero of Gogol's novel *Dead Souls*. The Grand Duke Vladimir Alexandrovich, who had financed *Boris Godunov* of the year before, now promised some of the money for the new enterprise. Diaghilev intended to get the outstanding, and greater, amount from a certain manufacturer of galoshes. This fellow was certainly not enthusiastic about Diaghilev's propagation of the Russian theater abroad, but he dreamed of becoming a member of the nobility. And the grand duke had promised to cooperate in this matter if he (the manufacturer of galoshes) would donate a substantial sum of money to this worthy cause. But these subtle machinations almost collapsed because on 9 February 1909 the grand duke died, and Diaghilev was forced to go to great lengths to stop his widow from breaking the unwritten contract.

Still, the rehearsals began and, as in the previous year, took place in the Hermitage Theater. They differed markedly from the state theater rehearsals. Diaghilev gave Fokine carte blanche in choice of performers, and Fokine selected those who supported his reform (as he had come to call his own experiments). Almost all of them were the same age as, or younger than, the twenty-seven-year-old ballet reformer. The main thing was that all of them believed in the artistic truth of Fokine's productions. They looked on them as an escape from the stagnant atmosphere of the official theater. Even though Fokine was a stricter taskmaster than some equable régisseurs, this only served to inspire their enthusiasm.

Nijinsky seemed to stand aloof from this mood of enthusiasm. What he picked up straightaway he repeated constantly and without question so that the less intelligent dancers could attain the harmony of the ensemble. He was always like that, everywhere. But the excitement at rehearsal seemed not to touch him. He would have nothing to do with the lively groups that always spring up spontaneously among theater people, so contented with themselves and their affairs. During breaks he would wander backstage, or he would go down into the auditorium where the amphitheater of coral-pink velvet seats rested beneath the yellow marble columns reflecting warm shadows in the light from the lamps concealed behind the cornices. Down in the foyer Nijinsky had to blink his eyes in the March sun crazily refracting the ice on the Neva and reinforcing the gilded spire of the Peter and Paul Fortress. Once he bumped into Benois, Diaghilev, and other strangers who were all arguing about something heatedly. Diaghilev noticed him and, so Nijinsky thought, strode over toward him dissatisfied with something. The dancer stepped back, shut the door, and ran down the amphitheater stairs back to the stage. This wasn't the first time that he had caught the imperious gaze of the master of all these people, of these rehearsals, of everything that was going on around him.

The rehearsals continued. Because of the fabulous expense, Diaghilev canceled all the operas except *Ivan the Terrible*, but, in the case of *Prince Igor*, he retained the scene of the Polovtsian camp. The only piece that Nijinsky did not perform in was the *Polovtsian Dances*. He danced in *Sylphides*, *Nuits d'Egypte*, and *Armide*; in the hastily compiled divertissement called *Le Festin* he had to perform the lezghinka and the part of the Bluebird (with Karsavina as Princess Florine). Actually, this well-known duet from the last act of *The Sleeping Beauty* was called *The Firebird*. When Karsavina and Nijinsky tried on the costumes designed by Bakst, they stared at each other in astonishment—the fiery brocade, the semiprecious stones, the whole cut of the oriental costumes were a far cry from what they had been used to wearing.

Fokine heeded Diaghilev's advice and did not touch the dances in *Les Sylphides*. But he did change a bit in *Le Pavillon d'Armide* and almost recomposed *Les Nuits d'Egypte*, renaming it *Cléopâtre*. During the course of rehearsals Nijinsky suddenly felt that both his Slaves had changed imperceptibly, although he could not explain why. No doubt Fokine couldn't have explained it either, although intuitively he perceived a shift of direction in the general conception of the spectacles: the theme of fate had become more intense, at Diaghilev's request. Armida's yearning for her knight was now overshadowed by the motif of insidious seduction. Pavlova, who was very sensitive to any human expression both tragic and comic, suddenly began to shun the role that she herself had created. Her heroine, who in the present *Cléopâtre* had been renamed Ta-hor instead of Véronique, simply evaporated in the presence of the Cleopatra of Ida Rubinstein—the Rubinstein who, as Benois once said, was as frigid as Astarte. The idea of a destructive, voracious beauty, eulogized by the poets of that time, now became the measure and the symbol of the two sovereigns, the mistresses of Nijinsky, the White Slave and the dark-skinned Slave. Both Slaves now lost their former spontaneity and took on an elusive nuance of sensuality, something that had previously been imperceptible.

At the height of the preparations a big problem developed. The bureaucrats were very worried by Diaghilev's independent actions, this Diaghilev who, on his own initiative, was contriving to export the Imperial Ballet beyond the frontiers of Russia just as if the powerful bureaucratic system was nonexistent. Almost every evening Teliakovsky, the director of the Imperial Theaters, took out his ruled notebook (the current addition to his diaries) and made a note of the latest "insolent" threat to the well-being of his theaters, the

Nijinsky in *Le Festin*.

(*right*) In costume for the pas de deux billed as *The Firebird*. The costumes were unusual, but Petipa's choreography and Tchaikovsky's music were familiar. The Bluebird pas de deux, by any of the several names that Diaghilev gave it, always caused a sensation when it was danced by Karsavina and Nijinsky.

(*below*) In the lezghinka, a Georgian character dance to music by Glinka.

Mariinsky and the Bolshoi. He forbade everything he could. On the other hand, Kschessinska, although on bad terms with Teliakovsky, was annoyed that Diaghilev and his friends had passed her by and began to set her own powerful connections in motion. So one fine day as the rehearsal was in full swing the performers were ordered to vacate the premises of the Hermitage Theater as quickly as possible.

But it was not easy to deal with Diaghilev. The workmen had hardly taken down the scenery, the seamstresses had hardly packed away the costumes, the actors had hardly removed their makeup when Diaghilev informed them over the telephone that he was waiting for them in the German Club on the Ekaterina Canal. A string of carriages was soon winding its way through the streets of St. Petersburg; Benois and Diaghilev's secretary sat in the first *drozhsky*, the artists and staff in the others.

Within an hour or so, a steady procession of Konchak's prisoners was lining the tiny stage of the German Club. Then came the romp of the Polovtsians. Fokine shouted angrily from the orchestra, giving order to that ecstatic chaos of dance that he himself had created.

No, it wasn't at all easy to deal with Diaghilev.

Whether by intent or by accident Diaghilev bumped into Nijinsky in the doorway of the German Club. Holding the startled dancer, he suggested they have a snack together during the break between rehearsals. He took him to a restaurant, fairly empty at that time of day, and while the obsequious maître d'hotel fussed about their table, he began to talk about the strict routine that a dancer like Nijinsky ought to observe. Without asking for a yes or a no, Diaghilev took charge of Nijinsky. He did so with that same sense of prerogative that he exercised when he had collected ancestral portraits from their owners' estates for his exhibitions. But in appropriating this "animated artifact," Diaghilev made an attempt upon another man's soul. He wished to attach it to himself, but in so doing he broke his rule of being superior to normal human feelings. He paid for this dearly, for, in tying Nijinsky to himself, he tied his own hands. And this happened very soon. Until his dying day, Diaghilev was troubled by the impossibility of undoing what had once been done.

In any case, was it not because Diaghilev found the solitary pose of his superhuman arrogance unbearable that revengeful fate brought him to Nijinsky? In this talented but unsociable fellow, Diaghilev suddenly discovered a malleable piece of material out of which he could fashion the ideal model of a pupil, a friend, and a first-rate artist. And, like the impresario, the dancer too was alone. But, in complete contrast to Diaghilev's arrogant isolation, Nijinsky's was a solitude not of pride, but of helplessness and timidity.

With his wisdom and perspicacity, Diaghilev immediately perceived many things in Nijinsky. He realized that the high life of a bohemian was beginning to exhaust the dancer, that it was burdensome to him, and that he would give it up without regrets. He saw that the serene depths of Nijinsky's enigmatic personality concealed turbulent currents. He understood what had to be done so that these invisible springs would burst forth in a mighty fountain. The key was to give Nijinsky the opportunity to associate with modern artists of genuine talent, and the main thing was to allow him the freedom to create, which Diaghilev, mentor and miracle worker, would encourage with an intelligent and delicate solicitude.

Diaghilev never retreated from this position. It was he who opened up the Elysian fields of artistic creativity to Nijinsky. And it was he who took away Nijinsky's sense of inner freedom, his independence. From the very beginning the relationship was an unequal one; Nijinsky (to quote the proverb) had to eat out of his hands. The more clearly Diaghilev revealed, both for himself and for others, the dancer's precious artistic nature, the more he constrained Nijinsky's human nature, and, involuntarily, stimulated the seeds of a disease that perhaps need not have taken root.

Diaghilev's attachment proved to be dictatorial, unbending. With one hand the master of Nijinsky's fate did good, but with his other he did evil. Was this freedom from the tedium of domestic life—and this new personal dependence—a blessing or not? The latter seemed paradoxical and antiquated in this camp of artists striving to become the free avant-garde of the twentieth century.

At the beginning of May, as the Russian company set off for Paris, Nijinsky boarded the railroad car accompanied by Diaghilev's servant Vasili.

This Vasili Zuikov was a remarkable person. He and an old nanny were the only servants Diaghilev had. Diaghilev was rarely at home

(*left*) The German Club, St. Petersburg.

(*below*) Participants in the first Saison Russe, at rehearsal in the German Club. At the piano: Nicolas Tcherepnin, Igor Stravinsky, and Michel Fokine. Tamara Karsavina in the center.

(*right*) In the German Club's canteen. Karsavina and the balletomane Nikolai Bezobrazov on the left. Nijinsky is standing on the right, at the end of the table.

and hardly ever dined there, regarding the St. Petersburg restaurants as suited for that purpose. When his friends met at his apartment, tea was served. His nanny used to sit by the samovar and everyone would shake her hand, except Benois, who would kiss her. She adored Diaghilev, and he returned her feeling with a most tender love, even though he maintained the attitude of a spoiled *barin*'s son with her. In her simple dress and dark headscarf, she would sit by the hours as they argued about painting, music, philosophy, and literature. These disputes were totally incomprehensible to this illiterate peasant woman, but it was she who created the cosy and intimate ambience in which they were conducted.

Unlike her, Vasili was independent and in his dealings with people manifested a certain bold aplomb. He was short, had a very ordinary although intelligent face, and his black moustache gave him a military aspect. In addition, he was a born servant. Not in vain did someone once remark that Diaghilev's gift for divining talent also helped him in his choice of servants. Vasili, appointed to look after Nijinsky, be-

"S. Diaghilev Dispatches His Company Abroad." Caricature from a Russian newspaper. The caged "birds" are Pavlova and Nijinsky.

came his bodyguard, almost his prison warden. He anticipated the dancer's slightest desire and watched over his every step.

Was Nijinsky really ever free?

Perhaps now, in retrospect, the restrictive discipline of the Theater School seemed a humane one to him. The routine of that intimate establishment had equalized everyone, even though this equality had freed no one from his solitude.

Perhaps he now remembered his first months as a professional dancer as a time of joy, even though he had been poor. And then had come his bohemian days, an empty life that had exhausted him and stupefied him with its intoxicating fumes.

Perhaps he at first regarded his meeting with Diaghilev as a road to salvation. Probably so. His every wish was catered to. He was delivered from his imaginary but burdensome independence. Only gradually did he come to realize that, at the same time, he had been cut off from the world, that he was living in a cage or, more exactly, an aquarium. Because now he looked at life only through glass walls erected by Diaghilev's hand. Beyond these walls everything was in a state of flux, but he now enjoyed a permanent and artificial tranquility and comfort.

Outside the car window he could see the crowd of travelers and their dear ones bustling on the platform. Vasili unpacked the bags. Then the spring meadows drifted past, with their fragrance, with their birds chirping, and with their sunshine—images unfelt, unheard, but so evocative. Bridges flashed by, railroad crossings, stations.

The panorama of Paris unfolded outside the windows of the motor-car. Nijinsky saw it as if on a screen. Diaghilev, who had met the company at the station, now sat next to Nijinsky in the car, naming the streets, the boulevards and buildings, pointing out the gigantic Serov posters depicting Pavlova in flight and explaining to Nijinsky that he too was worthy of such publicity—and that he would receive it.

Everything swished past, danced in circles, rang out, and then stopped and died away when Vasili closed the window and drew the heavy curtain. The shaded lamps illuminated the satin on the walls and furniture of an expensive suite in one of the best Paris hotels. Of the entire company only the head was residing here. Vasili went off into the bathroom and, a moment later, to the splash of water gushing from the tap, handed Nijinsky his dressing gown. Tomorrow there would be a rehearsal in the Théâtre du Châtelet. Diaghilev had said that he would turn this old "stable" into a "candy box." He was obviously pleased with the way things were going, although he was agitated.

The next morning Parisians saw a rather entertaining sight. A lot of people, most of them young, issued forth from their tiny hotel on the Boulevard St.-Michel. Chatting excitedly in a peculiar language, they made their way along the boulevard, crossed the Pont au Change and entered the Théâtre du Châtelet. Moving vans were parked in front of the doors; decors, piles of baskets, and trunks were being unloaded. A crowd of idlers soon gathered. Even those who were in a hurry paused to take a look; housewives and cooks from families of modest means with their shopping bags, mill girls, shop assistants, foot soldiers known by their nickname of "Pioupiou." They were all part of the regular clientele of the Châtelet, and many of them had just seen a "melodrama with a shipwreck" entitled *Les Aventures de Gavroche*. This melodrama had run 128 times because it was such a success—you could have a good laugh, have a good fright, shed a tear over the fate of the popular "poor Gavroche," and in the intermissions you could feast on oranges and lollipops. The crowd of bystanders now hazarded various guesses as to what kind of productions these foreign artists had brought with them. Alas, those who thought of coming to their spectacles were mistaken. This new presentation was intended for a very different kind of audience.

At the moment inconceivable commotion reigned in the theater. The newcomers fussed about like ants awakened by the joyful Paris sunshine. They scurried here and there, dragged along huge trunks, banged things together, sawed things up, scraped, polished, hung up the lights. They unrolled carpets and put potted plants all over. There was a frightful racket in the auditorium. Ten rows of seats were being removed to widen the orchestra pit. The noise was just as bad on stage. A disheveled and imperious little old man issued orders left and right. This was Karl Fedorovich Valts, who for many a decade had been in charge of effects in the Bolshoi Theater. And now he was supervising the workers mending the traps, raising and lowering the curtain, checking out its machinery and planing down the floor, so unsuitable for

The Théâtre du Châtelet, Paris.

dancing. Valts was very worked up, and he was annoyed as much as alarmed when Alexandre Nicolaevich Benois, who only confused everyone with his advice, stepped on to a trap that had just been summoned to open. Benois almost fell into emptiness but, thank heavens, just managed to catch the edge of the boards and held on, suspended.

Amidst all this hustle and bustle, Fokine introduced the Bolshoi dancers to the parts of *Armide*. Pavlova had gone on tour to Berlin, and the première was going to be danced by Vera Caralli and Mikhail Mordkin. Caralli was an ox-eyed Eastern beauty; Mordkin was strong and mighty like a Roman gladiator. Their Petersburg colleagues seemed rather puny in comparison. The Moscow couple did their very best to master the movements demonstrated by Fokine to the scarcely audible sounds of the piano. Nicolas Nikolaevich Tcherepnin, seated next to the pianist, was preparing to conduct his ballet.

Nicolas Tcherepnin,
conductor for Diaghilev
from 1908 to 1912,
composer of *Le Pavillon
d'Armide* and *Narcisse*.

Yet another Muscovite stood a little way off, wrapped in a gypsy shawl and leaning against the wings. She was not particularly beautiful, but there was something in her face beneath her mass of black hair that involuntarily attracted one's interest. Her eyes were downcast but they seemed to conceal passion. The sallow pallor of her sunken cheeks betrayed a kind of morbid tension. Here was an extraordinary character, a sister to Dostoevsky's "possessed women." It was on stage that Sophie Fedorova released her fire and passion. She would soon shock Parisians with her performances in the *Polovtsian Dances* and in Glazunov's bacchanal, which, after all, Fokine had inserted in *Cléopâtre* at Diaghilev's insistence. But among all those people thrown together by the risk, the lofty aims, and the delight of that first season (which quickly faded), Fedorova, like Nijinsky, kept herself to herself. In fact, they had a lot in common. Both had only just begun to taste the excitement of fame. But neither accepted it with enthusiasm, for they did not seek it, and in any case neither of them would awake from their world of dreams just for the sake of fame. Both of them later escaped into insanity. He was more fortunate in that he took shelter there forever, whereas she was forced to return and to live a long time forgotten in a foreign world. Still, neither of them recognized their spiritual kinship, even though they both blushed when they were introduced—which happened whenever they met someone they did not know.

Nijinsky appeared at the rehearsal separately, accompanied by Vasili, who then set off to find the *barin*. It was difficult to find him even though he managed to be everywhere at once. One moment he would be seen in the auditorium, the next he would be surveying some of the light fixtures somewhere in the flies. Actually, at this very moment he was settling an argument between Fokine and Robert Brussel. The venerable music critic, together with other influential friends of Diaghilev, had been allowed to attend the first rehearsal of the Russian company. He had got into conversation with Karsavina and she had missed her entry. This enraged Fokine, and he flew at them almost resorting to cursing. Diaghilev arrived on the scene just at the height of the polyglot argument and, with the chic of a Paris habitué, smiled and said that, obviously, Fokine did not know that M. Brussel had been given permission to "divert" the dancers. Brussel burst out laughing at this double meaning, spread his hands, and, bowing to Fokine, took his leave. Still, Vasili didn't interrupt the *barin*, for he realized that he could get into trouble and pay dearly both for Brussel and for Fokine.

Quite a lot of people had assembled in the orchestra seats of the auditorium, poorly lit by the work lights. Diaghilev had deliberately allowed the arbiters of modern taste to come to the rehearsal. Some of them were old acquaintances from the time of the Salon exhibition and the concerts, and Diaghilev was on friendly terms with one or two of them. Paris was witnessing a strange paradox, one that fully enacted the proverb "No one is a prophet in his own country." In St. Petersburg only a very small circle of people, mainly artists, understood and appreciated Diaghilev to the extent that he really deserved. The public at large either regarded him as an upstart, a sly fox, an imposter, or they'd never heard of him. On the other hand, Paris society, so capricious and exacting in matters of art, was conquered immediately, and in the most diverse sections. Everyone was trying to make Diaghilev's acquaintance: celebrated littérateurs, musicians, and artists, newspaper publishers, financiers and high society dames, the dictators of fashion. Some did this out of snobbery, simply wishing to keep up with fashion, but the most worthy people wished to make his acquaintance because they sincerely believed in him. Diaghilev, a Russian *barin* through and through, amazed them all with the range of his talents, and with his irrepressible spirit, which knew no impediments to achieving its aim. And although Diaghilev was not always scrupulous, he was enticed by the noble character of his aim.

Parisians saw a very calculating and very sophisticated Diaghilev. Fellow Petersburgians could well remember his vain attempts to be proficient in at least one art. But they also felt guilty at neglecting Diaghilev's latest undertakings. Certainly, he had got nowhere with his composing and had long since given it up. Diaghilev's trump card consisted in his gift for divining, anticipating, and revealing artistic talent. It was a versatile gift and could already be recognized in its different manifestations. It was now, at this very moment when so much had to be done, that Diaghilev's trump card brought him into contact with the most important personages of his time.

Indeed, beginning with his art exhibitions, Diaghilev had demonstrated his extraordinary panache. He had traveled the length and breadth of Russia collecting her pearls of painting from forgotten and decrepit estates. He had soon exhibited the canvases of the World of Art artists together with those of Finnish artists and, in his selection, had revealed his understanding of, and sensitivity toward, new and undiscovered artists.

The same with music. For the moment, Diaghilev limited himself to presenting the West with the great composers of Russia, presenting them in all the contradiction and diversity of their talent. For the future there was Stravinsky. At first Diaghilev would show him to Paris in forms that the contemporary public would understand, but later on he would do valiant battle on his behalf, seeing him as the creator of a new music.

At length Diaghilev had ventured to bring Fokine's ballet repertoire to Paris—a repertoire that had had a very moderate reception at home. And in Fokine's case, Diaghilev had understood something of vital importance, Fokine's dependence on stage pictorialism, on the spectacle in its final product, on the dazzling picture animating and exciting by its kaleidoscope of moving forms.

He also perceived the genius of the foremost dancer of the twentieth century. True, Fokine had already discovered Nijinsky and had valued him as ideal material for his (Fokine's) own compositions. True, Nijinsky immediately acquired recognition by the entire company, knew the audience's applause, and tasted the praises showered upon him by the newspapers. But he knew these things only in a very limited context, one that promised no prospects. All he could expect was a series of roles mastered by generations of dancers and a few of Fokine's experimental projects. But, before you knew where you were, these experiments at the Mariinsky might stop short or dry up if there were no other stimuli apart from Fokine's own enthusiasm. Diaghilev saw that Nijinsky's individuality was very promising. And he concocted such fantastic schemes that for the moment he would not divulge them to anyone, let alone Nijinsky.

Diaghilev realized his plans by revealing to the world, first, Nijinsky the brilliant dancer and, then, Nijinsky the brilliant choreographer. But in realizing his plans, Diaghilev committed a fatal mistake, perhaps the most terrible mistake of all, and the most terrible, although unconscious, sin in the whole of his sinful but glorious life. He overestimated Nijinsky's strength; he did not take account of the vulnerability and frailty of his nature. Circumstances took a fatal turn.

But all this occurred later. Right now Diaghilev was showing Nijinsky at rehearsal to the people he had invited here. He smiled, understanding why his guests were so slow to give themselves to the delights that he was instigating. They maintained a polite silence. Strange as it may seem, the reason for their reserve became clear from a conversation that some Russians were having a little way off. They were among the highlights of the season, they were Diaghilev's closest assistants, and they knew Nijinsky.

Benois was doing most of the talking. As always, Leon Samoilovich Bakst deferred to his erudite and voluble friend. Benois was surprised that even before the première the Parisians were asking more questions about Nijinsky than about Pavlova, even though her posters were all over town. He sensed one of "Seriozha's maneuvers" here and, not without a certain good-natured sarcasm, commented on the Frenchmen's perplexity. They were observing Nijinsky and, of course, saw nothing exceptional in his impeccable but also mechanical and automatic execution. He had no doubt that this apparently premature demonstration also concealed one of Diaghilev's "maneuvers"; the lad would surprise them all the more later on. Usually something happened to Nijinsky on the night of a performance. He seemed to cast off his lethargy—began to feel and, moreover, to think. What a metamorphosis that had been at the very last moment in *Armide* in St. Petersburg! At first he had been nervous and capricious; something was wrong with his costume—it hadn't corresponded to the design. But then, when everything had been put to rights, he stared at himself in the mirror and, before his very eyes, literally, he had transformed himself into that phenomenal and fantastic being. He had simply turned into poetry.

Bakst, so ridiculously ungainly but uncommonly charming, continued to blink his red eyelashes and to lisp and then, suddenly, remarked that he could understand that. He also knew that moment of joy when you step across a certain boundary and seem to enter a different dimension. Interestingly enough, for him (Bakst) this moment was definitely connected with the dance. It was essential for him "to see the music of the dance, so to speak" in order to dress it—to dress it so that the fabric itself would dance, so that the fabric would extend the movements of the dancing body and even anticipate them.

Benois grew silent and fell to meditating. He knew both music and the ballet much better than Bakst did. But his rational spirit, alas, was not capable of such revelations. Rarely did he experience moments of poetic inspiration, although he loved art with his intellect, and loved it perhaps a thousand times more than all these geniuses with their inexplicable tricks of the subconscious.

A very casual and very Russian voice shook him out of his reverie. A just as casual Chaliapin had quietly installed his huge body in the chair next to Benois. He said that "Vatsa is a fine fellow. He'll show these little Frenchmen how we can dance. As for nerves, you can't do a thing about them." Last year, the night before *Boris Godunov*, he himself "had been such a downright coward that he hadn't gone to bed in his own room but spent the whole miserable night at Sergei Pavlych's on the uncomfortable little divan." [17]

On stage, Fokine had become completely hoarse, but he went on to rehearse *Cléopâtre*.

3

ON 18 MAY 1909, JUST WHEN EVERYTHING seemed to have fallen to pieces, the Théâtre du Châtelet filled with an elite audience in readiness for the final dress rehearsal.

The auditorium looked like a gigantic salon where everyone was more or less acquainted. Here was a cross section of Paris representing the castes and circles of this buzzing beehive.

Perched in a good vantage point, one reporter quickly wrote down in his notebook, whispering the words to himself so as to get them right: "The Minister of Foreign Affairs, the Minister of Education, the Minister of Finance, the British Ambassador, the Greek Ambassador, the Russian Ambassador. . . ."

Another reporter was more concered with literary celebrities and made a note referring to a rather solid gentleman with a splendid moustache à la Wilhelm—Octave Mirabeau; and there was another gentleman, balding, but elegantly dressed, and playing with his monocle on its silken chain—Henri de Regnier.

The theater critic Roger Marx accompanied Auguste Rodin down the central aisle of the orchestra. The famous sculptor was already well into his sixties and his thick locks of hair thrown back from his forehead were white, but his glance was still youthful and perspicacious. The music critic Pierre Lalo was chatting with an imposing old man, the composer Camille Saint-Saëns, and with the latter's pupil, Gabriel Fauré, also of a venerable age.

The singer Lina Cavalieri adorned one of the boxes, brilliant in her beauty and her toilette. In an adjacent box, the actress Gabrielle Réjane exchanged greetings with her Russian admirers—those who had seen the French troupe in the Mikhailovsky Theater in St. Petersburg. Carlotta Zambelli, ballerina of the Opéra, raised her eyebrows sarcastically as she examined Isadora Duncan enveloped in something resembling a Grecian peplum. Yvette Guilbert, the unique music hall singer, the darling of Paris who had once been Toulouse-Lautrec's model, smiled affably at the head of Paquin, a woman who dictated world fashion.

Among all this society an eccentric but elegant young man was attracting particular attention. This was Robert de Montesquieu, poet and arbiter of artistic taste in this capital of the world. In a sonorous falsetto voice he explained to the very young Jean-Louis Vaudoyer (just beginning his poetical career) that his friend Marcel Proust was not going out anywhere because he was completely immersed in his novel. But Marcel would have been so impressed here! He, Montesquieu, was sure of one thing: the Russians were beginning a new era in art and this day would go down in history.

Not long before the lights went down, Diaghilev dropped into the box of Misia Edwards, wife of the editor of *Le Matin*. This refined, intelligent woman, whose salon was the center of musical and artistic life in Paris, had understood Diaghilev from the very first, and Diaghilev, ever surrounded by people, but still solitary, maintained his friendship with her until his dying day. Misia also liked to discover talents, and right behind her, apart from her honored guest, Claude Debussy, and the Spanish artist José-Maria Sert, soon to become her second husband, sat a young man whom she called "mon petit Ravel."

Diaghilev was reserved but excited, like a general before a battle. He glanced around the crowded auditorium, took out his pocket watch, nodded to Misia Edwards and went off into the wings.

In a box at the Théâtre du Châtelet: José-Maria Sert, Jean Cocteau, Misia Edwards (later Sert), and Sergei Diaghilev. Caricature by Jean Cocteau.

The curtain rose. A murmur of approval went through the auditorium. Whatever was to come, the French audience appreciated the taste and the faithful rendering of their antique architecture. Then came an attentive silence, broken once again when a dazzling light suddenly filled the stage, contrasting with the semidarkness of the pavilion. Now could be seen a castle framed by greenery, tall fountains splashing their waters, and the personages from the animated tapestry began their sumptuous masquerade.

Diaghilev returned to his box. He stood there gripping the back of one of the chairs with such force that the white joints of his fingers could be seen distinctly. He waited in suspense.

Meanwhile everything was going smoothly; the audience had not lost interest. At length, Armida's two confidantes appeared on stage,

THÉATRE DU CHATELET
Mai - Juin 1909

SAISON RUSSE

avec le Concours

DES ARTISTES. L'ORCHESTRE & LES CHOEURS

DES THÉATRES

DE SAINT-PÉTERSBOURG & DE MOSCOU

Le 19 Mai 1909

PRIX : 50 CENTIMES

Program cover, opening night of the first Saison Russe.

dressed in their exqusite yellow and gold costumes. They were brought on by a dancer, the slave of the enchantress of this celebration. His white and yellow costume was embroidered in silver; a turban adorned his head; a band around his neck flashed with precious stones. Like a bird of paradise, this exotic personage attracted everyone's attention. The male dance had gone out of fashion in Paris. Its place had been usurped almost fifty years ago by the dance en travesti. And here you had this man—or, rather, boy—whose graceful appearance clearly surpassed that of any girl dressed up as a prince or shepherd. His smile concealed a secret as he invited the audience to admire the dancing of his ladies. But he revealed his secret when, his hands encircled above his head, he took off into the air faultlessly, weightlessly, in a leap that did honor to his teachers, now so very far away.

The audience at the Châtelet gasped, almost groaned, in response to the flight of the White Slave. Diaghilev also sighed with relief, unclasped his benumbed fingers and straightened his shoulders. He made his exit, knowing that this performance and, therefore, the whole season would be the subject of general admiration.

Every morning Vasili would now bring in a pile of morning newspapers and unfold them on the bed of the still drowsy Nijinsky. Photographs of *Armide, Les Sylphides,* and *Cléopâtre* on every page, the two names *Nijinsky* and *Vestris* linked together in the columns of incomprehensible French words. If he wasn't rushing to keep one of his ceaseless appointments, Diaghilev would meet Nijinsky after the daily class and rehearsal, take out the newspapers, and translate at random: "In our view the most noteworthy aspect is the important role that has been given to the men in Russian choreography. They display a harmony and grace, a simple elegance as they dance their parts, whereas their colleagues over here have caused us to smile many a time. Among these dancers is one, M. Nijinsky, who has been called the new Vestris and who certainly deserves this title."

Did Nijinsky suddenly remember that quote from Karamzin— "Vestris galloped like a frisky goat" [1]—that he had heard at school? Actually, there wasn't much that was goatlike in the friskiness of his two Slaves. Their soft, stealthy, and cunning grace echoed what many modern poets were saying about the "animal element" in Man; their "bestiality" indicated not open-heartedness but heartlessness. This kind of analogy was less valid when applied to the Youth sporting among the sylphides. His animation, his "friskiness" revealed another side of modern art, for it dispensed with the carnal element of human nature.

Reporters of the Paris press eulogized Nijinsky's "acrobatic ease" and the "height of his leaps" but did not proceed further than the "delightful grace of his pose" or the "elegance of his gait, his gestures" that brought forth a "cry of delight" from the "ultra-blasé and ultra-elite" audience. Nijinsky chased after an elusive dream; he ran from the inevitable. But the Paris audience scarcely understood that, in his own way, he embodied the complicated, spiritual endeavor of a large section of the Russian intelligentsia. His audience simply accepted what corresponded to their own intellectual life. Still, they felt the onslaught of an imminent catastrophe no less clearly than their Russian counterparts, and this realization inspired dreams of escaping from reality; it engendered the same refinement, the same haziness, the same vacillation of feeling that Nijinsky expressed.

The audience was intrigued by the personality of this dancer. As the partner of Pavlova and Karsavina, as the friend of Diaghilev, he had immediately conquered Paris; the doors to the most inaccessible salons were flung open before him. But, as before, no matter how sympathetically people behaved toward him, he always found it burdensome to be with them. But he was forced to plunge into the social round—such was Diaghilev's wish.

Nijinsky knew very well that he disappointed many people's expectations because of his morbid reserve, his interminable habit of blushing and stuttering each time somebody addressed him. He also knew that many people found his "plebeian" appearance to be something of a disappointment. But beneath his outward nonchalance Nijinsky was deeply troubled. Diaghilev's society friends shrugged their shoulders after trying to make contact with him and coming up against his cold unsociability. The general opinion of him was, therefore, an unflattering one. Misia Edwards summed it all up when she called this individual who was on everyone's mind an "idiot of genius."

Nijinsky himself probably suspected something of the kind, because ten years later he wrote in his diary: "I now understand Dostoevsky's 'idiot,' because I am myself being taken for an idiot." [2]

And so this tragic division between "serving the muses" and lead-

116

ing a normal, everyday life deepened, and Nijinsky's realization of this only undermined his psychological condition. It was his fate to remain misunderstood. Only once did Nijinsky meet another great artist whose art, essentially democratic, might seem to have been very distant to Nijinsky's refined transubstantiations. But this other artist esteemed them just as he esteemed Nijinsky's total personality. The creative paths of Nijinsky and Charlie Chaplin intersected deep down to the original foundations of their art.

During their acquaintance both men were already famous, although Nijinsky's star was descending. Chaplin, on the other hand, was still being regarded only as a unique comedian. He invited the dancer to come and see the shooting of one of his movies, and anxiously saw how Nijinsky became more and more depressed as the acts became more and more comic.

The shooting came to an end. The guest, looking like a "monk dressed in civilian clothes," struck Chaplin as being "beautiful-looking." Nijinsky, almost reluctantly it would seem, murmured, "Your comedy is balletic; you are a dancer."

Nijinsky. Detail of a drawing by Valentin Serov, 1909–10.

A few days later Chaplin was charmed by Nijinsky's dancing, by his "flight into strange fancy," by his "somberness suggesting moods of other worlds." Chaplin went backstage but was too timid to say anything to Nijinsky.

Many years later Chaplin declared in vexation to himself as much as to his reader that "one cannot wring one's hands and express in words one's appreciation of great art." [3]

Actually, it was more complicated than this. Both men were unable to express themselves freely in life, to enjoy the banalities of life, and this reflected a spiritual condition germane to their art. Charlie Chaplin, in his baggy suit, and Nijinsky, in the clown costume of Petrouchka, in the clumsy automatism of their movements, expressed the theme of their time: the struggle between spirituality and the stagnation of recalcitrant matter. They created a stereotype mask behind which could be seen the suffering face of humanity.

Both men understood each other, but their paths soon divided. It could not have been otherwise. Their meeting was a fortuitous one. Moreover, Diaghilev insisted that Nijinsky accompany him on his social rounds and jealously guarded his property from any encounters that threatened to develop into friendship. The only outside influence that Diaghilev permitted was his own.

But Diaghilev did try to stimulate and to educate Nijinsky; and he did try to bridge the gap between the dancer's imperfect "secular" visage and his perfection as a theatrical creator. Sometimes these truly heroic efforts achieved very little, other times their impatience and insistence merely knocked Nijinsky off course.

Nijinsky followed Diaghilev everywhere, obediently. Together they attended aristocratic receptions, concerts, the theater, museums. The dancer at once retired into his solitude whenever he found himself in a crowded and brightly lit concert hall or in a museum amidst loquacious people surveying each other as they passed by the pictures. At such moments a chance musical phrase would transport him into a sphere of sonorous images. He would forget himself, half open his mouth, and take on the appearance of a stupid schoolboy who has angered his teacher by not paying attention. At such moments, painting would become more real for him than the surrounding and formless mass of people (as, for example, when Diaghilev showed him Gauguin's works) and would infect him with the mysterious harmony of its world. Occasionally, in his faltering speech, substituting clumsy interjections for real sentences, he would try to explain to Diaghilev the vision that he had had. And Diaghilev, overjoyed, would help him, trying to encourage his creative development. But Diaghilev was the only person who could perceive this gift in the dancer.

On 19 June the curtain came down for the last time on *Le Festin,* and the organizers of the "season" congratulated themselves on their triumph. Paris had been vanquished, and Diaghilev was already planning future victories. For the moment he had gone off to Venice, taking Nijinsky with him. The sweet moments of their holiday went by on the canals and squares of Venice, so reminiscent of a St. Petersburg that magically had thrown off its official severity. Diaghilev hoped to achieve a great deal in the education of his pupil, but the latter, while seeming to be tame, remained withdrawn and on his guard. Diaghilev never left his side. The only times he let Nijinsky out of his sight were to take his daily class and to write his regular letter to his mother. Nijinsky had never been away from her so long.

They returned to St. Petersburg via Paris. Diaghilev was preparing the ground for a new "season" and was in no particular hurry to get home, although it was already the end of September and performances at the Mariinsky had long been underway. On Diaghilev's advice, Nijinsky sent off a doctor's note to the Theater Office and then, as if on purpose, bumped into Krupensky at the Opéra. Krupensky wrote Teliakovsky about this meeting, mentioning how Nijinsky had been embarrassed on seeing him, "had gone as red as a beetroot," [4] and had then disappeared. Quite rightly Teliakovsky was furious and made a mental note of the incident in readiness both for Nijinsky and for Diaghilev.

Meanwhile the St. Petersburg press was giving a rather dull coverage to the "Russian Vestris."

"What do the French like best?" asked one reporter, who wrote, quite perplexed: "It turns out that it wasn't so much our ballerinas as our male dancers with their dizzy flights and jumps that struck them." For clarification of this matter the reporter was forced to address himself to Gerdt, who affirmed that the reason for this was, indeed, "leaps and flights": Nijinsky "manages even to stay in the air for a moment."

Diaghilev visiting the sick Nijinsky. Drawing by Mikhail Larionov. Nijinsky suffered a bout of typhoid fever immediately after the first Saison Russe, in June 1909. This drawing, perhaps done several years later, may depict a scene from that time.

This veteran of the Mariinsky stage had no intention whatsoever of belittling the importance of his younger colleague. On the contrary, he confessed quite frankly: "In my youth I also had occasion to jump like that, although I never attained the level of Nijinsky's art." [5] But neither Gerdt's nor his interviewer's imagination went any further than the notorious leaps.

A little later, another reporter entertained the idea that after

Nijinsky's "successes abroad" the theater administration would risk putting on a ballet for him, one that would enable the "artist to demonstrate the best part of his talent to the full." And, by "best part of his talent," this reporter meant what everyone pointed out: "the extraordinary ballon and uncommon elevation." [6]

On 6 October an interviewer from the *St. Petersburg Gazette* described his impressions of a meeting with the "contemporary Vestris," who had just returned the night before: "Dressed modestly, shy, with a very boyish appearance, Nijinsky did not look like the hero of the brilliant Russian season in Paris, which scored such a success in that contemporary Babylon. He speaks just like a child. He gets worked up and blushes just as if he is embarrassed by his position of celebrity."

The celebrity's replies were indeed laconic.

Yes, he was late arriving at the Mariinsky because of illness. No, he had not expected such success abroad. Yes, the realization that the success of the Paris season had owed a great deal to his dancing had given him new strength. He listed the ballets in which he had taken part. No, he had refused to dance in music halls because that's "no place for an artist of the Imperial Theaters who values his reputation." He did not conceal the fact that in the state theater he received 900 rubles a year, at which his interviewer exclaimed: "In comparison with salaries abroad that's peanuts." [7]

The theater administration took note of all this newspaper talk, but it intended neither to give Nijinsky a raise nor to put on ballets for him. The *St. Petersburg Gazette* maintained its reputation as the city gossip when it reported in December that the money collected from the coming benefit performance would as usual be divided among those dancers who received less than 1000 rubles per annum, so Nijinsky would also get a piece of the "benefit pie." [8] In issue after issue, the *St. Petersburg Gazette* printed banal eulogies to the "dancer who stands above competition"—Nijinsky.[9] In his pas de deux with Egorova in *Le Roi Candaule* he amazed the reporter by his "gigantic leaps almost across the entire stage"; in his pas de deux with Karsavina that Legat had inserted into *La Fille Mal Gardée* he flew, so to speak, "to the skies." [10] Indeed, what else could you say about these pas de deux?

There were various circumstances that caused the striking contrast between Nijinsky's fate on the official stage and his fate as star of the Diaghilev tours. Both subjective and objective reasons were at work.

Subjective factors made him a bone of contention between Teliakovsky and Diaghilev. Their hostility became more intense after the Paris success, and both openly and in secret Teliakovsky vented his displeasure with mighty Diaghilev on Nijinsky. In his diary he now called Nijinsky nothing less than "Nezhinsky,"[11] and he was quick to pick up the slightest gossip pertaining to him. At work he hauled him over the coals for the slightest misdemeanor. Scandal-hungry newspapers published the fines that Nijinsky had to pay each time he was late for rehearsal and speculated on the delays in his promotion up the ladder of the ballet hierarchy.

Objective factors concerned the general condition of the St. Petersburg ballet. For a long time it had been stagnating. Legat, its official ballet master, was demonstrating his conservative position more and more patently. In regard to Fokine, the authorities kept checking up on him and were afraid to give him a full rein. Many hated this routine. Anna Pavlova mentioned more and more often that she was sick and tired of repeating the same old roles, even though they were principal ones. In January 1910 she left the Mariinsky, to return to it only as a guest artist. Most of the company, however, supported the traditions, which, undoubtedly, were magnificent and, of course, were much appreciated by the public. Not without valid reason did people say that you couldn't beat the old way, whereas with the new—well, it might misfire.

Hence, Legat's productions were presented once a year as "novelties," but dubious ones. Legat had long realized that an ability to perform and to teach, even extremely well, did not presuppose an ability to function as a ballet master. Actually, Legat was a very decent person. But even decent people do not always find the strength to refuse something that is foisted upon them. And nothing more nor less than a ballet company had been foisted upon Legat. But he loved this company above all and, by occupying his post, he hindered the progress of his talented but unorthodox rival. So Legat trod more and more carefully and for his own original productions began to turn to

restoring the classics. But since the best classical models were always being performed on the Mariinsky stage anyway, he began to restore weaker ballets, second-rate classics, so to say, which, strictly speaking, were no longer classics. This appealed to the more academic wing of the company, to the administration, and to those who controlled the administration.

For Preobrajenska's 25th Jubilee on 29 January 1910, Legat resurrected Petipa's ballet *Le Talisman*. Although Drigo's music for it was not too bad, this ballet had not had a great success even at its première in 1889, and the late Leikin, the humorist, had commented at that time through the mouthpiece of one of his characters: "It's a ballet, sir. But what it denotes . . . is quite impossible to understand. Okay, in a play people talk with their tongues, but in the ballet they do so with their legs. So just try and make out what these legs are saying! Even if everything were as clear as day, you still couldn't make it all out; everything's been obscured on purpose." [12]

The theme of *Le Talisman* was indeed obscure and extremely stupid. The Daughter of the Air descended to earth, fell in love with a mortal, and lost a talisman, a star, with the aid of which she could have returned to the sky. In her wanderings, she was accompanied and protected by a hurricane. At the première the part of the Hurricane had been taken by Cecchetti; Legat now gave it to Nijinsky.

In his own undemonstrative way, Nijinsky was fond of Legat. Nijinsky had grown to like him the day Legat had decided the dancer's fate by accepting him into the Imperial School. But at rehearsals, Nijinsky found it difficult to believe that his old teacher was seriously proposing these assignments. The Hurricane was now called Vayu, God of the Wind. In carrying out his duties as watchman during the many acts, Vayu had occasion to disguise himself as a Brahmin. The Rajah, who had fallen in love with the Daughter of the Air (the Rajah was played by an obviously dissatisfied Fokine), ordered his servants to kill the Brahmin, who had got on his nerves. With regard to the servants' stratagem, one of Leikin's characters reported that it was a "special kind" of murder and explained: "No revolver, no dagger, none of these things—they simply inebriated him and he drank himself to death." [13] This was not altogether accurate because after a sound sleep the Brahmin returned to life.

125

Nijinsky as Vayu in *Le Talisman*.

The twentieth-century dancer tried his best to justify the ponderous naïvetés of a nineteenth-century ballet. With his faultless instinct, Nijinsky guessed that this character (which Cecchetti, dancer of the grotesque, had created the year Nijinsky was born) could be changed a bit in accordance with the poetics of modern ballet. In any case, the white turban bedecked with strings of pearls and the white satin with gold stripes that constituted Vayu's costume (designed by Shervashidze under the influence of Benois' design for Armida's White Slave) helped Nijinsky's intention. As the dark-skinned Indian youth he was seductively handsome, and, thanks to him, the academic stereotype of Legat's dance suddenly assumed an angular, and at the same time, smooth design. The awfully ridiculous Hurricane now turned into an enigmatic being, the embodiment of the wind. Naturally, Fokine was jealous that Nijinsky had transferred aspects of his own images to Legat's ballet. But even though he was indignant, he did not forget that he was an artist, and, evidently, something of the ballet left its mark. Two years later, in the ballet *Le Dieu Bleu*, which he composed to music by Reynaldo Hahn, he took the image of the Hurricane that had so annoyed him and stylized it after Indian sculpture. In vain did Fokine try to erase the memory of what had so delighted the audience of *Le Talisman*—Nijinsky's flying leap, which Legat had made ample use of.

To a certain extent, Nijinsky saved the première of *Le Talisman*. Vayu–Hurricane appeared in the form of such a violent whirlwind that, according to one reviewer, Nijinsky "it seemed, found the Mariinsky stage too small." [14] Vayu the Brahmin gracefully yielded to the intrigues of the Rajah's servants, drained the last cup, and fell asleep with picturesque languor. Another reviewer expressed his enthusiasm for the expressivity of all the mime scenes done by Nijinsky. [15]

But the role of the Hurricane was followed once again by endless pas de deux. By the middle of the official season something had begun to go wrong with Nijinsky.

He began to miss his classes with Legat, more and more often professed to be ill just before a performance, and danced capriciously and sluggishly in the academic repertoire. Critics noticed this at once. Some feared that his illness would "impede the development of his wonderful talent." [16] Others complained that the dancer "for some reason now appears on stage very rarely," that he was constantly "out of sorts," that his dancing seemed "somehow rickety." [17]

But from time to time Nijinsky would mix them all up. If *Le Pavillon d'Armide* or *Chopiniana* was billed, then his illness would disappear like magic. He rehearsed with the utmost vigor, demonstrating unexpected technical feats and skill. The next day the newspapers would admit that the dancer "was in very good form yesterday" and would sing their praises of his "vitality" and his "remarkable lightness and softness," describing how the "air supports him and keeps him from descending to earth."

The key to this riddle lay in the fact that Nijinsky had begun to work with Cecchetti. Cecchetti gave private classes and many leading dancers of the Imperial Ballet had gone to him. Diaghilev persuaded Nijinsky to follow their happy example and often used to accompany him to the little hall that occupied half of the Italian maestro's apartment.

At these moments no one else was around except for Cecchetti and his wife. They were a very curious couple. Cecchetti was completely gray and, as old age approached, he became even shorter, or so it seemed. But he retained his vivid temperament. Normally affectionate and cheerful, he turned into a real demon at his classes and was quick to apply his stick if the "first subjects" of the Mariinsky were slow on the uptake. Signora Cecchetti, whom the maestro honored as "Madame" when talking to her in the presence of his pupils, matched her husband's fiery temper with her own serene character. She was accustomed to their nomadic way of life and was always trying to create the necessary atmosphere of comfort.

Diaghilev loved to sit with his back to the mirror and, leaning his large head against the high back of a wooden chair, watch the class. The terrifying teacher became unusually meek and mild with Nijinsky. Whistling the dance tunes, with his black eyes shining, he would devise more and more difficult exercises for his pupil, this pupil who so miraculously embodied his dream of the perfect dancer. And the pupil felt himself free as with no one else. He even became talkative and began to discuss this or that exercise. This made Diaghilev think that perhaps there really was trustfulness, openness, and responsiveness to human sympathy in Nijinsky's nature.

At that moment the history of ballet was performing a very clever trick. Nijinsky, who had resurrected the classical male dance, would soon have to renounce it. It was precisely when he was attaining the heights of technique with Cecchetti, the last of an ancient line of virtuosi, that Nijinsky began to neglect the models of the "pure classics" on stage. Diaghilev encouraged Nijinsky's scorn for the repertoire on which he had been nurtured. But Diaghilev did not do this merely to hit back at the Office of the Imperial Theaters. He sincerely believed that the repertoire was dead. Consequently, he urged Fokine to experiment with his pictorial, natural movements in which there was no place for those bravura flourishes that Nijinsky exercised under Cecchetti's supervision and that Diaghilev actually liked very much.

In his own way, Diaghilev was right. As always, he sensed, he *knew* what was needed at a certain moment in time. Time had caught the academic ballet theater napping, and time demanded the wholesale abolition of many of its aesthetic conventions. But the demand was not in effect for long. The classical dance was resurrected so quickly that, a decade later, Diaghilev was forced to take the young dancer Serge Lifar to Cecchetti. As Lifar himself admitted, at that time he was a complete ignoramus as far as the classical dance was concerned. By then Nijinsky had turned thirty and was already a legend. However, time and Diaghilev once again came into their own. Time brought forth new talents from the Russian school, and they, in turn declared Fokine's aesthetics to be moribund. Diaghilev gave these talents the opportunity of establishing counterreforms. Lifar was, as it were, remolded by Cecchetti to embody the ideas advocated on the foundation of the restored classical dance. And like a phoenix, the dance arose from the ashes of its victims. Ashes could not be avoided. The altar fires were used to melt down the elements from which the new classical dance was created. The purveyor of these elements was Nijinsky the choreographer, who refused Nijinsky the dancer even those few classical conventions that had been essential to Fokine.

The season at the Mariinsky was coming to an end. Preparations for the 1910 Paris tour were underway.

The members of Diaghilev's "committee" assembled once more at his apartment and took their seats at the round table by the boiling

Enrico Cecchetti

samovar. They were knights proud of their victory and ready for new crusades, new adventures.

Next to Benois sat the very proper and silent Walter Fedorovich Nouvel. A first-class musician, he had been one of the founders of the World of Art group. Nouvel and Benois had been friends since their schooldays, and they called each other "Valechka" and "Shura." Bakst installed himself more comfortably, laid a sheet of paper in front of him, and immediately began to sketch. The gray-haired, kindhearted General Nikolai Mikhailovich Bezobrazov smiled about at everyone. He had already been an experienced balletomane when the young Benois was just being initiated into the secrets of Terpsichore, and he attended these meetings as a much esteemed patron of the new art. His eyes flashing, Fokine ardently whispered something to Sergei Leonidovich Grigoriev. The latter tried to keep in the background. He had been a member of the corps de ballet and not a very good one, but Diaghilev divined an administrative talent in him. As always, Diaghilev was not mistaken, and Grigoriev kept his position as régisseur throughout the twenty years of the Diaghilev ballet.

Nanny poured out the tea. Diaghilev opened his black book full of odd notes and jottings,[18] and began to speak.

He said that after the phenomenal success of the previous summer, they had to formulate a clear campaign plan. The ballets of the next season would have to be no less novel and no less interesting. It would be wonderful to show the Parisians something Russian, a fairy tale. Actually, he had already asked Anatol Konstantinovich Liadov (who had been his teacher in the harmony class at the conservatory) to compose a piece of music based on the Firebird theme.

Nouvel interpolated delicately that Liadov was not exactly famous for his speed of execution; he might let them down. But Diaghilev interrupted him.

For the second ballet, Diaghilev continued, they could take Rimsky-Korsakov's *Schéhérazade*. He paused and then added that he was just a bit troubled by the third part of this symphonic poem. It wasn't very interesting and, the main thing, couldn't be danced. It would have to be cut.

Nouvel mumbled something about "barbarity," but simply shrugged his shoulders and went over to play *Schéhérazade* as a duet with

Diaghilev. Fokine leaned on the piano while they played and was soon nodding his head in time.

Coming back to the table, Diaghilev said that they needed two more ballets. He looked about at everyone and his eye alighted on Benois. Benois faltered and then declared unexpectedly: "*Giselle.*" Diaghilev raised his eyebrows. "Yes, I mean *Giselle,*" Benois went on, unruffled. "How great it would be to give back to the French their own classics . . . and, besides, Adam's music is charming."

Diaghilev continued to frown. He thought that the French would expect a surprise. But how could you surprise anyone with *Giselle*?

He wrote down *Schéhérazade* and *Firebird* in his black book and left the matter of the two other ballets open.

That evening Diaghilev told Nijinsky about the committee meeting. The dancer was silent. Diaghilev wanted to know his opinion. Then, choosing his words awkwardly, Nijinsky mentioned that ever since ballet school he had dreamed of doing *Giselle.* He felt that no one who danced it understood the part of Albrecht. Albrecht wasn't just a . . . he didn't just deceive a girl so as to have a good time. He was in search of something. He needed to find beauty.

At the next committee meeting, Benois again brought up the matter of *Giselle,* but Diaghilev appeared not to hear him. Bezobrazov, whose bass voice could not fail to be heard, gave his support to Benois, remarking that this pearl of the old classics would shine brilliantly in contrast to Fokine's innovative effects. Grigoriev then added cautiously that the company knew *Giselle,* so they could save time on this and give it to rehearsing other ballets. Diaghilev looked from Grigoriev to Bakst.

Bakst forced his attention away from the female figure that he was drawing. He had been adorning her tiny waist (as if she were wearing a fashionable corset) and her luscious hips in a see-through blouse and stylized trousers. He began to talk hurriedly, not about *Giselle,* but about a shah (and now Bakst began to describe a whole pantomime) who, having found his unfaithful wife in the arms of an "unbelievable, unbelievable" Negro, ordered the whole harem to be massacred.

Everyone laughed. Diaghilev gave up and turned to Nouvel. The latter suggested that, given such great talents as Pavlova and Nijinsky,

131

it was worth taking the risk. Everyone knew how good Pavlova was as Giselle. As for Nijinsky, so little appreciated on the Russian stage— well, he might just astound everyone in the role of the hero (Grigoriev supplied the name, "Albrecht"). Nouvel emphasized that he might even astound the French—and everyone else for that matter.

Diaghilev, deep in thought, was playing with his monocle. Benois, knowing how "Seriozha loved to be theatrical," immediately suspected that everything had already been decided: *Giselle* was already part of the season's repertoire, but for some reason or other this was still being kept a secret.

Diaghilev quickly changed the subject: *Giselle* or no *Giselle*, they still didn't have a fourth ballet.

Thanks to Bakst, the fourth ballet was found on the spur of the moment. For about two years the journal called *Satirikon* had been coming out in St. Petersburg.[19] Among the hundreds of journals that had been in existence for decades and others that had come and gone overnight, this one had immediately attracted the attention of the reading public. Its very title, reminiscent of Petronius's *Satyricon*, was intriguing. It promised to maintain a skeptical attitude to reality and, therefore, a freedom of form and a free choice of diverse themes. The editors were for the most part young, although they already included quite a number of talented people: the prose writers Averchenko and Teffi; the poets Sasha Chernyi, Potemkin, and Agnivtsev; the artists Re-Mi and Radakov. The first issue promised its subscribers much scathing satire and venomous laughter for the future. For its cover Bakst had depicted Zeus casting bolts of lightening down to the streets of a mournful modern city.

Satirikon kept its promises. But a lyrical element could also be detected among its sharp political attacks and taunts at everyday philistine life; and this element concealed in turn a desire to escape from politics and the hateful tedium of everyday life—into laughter. Sasha Chernyi declaimed this in his poem called *The Oasis:*

> And laughter is a magic alcohol,
> That counteracts our earthly hell,
> Sonorously it lulls our pain to sleep,
> As the waves do a dead Naiad.

The World of Art artists had also dreamed of magic "oases." So it was natural that, when the *Satirikon* editors decided to give a ball in the Pavlova Hall [20] on Troitsky Street, they should have turned to Bakst (who brought Fokine in) for the "magic alcohol." True, it was the "magic alcohol" not of laughter but rather of an illusory smile.

The organizers of the ball expected the atmosphere to be very free and easy, as in a Paris cabaret. But when the visitors came up the stairs into the main hall with the stage and into the adjacent foyers, they were confronted with gigantic caricatures on the walls and with various platforms erected in odd places. Their impression was a despondent one. The MC's bustled about on the platforms, appearing, disappearing, changing their costumes and masks. But, like waves pounding a cliff, all this merely smashed against the indifference of the guests.

Toward morning the waves brought up an entertaining number devised by Bakst and Fokine.

In the main hall a pianist started to play Schumann's *Carnaval* and the curtain parted on stage: ladies in crinolines and bonnets, gentlemen in white top hats passed in glittering array about a tree and a bench beneath. As one of the guests said, "It was like a dream." [21]

Pierrot intruded into their elegant promenade. The spectators could recognize the narrow, hook-nosed, nervous countenance of a famous producer beneath all that powder. They whispered, "That's Vsevolod Meierkhold." Pierrot waved the long sleeves of his white smock in an awkward, un-balletlike fashion as he ran after the girls. But they just laughed and slipped away on the arms of their escorts.

Suddenly Papillon, a young girl disguised as a butterfly, darted out on the stage and began to tease Pierrot, flying around him in circles. Thinking he had caught Papillon in his wide-brimmed hat, he began to lull his captive to sleep. But when he saw that he was caressing only a phantom, he burst into tears.

A new couple started in, quickening the pace of the melancholy action: Harlequin, in a half-mask looking like his second face, and Columbine, bedecked like a china doll. They ran in as if they had been wound up by an invisible mechanic. She minced daintily on the tips of her toes. He embraced her and ran beside her, jumping about like a candle flame. The fantastic run ended in a fantastic confession of love. The jesting but gentle Harlequin pulled his heart from his breast and threw it at the feet of Columbine. Then he played out his jealousy by turning into a rainbow-colored top: the many-colored lozenges of his tights fused into one and then became distinct again as Harlequin rotated slower and slower, subsiding on the floor with the final cadence.

The spectators thought they also recognized Columbine and Harlequin, mentioning the mysterious charm of Tamara Karsavina and the bubbling gaiety of Nijinsky.

The couples in the carnival mingled in a waltz. They ran off the stage, down the side stairs, and dragged the audience into their dance.

But Harlequin, who had so intoxicated the *Satirikon* artists and their guests with dancing "that counteracts our earthly hell," took Papillon and Columbine by the arm and escaped with them behind the scenes. Later, Nijinsky and his sister Bronislava escorted Karsavina home.

(*left*) Karsavina as Columbine and Nijinsky as Harlequin in *Le Carnaval*. Drawing by Ludwig Kainer.

(*right*) Nijinsky as Harlequin in *Le Carnaval*. The original casting of this ballet has been disputed in several conflicting accounts. Nijinska, who danced Papillon, says that Nijinsky was Harlequin. In any event, he later scored great success in the role.

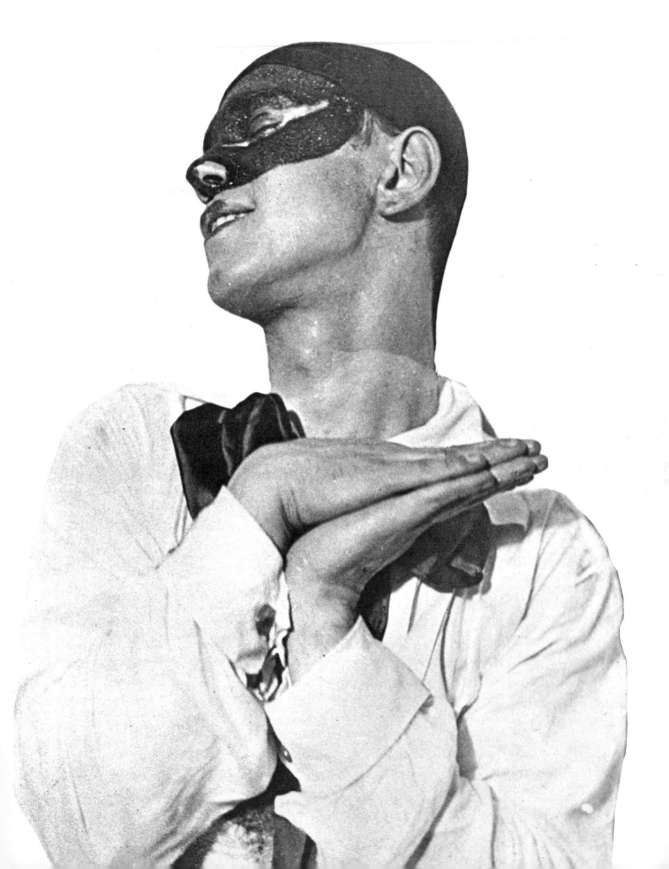

Nijinsky was now calling Karsavina "Tatochka." They were joined by the friendship of partners, a friendship developed by habit. They were always dancing together, and it seemed that they would soon be leading future tours, because it had become obvious that Pavlova was going to break with the Diaghilev enterprise.

There were various reasons for this, but two of them were directly related to the enterprise itself. First and foremost, Pavlova had become more and more put out by the Fokine repertoire, by the constant theme of fate and lifeless beauty. Furthermore, however much Pavlova was enthusiastic about innovative experiments, the classical dance remained the air she breathed. But Fokine was rejecting the classical dance in its pure forms with more and more insistence. The second reason was not a programmatic one, but for Pavlova it was important: the ballerina did not like to share success. Alas, Pavlova was jealous of Nijinsky; she regarded him as a rival, as a usurper of her primary position—something that Nijinsky did not understand in the least.

After her departure for America, the newspapers ran numerous accounts of her triumphs. Gradually rumors appeared in the press that she was preparing to dance in London and that she had invited Mikhail Mordkin to be her partner.

Karsavina, on the contrary, revealed her personality by performing in Fokine's ballets. She was particularly attracted by the variations on the theme of fatal temptation and by dance movements that left the academic conventions far behind. Moreover, Karsavina was not one for putting on airs, something of which even the best artists can be guilty, and she was not prey to outbursts of arrogance and childish pouting. (Who knows? Perhaps such outbursts are really only the reverse side of creative inspiration.) The noble and languid beauty of Karsavina, star of the second and of many subsequent Paris seasons, shone with a constant light. Even when she lost her patience in some dispute over some point of performance, Karsavina (unlike Pavlova) was quite incapable of breaking down or bursting out in hysterics, although there were times when she retreated in tears.

Later on she could recall the tears she had shed at rehearsals for *Giselle,* which did become part of the program for the second Paris season, along with *The Firebird, Schéhérazade,* and *Le Carnaval.*

Apart from *The Firebird*, Nijinsky was involved in everything. He was particularly enthusiastic about *Giselle*, which he approached in a new way. That unconscious ability to assimilate a role (something that Benois had noticed in the dancer) now gave way to perplexity and hesitation long before the rehearsals. Incidentally, *Giselle* was rehearsed very little. Fokine was totally absorbed by the production of *Schéhérazade* and *The Firebird* and the alterations for *Le Carnaval*: in these he revealed his amazing fantasy and tenacity. But he worked on *Giselle* only because he had to.

On the other hand, Nijinsky, whom Diaghilev had advised to attend a recital of Romantic composers and to read Hoffmann, Shakespeare, and Maeterlinck, suddenly started to write.

Not one line has survived from these writings, and later on, in his diary, Nijinsky made no mention of *Giselle*, although many incidents were connected with it. His appearance in *Giselle* on the Mariinsky stage was almost the occasion for police reprisals.

However, *Giselle* was not at first understood in Paris and, in contrast to Fokine's exotic ballets, did not receive its due. But Nijinsky used the role of Albrecht as a nucleus for the development of his poetical designs, as a beginning of his own independent art. There were neither obstacles to this nor external influences. Fokine concentrated on his own work and did not interfere. Diaghilev watched with interest how this artistic embryo was maturing in someone who, thitherto, had been the timid executor of other people's wishes. Nijinsky, who had known various Albrechts since his childhood, set out to find his own interpretation.

He did not take to the image of a spoiled and pampered count who was supposed to have seduced an innocent peasant girl for the sake of his own amusement. Neither did he like the hero's repenting and asking the forgiveness of his dead sweetheart. The Romantic theme of the nineteenth-century ballet, the expiatory agonies of all these Albrechts, Siegfrieds, and Solors, seemed rather simple-minded, even obsolete, in their traditional form. The actor did not need sin and moral expiation. Sin was to be understood as a necessary condition for the discovery of oneself.

Nijinsky's hero saw beauty as the only value in the world, but he did not imagine that it could save the world and he did not intend

(left) Karsavina and Nijinsky in *Les Sylphides*, advertising the second Saison Russe.
(above) The Avenue de l'Opéra, Paris.

to save beauty. He loved beauty passionately, but he remained a dreamer, searching idly for its secret meaning. He found here, so to speak, a fragmentation of the soul, and, unexpectedly, came close to the lyrical heroes of Symbolism. Nijinsky's Albrecht saw Giselle in more or less the same way as the Poet sees The Stranger in Blok's play,[22] that is, merely as the alienated embodiment of his own spiritual discord.

But, in transforming the concrete heroine of a traditional ballet into an abstract symbol, the dancer encountered desperate resistance from his partner.

As soon as the rehearsals for the second season began, quarrels broke out between Karsavina and Nijinsky, normally so accommodating. Mindful of Benois' design, a Giselle bedecked in a costume from the epoch of Gautier and Carlotta Grisi, Karsavina followed the

139

long-established staging. She thus expected Albrecht to respond to her childish coquetry, to her sudden palpitations during her dance, and then to her insanity caused by his unfaithfulness. But Nijinsky just bit his nails absent-mindedly. As if contemplating her from afar, he did not hasten to involve himself in this pantomime dialogue.

She tried being insistent, tried to remind him that at this or that place Albrecht was supposed to approach Giselle. He responded by mumbling reluctantly that he knew the role quite well.

The result was that Karsavina burst out crying, although her bitter tears in no way mollified Nijinsky. Diaghilev had to go up on stage and, putting his arm about Karsavina, lead her offstage. Having little time for sentiment, he nevertheless tried to console her and even furnished her with his own handkerchief. "Nijinsky is not being capricious," he said, "he's not being capricious. He is searching for something. He has volumes of notes concerning the role of Albrecht." This did not make Karsavina feel any better. She dried her tears but, at heart, she was not consoled.[23]

On 4 June 1910 the second Saison Russe opened at the Paris Opéra. The public had snatched up the tickets and was now waiting for surprises. It was now a matter of honor for many snobs to be seen at the première of the Russians. (Indeed, even Marcel Proust forsook his voluntary imprisonment for it!) And Diaghilev certainly provided a surprise by firing his first salvo through that vast auditorium—the dazzling *Schéhérazade*. Even after many years, French tourists who set foot on Eastern shores would think of Bakst's "barbaric" colors and exclaim, "It's just like the Ballet Russe!" But the multicolored spectacle of *Schéhérazade* was not simply that of an oriental bazaar. The emerald green, gold, and black draperies on stage, the sultry patterns of orange, blue, pink, and dark red costumes gave off an aura of fateful passion. The action unfolded in the tensely dramatic contrasts so beloved by Fokine.

Odalisques began to dance before the Shah, their bodies swaying in languid rhythms. Shah Shahriar (Alexei Bulgakov, one of the most celebrated mimes of the Russian ballet) was majestic and valorous, but he seemed to be consumed by some gloomy thought: he was loath to depart for the hunt and took his solemn farewell of the Sultana, Zobeide. Luxuriating among her pillows, she also tarried long. The audience recognized Ida Rubinstein, the Cleopatra of the preceding season. They recognized her peculiar immobility and the still more peculiar "reticence" of movement when she arose and walked; at every step she swayed her narrow body slightly as she threw back her small but proud head. She stepped resolutely—her legs clad in *sharovary* tied at the ankle with precious stones—and she held her elbows firmly to her hips, thereby rejecting balletic convention by her very angularity.

"She is excessively beautiful, like a liqueur from poison fragrances," thought the poet and artist Jean Cocteau, memorizing these words for a future review. A contemporary of Nijinsky, he passed initiation into the Ballet Russe circle and was soon appreciated by Diaghilev.

The Shah left his harem. Now, as the melody twisted and turned in its supple repetitions, his wives danced before the Eunuch, danced as they would to entertain their lord and master. They beseeched, they commanded the Eunuch, whispering to him of their desire. At last he threw open the bronze door. The languid rhythms were broken as Indians dressed in bronze costumes rushed in, seized the eager maidens, and bore them away to the pillows. From the silver door appeared black slaves dressed in silver, and the stage was filled with new couples. And then, slowly, imperiously, Zobeide gestured the Eunuch toward the golden door. He reluctantly turned the key and, on the threshold, contrasting to the bronze and silver torrent, appeared but one slave—an "unbelievable" Negro, as Bakst had dreamed of.

Dressed in light gray and in *sharovary* of a golden, flowing fabric, he flew to Zobeide's couch in a single leap. From the length of the leap it was clear to all that this was Nijinsky. Moreover, the dancer was once again representing a slave, his third after *Armide* and *Cléopâtre*, and, like the others, this Slave was also the whim of a royal mistress. But now he was not a mere page or a kitten. "A beautiful beast, like a tiger, strong, stealthy, and with a childlike smile," wrote Levinson of the Golden Slave.[24] Levinson, a champion of the Russian classical school came regularly to every Paris season.

The Golden Slave became the center of an orgiastic dance, the protagonist of Fokine's beloved bacchanalia. The dance weaved in and out, blazed up, grew broader, and attained incredible heights,

Nijinsky as the Golden Slave in *Schéhérazade*. Jean Cocteau was so moved by this ballet and by Nijinsky's dancing that he missed few chances to praise them, whether in drawings (as at right), in articles, or in poems. Marcel Proust, usually not a man of few words, was, for once, surprisingly succinct: writing to Reynaldo Hahn about the première of *Schéhérazade,* he declared, "I never saw anything so beautiful."

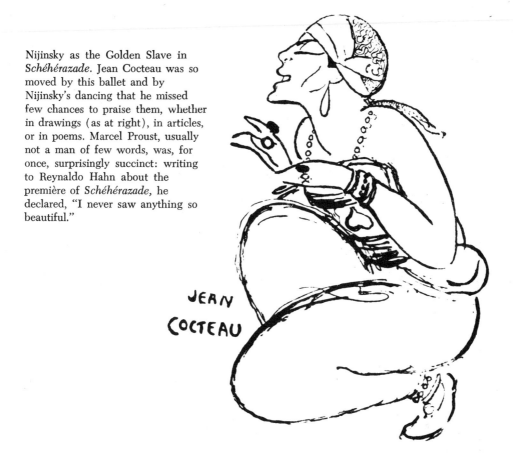

JEAN COCTEAU

to be suddenly broken off. After a deathly pause in the music and on stage, Shah Shahriar entered his harem. The hunt had been a trick suggested by his brother. And now, enraged, he gave the sign to his warriors.

The bodies interlaced once more, but in embraces of death, not of love. Among them, true to his instinct, the Golden Slave took to flight in gigantic leaps. He hid himself behind a huge incense burner, leaped out, and, like an ambushed hare, rushed back and forth, surrounded by the warriors. Struck by the curved blade of a scimitar, he made one last convulsive leap—an animal struck down at the height of its spring.

During the intermission those fond of metaphors spoke of a "tiger" and a "hare," of a "reptile glistening in its coils," and of a "bird beating against the bars of a cage." Cocteau, who was full of youthful ardor not yet spiced by the poison of sarcasm, soon provided the readers of *Comoedia* with an entire bouquet of such analogies. He wrote in one passage: "[Nijinsky] jumps like a young beast of prey that had been kept locked up in darkness and is now intoxicated by the light. His movements are sudden, like a tiger's; he reels from happiness; he gives out mute cries; his dark face is illumined by his white teeth; sensuously, he stretches out on the pillows where his golden *sharovary* undulate, like a fish gleaming in the sun." [25]

This was all very true, but it was a superficial truth. The Paris cultural elite did not understand that the themes of Russian poetry had penetrated their ancient theater, that Bulgakov's Shahriar and Nijinsky's Golden Slave were the echoes of Acmeism. [26] One was the victim of introspection, the other was the servant only of his instinct, and both were toys in the hands of fate; neither was given to taste the full secret of beauty. In any case, neither the authors nor the dancers had set themselves any conscious aims. The theme had arisen spontaneously.

In *Schéhérazade* Nijinsky submitted to each and every command of the producers. He submitted to Fokine in his rendition of the Siamese Dance to Sinding's music that Fokine had composed as a divertissement under the title of *Les Orientales*. Fokine used Nijinsky as if he were malleable clay, molding various poses, each more whimsical than the last. Bakst observed what was going on, smiled to himself, narrowed his eyes, and proceeded to sketch the pattern being woven before him. Trying it this way and that, he colored in this ornamental pattern of Nijinsky's movements.

At the performance of *Les Orientales*, the audience was confronted with a figure looking like the statue of an ancient oriental god in the midst of the empty stage, but the statue was too small for such a big space. A golden *kazakin*, pink *sharovary* down to the knees, blue stockings, and a tassle of green silk hanging from a golden cap onto berouged cheeks began to fuse and to blaze in a game of tortuous gestures. The neck of this dancer was long and stretched out; his eyes extended to his temples beneath the painted arches of his eyebrows; his lips were compressed to hide some mystery; and his fingers, bending and coiling, created a pattern as if to entwine the angular and plastic lines of the slow dance.

(*left*) Nijinsky in the Siamese Dance in *Les Orientales*.

(*above*) Nijinsky in his Siamese costume, photographed in the garden of the artist Jacques-Emile Blanche.

After the second program had been given, it became fashionable to speak of the "bestiality" of Nijinsky's creations. Harlequin was described as "supernatural," and this creature "with a body resembling a steel spring" and embodying the "soul of knavery" was declared to be "very unlike a human being." Spectators extolled the Slave's "bestiality." They were enchanted by the strange indifference of the Siamese god.

Such enthusiasm was oppressive to Nijinsky. His fear of people did not destroy his hopes of communicating with them more closely. But the possibility of doing so became more and more remote. He was admired from afar as if he were an expensive toy. People took great pains to meet with him so as to boast their acquaintance with a celebrity. Furthermore, he was accessible only through Diaghilev, and Diaghilev was the one who picked and chose.

Diaghilev ordered Vasili to take Nijinsky to the artist Jacques-Emile Blanche. When they got there, Vasili dressed him up in his godlike costume and, while a photographer was setting up his tripod on the lawn of the English garden, Blanche did a few sketches. Diaghilev took Nijinsky to Misia Sert's five o'clock, where the dancer was seated at the piano next to Ravel so that, once again, a photographer could record the two artists together. Diaghilev brought important gentlemen and sumptuously dressed ladies to Nijinsky's dressing room. They spoke as if they were dealing with a child who couldn't talk properly yet, and, smiling wearily, Nijinsky felt his human face turning into a mask. Gradually the consciousness of his inescapable solitude became more intense, and so evolved the idea of the mask of the eternal clown. An oppressive and importunate idea that later made itself known in his diary—in Nijinsky's transformed interpretation of himself as the "clown of God."

People grew accustomed to looking for traces of theatrical masks on Nijinsky's face. What else could one expect? So then he tried starting from the other end. In *Giselle* he came on without a mask.

This was the first time that Nijinsky failed to identify completely with Benois' design for Albrecht's entrance. This design was for a handsome but affected curly-haired youth in a Romantic costume (known in ballet terminology as a "troubadour" costume). Unquestioning, Nijinsky tried it out for size, and on the evening of the per-

Nijinsky and Maurice Ravel.

formance he put on the yellow tights, the shirt with its rounded, turn-down collar and soft, lace cuffs and sleeves. Over this he put on a dark doublet with a pocket-bag at the hip. Then, quite arbitrarily, he ruffled up the curls of his dark wig and carelessly threw them back in long locks. Onto the stage walked not a pampered, neat, and tidy dandy, but a poet obsessed by a dream.

As usual, Albrecht called Giselle to a rendezvous. But the abrupt shifts in their amorous dialogue immediately conveyed the extraordinary behavior of Nijinsky's hero that Karsavina had had to resign herself to. This dancer who so very recently had delighted in his primitive and unbridled passions in *Schéhérazade* now seemed to fear touching his partner. Thereby he indicated that his hero could perceive in Giselle a world both attractive and frightening in its purity. Albrecht smiled pensively as he watched Giselle telling her fortune with a daisy and as, surprised by Hilarion, he puts off the encroachment of his rival. The madness and death of Giselle occasioned his despair: he was like Hamlet, the innocent perpetrator of Ophelia's madness and death. This lyrical hero of the French ballet of the 1840s had survived for more than fifty years in Russia. Behind the impregnable walls of the Imperial Ballet he had preserved his unchanging character, his behavior, and his worldview. But in the guise of Nijinsky, this hero had now brought the complexity of modern Russian lyricism onto that very stage on which he had been born. He seemed to embody the idea that Blok had just expressed: "In our own time it is in lyricism that the experiences of our soul, of necessity so isolated, find strength. These experiences are generally complex and chaotic; to understand them, you have to be 'a bit like that' yourself." [27] Nijinsky was "a bit like that," and, consequently, in *Giselle* discovered a complex alloy of experiences.

While no less complex, Act II dispensed with the chaos of the "individual soul, its doubts, its passions, failures and degradations." [28] It is in this act that the action of *Giselle* leaves its dramatic form and becomes pure lyricism. Having changed his costume, Nijinsky's Albrecht now seemed to have thrown off his doubts. He entered in a cloak of mourning, oblivious to the fact that the white flowers he was carrying were about to fall and be scattered. Slowly he crossed the stage toward the cross on Giselle's grave. The square collar of his velvet jacket visible beneath his cloak revealed his neck, and his white shirt could be seen protruding from the sleeves of his cloak. He was once again the troubadour, but the knight–troubadour of the Beautiful Lady,[29] of an illusion born of his imagination. When the illusion appeared, Albrecht's face shone like that of the poet who had embodied the image soaring in his consciousness in sound and rhyme. Throwing up his hand in a gesture of astonishment and rapture, he tried to detain the phantom. He might have spoken the words uttered by Pelléas: "I was alarmed, I searched everywhere at home, I searched everywhere abroad. . . . I could not find beauty. . . . But here at last I have found you!" [30] Much more the hero of Maeterlinck than of Gautier, this Albrecht did not fear the vindictive wilis. They had also been created by his own poetic dream, created to accompany his flight of inspiration materialized in his dance.

148

Nijinsky as Albrecht in *Giselle*, Act II.

His dancing seemed like classical music, but was illumined from within by a new meaning and was, therefore, dazzling in its perfection of forms. Even the strictest pedant would have found no cause for quarrel here: the methods were correct, the postures of the body in the air and on the ground were impeccable, the pauses were firm and precise. But this masterful technique seemed to come of its own accord and, for the performer, seemed to have no meaning. The soaring diagonal of his cabrioles cut across the stage in a sudden burst of force and inspiration, his tours en l'air made the dreaming hero dizzy, and, suddenly, he ceased them and fell to his knees before the beautiful mirage.

Who could have known· then that *Giselle* would be the only ballet in which Nijinsky was able to free himself from his mask and express his individuality to the full in the pure forms of the classical dance? Because it was *Giselle* that played such a fateful role in the destiny of this social misfit, and it did so with the same degree of paradox that marked the whole of Nijinsky's life. True, part of the blame lies with the dancer, even if he was innocent of active perpetration.

Diaghilev again insisted on a long holiday in Venice, and just before the beginning of the season Nijinsky sent off a letter to St. Petersburg saying that he had had sunstroke and then angina. This annoyed the administration. Teliakovsky said that this time Diaghilev had really behaved impudently and that he'd soon be arranging it so that he'd put Imperial dancers on tour in the Imperial Theaters. Soon Teliakovsky issued an order to "terminate issuance of salary" and in no case to raise it when Nijinsky returned. He uttered a classic phrase, "No talent is irreplaceable," and added that a certain Pierre Vladimirov would be graduating from the school in the spring, and people were already saying that he could outdo Nijinsky by far.[31]

On 26 November 1910, a dark winter morning, Nijinsky arrived in the rehearsal hall straight from the station. He felt like a stranger. The season was at its height; the classes, the rehearsals, and the performances were all running smoothly. The inevitable friendships and hostilities, the merry and wicked intrigues had already formed. Furthermore, after the sharp change of climate, the dancer felt very weak, and this alienated him still further from people. It was no good pretending. As before, Nijinsky just could not take the part of a natural and sociable comrade.

Still, he was glad to get home. His mother had waited patiently, unquestioning, never referring to anything taboo. The unwritten conventions of the "Nijinsky clan" returned Vaslav and Bronislava to the cosy, serene dependence of their early childhood.

He didn't see Diaghilev very often. The latter was busy preparing the next season and contented himself with Vasili's regular reports. Gradually, the old theater routine reestablished itself. Nijinsky got involved in it again. The permanent rules that he was forced to obey along with any other member of the company soothed him, and the régisseurs ordered him about as if they knew nothing about his reputation as the "miracle" on tour.

The newspaper gossip columns reported regularly that "Mr. Nijinsky still does not consider himself prepared and spends all his time exercising his dances." [32] At long last his first performance in *Giselle* was announced. This was destined to be Nijinsky's last stage appearance in Russia.

On 23 January 1911, the hall of the Mariinsky shone as brilliantly as a gala performance. The royal box was occupied by the Dowager Empress Marie Fedorovna, two grand duchesses, several ladies-in-waiting, and Prince Sergei Mikhailovich (Kschessinska's eldest "patron"). The director's box opposite was empty. Teliakovsky was in Moscow.

Behind the curtain Nijinsky and Karsavina were going through their phrase from the main waltz. Taking each other's arms, they tapped the floor with their toes completely synchronized, then threw out their legs in high pas de basque, which Nijinsky moderated by conforming to his partner's leap. All around there was that same hustle and bustle as there had been ten years ago when the schoolboy Nijinsky had made his debut: the soloists were warming up, the members of the corps de ballet were chattering away in groups, someone peered at the audience through the "eye" cut in the curtain, and that same bowlegged prop man was scattering yellow rosin powder over the stage. Krupensky stroked his black beard beneath his snow-white cuff as he towered above a group of conferring officials. Alexander Yakovlevich Golovin detached himself from this group and came up to Nijinsky, saying that as a consultant artist for the administration of the Imperial Theaters and also "as a friend" (he emphasized these words) he considered it his duty to warn Nijinsky that it would be risky to appear in that costume: it might not appeal to . . . and, significantly, Golovin omitted to say to whom.[33]

Nijinsky lost his head. He had put on the costume with the administration's permission. It was Benois' costume, the same one he had worn in Paris, and it hadn't caused any embarrassment there. But the régisseur was already requesting all those not coming on now to vacate the stage.

Golovin shrugged his shoulders and returned to the affable and smiling Krupensky. The orchestra struck up the first phrase of the short overture.

As always, the music shut Nijinsky off from reality, transporting him into its own world. The decor that he had known since childhood, the choreography that he had already mastered in Paris, even the very floor of the Mariinsky stage, curiously springy—all these things helped Nijinsky immerse himself in the aura of the role he loved so much. After Act I, the dancer waited out the intermission, profoundly affected by the death of Giselle and not noticing that his clothes were being changed. He simply darkened his eyes a bit and put white powder on his cheeks. He noticed neither the whispering nor the smiles of malice (and of sympathy) of the people crowding about the stage just before Act II.

The next morning, Nijinsky suddenly felt very happy when Vasili brought in the newspapers with his breakfast. The *St. Petersburg Feuilleton*, whatever its reputation for vulgarity, pronounced: "He depicted a Count Albrecht with long hair and furnished him with a little purse, the kind that sweet ladies keep their handkerchief in. But what was really smart was in the 'inexpressibles'. . . ."[34] This newspaper always discussed art in this way. Still, it was pleasant to read, but in Russian, something that had already become a cliché with the French, that is, about the "noble and enchanting beauty of Vestris resurrected." And it was of interest to ponder the remarks of another reviewer who had been "touched and delighted" by Nijinsky's rendition of Albrecht, even though it would seem that this reviewer had not fully understood this rendition since he wrote: "He has not yet

Karsavina and Nijinsky in *Giselle,* Act II.

brought all the groups of elements out of which he creates his plastic image on stage into line or into total harmony."[35] On the other hand, it was wonderful to learn from one reviewer that he (Nijinsky) possessed a "rare gift for movement but an even more accomplished sense of style." Eagerly he read further: "Nijinsky's leaps and 'flights' take on an extraordinary purport, an essential artistry. He knows how to find the right movements of the arms, the necessary turns and inclinations of the head to go with them. He reveals the 'idea' of every form, of every element of the dance through subtle, almost imperceptible allusions." [36] This kind of talk required the most elegant descriptions, the most ingenious analogies. That is how they began to write about him in Russia.

Vasili interrupted his train of thought, announcing: "You are to report to the office."

When Nijinsky arrived at the Office of the State Theaters, Krupensky did not invite the dancer to sit down. He himself arose from his wide, solid desk and declared that Nijinsky had been fired from the Imperial Theaters—because of the costume he had worn in Act I of yesterday's *Giselle*.

Nijinsky could not himself remember afterward how he had blurted out to that repellent individual: "I am amazed by the St. Petersburg public. They go to the ballet as if it were a pub, and they have no appreciation of genuine costumes." [37] He said this, but then realized that the public had nothing to do with it.

Krupensky left the Office of the State Theaters and went up to Teliakovsky's apartment (Teliakovsky had just got back). He inserted the above words at the beginning of his report, adding that Nijinsky's claim was probably directed first and foremost at the royal box inasmuch as his costume "had caused a scandal there and the dowager empress had sent the Grand Duke Sergei Mikhailovich on stage to find out what kind of costume there would be in Act II. If it was to be a repeat version, then she intended to take the grand duchesses home immediately." [38]

The director suddenly flared up and proceeded to haul Krupensky over the coals: no sooner had he, Teliakovsky, departed from St. Petersburg than Krupensky had all this trouble, which he had to sort out now that he was back.

Nijinsky in the Mariinsky costume for Albrecht in *Giselle*, Act I. The costume designed by Benois for the Diaghilev production in Paris, which was the pretext for Nijinsky's dismissal when he wore it at the Mariinsky, was, basically, a pair of tights, a shirt, and a short jacket. The reason that it was allegedly so scandalous was that it lacked the short pants, or trunks, customarily worn by male dancers portraying princely characters on the Imperial stage. No photograph of this notorious costume is known to exist, but eyewitness accounts indicate that it was considerably more attractive than the severe Mariinsky version shown here.

He was worked up for good reason. It had all occurred, in fact, without his knowledge, and for many an evening thereafter he noted in his diary his various guesses as to why Nijinsky had really been made to retire so soon, and why the minister himself, Baron Frederiks, had sanctioned this without consulting him (Teliakovsky). One guess was that the "Nijinsky episode had been prepared by Diaghilev, Benois, and Co." who needed to procure the dancer permanently. Another guess was that that old fox Krupensky wanted it since "he hates anything to do with Fokine." [39] Yet a third guess was that the episode could be explained by Kschessinska's influence, although this was just gossip. Actually Kschessinska is supposed to have summoned the principal scandalmonger to her dressing room and to have told her that she was not the one who had driven Nijinsky out and that if she had had the power to fire people from the company, then, of course, she would have begun with this scandalmonger.[40] But for all these guesses, the mystery was never cleared up—although, actually, there probably was no mystery. It was simply chance that had made Nijinsky get caught up in the wheels of the bureaucratic machine, and the machine took him in its grasp, ground him up, and cast him out.

Teliakovsky soon turned to something else: he took to commenting in his diaries on the Russian and foreign press reports dealing with the "Nijinsky affair."

Teliakovsky was no fool, and he realized from experience that social opinion was not in his favor. Moreover, Nijinsky had to be replaced by Andrianov in the next *Giselle*, scheduled for three days later, for Wednesday, 26 January. On the Thursday following, even the reporter from the *St. Petersburg Feuilleton* described the "half-empty auditorium," confessed that the "performance was uninteresting," condemned the chastisement of the "administrative Arguses," declared Nijinsky to be an "innocent victim," and ended with these words: "There was the kind of tedious atmosphere in the auditorium yesterday that audiences generate when performers lack that divine light, the light of genuine talent."[41] But it was too late to do anything now. Teliakovsky was forced to "put on a good face." On 3 February he looked through various French newspapers and journals full of attacks on the bigotry of the Russian theater authorities and noted, "I think that Paris permits a great deal that Russia cannot." On 7 February he translated a sentence from the newspaper *Comoedia:* "Everything that is talented is trampled under foot in Russia."[42] He probably just shrugged his shoulders—he'd known that for a long time.

So Nijinsky left the Office of the State Theaters accompanied by the curious stares of all the staff. He dismissed the cabbie waiting for him and automatically set off for Nevsky Prospect. He stopped by the iron railing of Ekaterinsky Square and turned around. The building of the Alexandrinsky Theater hid Theater Street from him. He could see Apollo on his pediment, majestic, like Nicolas I, holding the reins of the four prancing horses drawing his chariot. Nijinsky stood there, his head raised, his mouth half-open like a child, and he contemplated this emblem of Russian art. His figure stood alone on the square, asleep in its eternal parade of statues, colonnades, and trees covered in hoarfrost.

He daydreamed. Deep in his memory he could hear the clatter of horses' hooves, the smirk on someone's bearded face leaning over him in a Cossack *papakha*. But then he had been wearing the coat of his uniform with its Imperial lyres on the collar. And now there were just ordinary people bustling about on Nevsky over yonder, and you could pass through them, and go wherever you wanted to. To the four corners of the Earth. Well, everything had turned out peacefully. Without whips, at least.

Turned out peacefully. But Nijinsky bore in his heart the scar of this Petersburg day throughout his life.

For a long time he wandered about the streets and embankments of this city of his childhood. He got home frozen stiff. It was warm and serene at home. A bundle of newspapers lay on the table in the sitting room.

He would have to explain things to his mother. No sooner had he begun his story than she burst out crying. As he consoled her, Nijinsky heard the inner door open and then close as if someone were creeping out. He thought that it was Vasili who might have gone to inform Diaghilev of the news, not trusting to the telephone.

The door flew open and then banged shut. Bronislava rushed in, still wearing her fur coat and hat. She had the slanting eyes of her brother, her mouth was rather too big, and she was shy and awkward like him, but she hid this beneath an affected devil-may-care attitude. Since childhood she had adored Vaslav. As soon as she had heard what had happened, she left the rehearsal and ran home. Embracing her mother with one arm, she shook her fist, declaring that she couldn't remain in a theater that could abide such abominations. No, not for the world.

She kept her word. Even though Teliakovsky ordered Krupensky to summon Bronislava and have a word with her, he was forced, ultimately, to stamp the word *Discharge* on the piece of paper beginning with the words, "In view of the dismissal of my brother, Vaslav Nijinsky, from the Imperial Theaters, I request the Office to remove my name from the list of Imperial Company." [43] She had not yet been in the company three years.

Reporters besieged the Nijinsky apartment. He himself would have liked to have been left in peace. But Diaghilev seized the opportunity of once more getting even with the enemy camp. So, wearily and reluctantly, Nijinsky told his story.

About how Alexander Dmitrievich Krupensky and Alexander Yakovlevich Golovin had at first "kindly agreed" to let him appear in the costumes that he had danced in "five times and not without success" on the stage of the Paris Opéra. How these costumes had been "made according to the designs of the famous Russian artist and art critic Alexandre Nicolaevich Benois." How he, Nijinsky, had always heeded the "authority of the art experts," and that his aim had been simply to "succeed artistically."

How he could not have disobeyed anyone, for the simple reason that no one had given any orders.

How, and here his voice fell flat and expressionless, he was "leaving the Russian stage prematurely," because he was only twenty-one. How he hoped that somewhere or other he would find a "position in which he would be judged according to his artistic activity and not according to a costume or dress that he happened to be wearing."

And finally, how he was baffled by the "official reasons that have terminated his artistic career in Russia so swiftly, so irrevocably—a career that he had only just begun." [44]

Nijinsky did not affect the indifference with which he told his story. He really couldn't have cared less. He was now even more dependent on Diaghilev. No longer would he be able to find a respite from his cares in the routine of the Imperial Theaters, even if it was a tedious routine. Of course, this wouldn't have given him freedom anyway. What freedom could there be with the Krupenskys of this world? But now, more than ever before, he felt himself to be a prisoner, albeit of his own universal fame. A young man who had scarcely attained the age of majority. A poor, helpless clown in the arena of the last masquerade of the Russian Empire.

4

DIAGHILEV GAVE NIJINSKY EVERY ATTENTION, as if he were recovering from a serious illness. He took him to his classes with Cecchetti. (Diaghilev was also negotiating with Cecchetti to try to engage him as teacher and mime for his company.) Diaghilev said that he had decided to organize a permanent company in which, of course, Nijinsky would shine amid a constellation of brilliant ballerinas. Now any dancer would agree to go on tour with Diaghilev at the slightest bidding. Kschessinska, for example, was already making strategic moves in this direction. Of course, these moves had to be encouraged, and Nijinsky could be promised as a partner. First, this would be a nice bomb to throw at Teliakovsky and his crowd. Second, despite her years, Kschessinska was still an excellent dancer. Third, and most important, she would help to attract others, bypassing Teliakovsky. A corps de ballet would be more difficult to assemble, but agents were even now looking for dancers in Russia and Poland; Cecchetti would give them polish. And next year Vaslav ought to try choreographing something. Yes, Diaghilev already had something in mind.

For the current season, Nijinsky and Karsavina had to prepare three new ballets by Fokine: *Le Spectre de la Rose, Narcisse,* and *Petrouchka.*

Diaghilev put great hopes on *Petrouchka.* After Stravinsky had played him his "Russian Dance" and "Petrouchka's Lament" (the basis of the music he still had to write), he offered to make peace with Benois. The latter was terribly angry. The previous season his name had not figured on the program for *Schéhérazade,* even though he had been the scenarist. But Benois became immediately enthusiastic with the idea of composing and designing a ballet on themes from the St. Petersburg fairground. Stravinsky and he finished the work in Rome in preparation for the arrival of the company.

Meanwhile, in St. Petersburg, in the same old German Club, Fokine was rehearsing *Le Spectre de la Rose.* Judged by the old concepts, this was not a ballet, but was really an expanded pas de deux for Karsavina and Nijinsky to the music of Weber's *Invitation to the Dance.* Jean-Louis Vaudoyer had suggested it after recalling the lines from Théophile Gautier's poem:

Je suis le spectre d'une rose
Que tu portais hier au bal.[1]

Bakst explained that this was the 1830s; that Karsavina should be dressed in a long, sumptuous gown with little sleeves, a sash, and a plunging neckline. Perhaps she would also wear at first a capacious cloak. Nijinsky appears to her only in a dream. He is more ephemeral than the young man in *Les Sylphides.* He is simply a perfume, the heady and intoxicating fragrance of a rose that has now begun to fade after the ball—where there had been such brilliance, so many amorous cavaliers, music. Bakst had not devised Nijinsky's costume yet; he'd have to see what Fokine would compose first.

Fokine listened, pulling at a lock of his thinning hair that had fallen on to his forehead. Image upon image crowded his mind. Taking advantage of a break in Bakst's monologue, he asked impatiently whether he might begin.

Soon all four were rejoicing in that rare happiness of artists captivated by a single idea and comprehending one another instantly.

Fokine demonstrated the entrance. Karsavina ran on. She glided smoothly on her toes, still enveloped by the music of the ball now resounding in her memory. She sank into a chair in the middle of the stage. Tired, she crossed her legs and then stretched them. She dropped her hands into the imaginary folds of her dress, bowed her head, and drowsily closed her eyes. The music entered a major key. Nijinsky took a run, soared up, flew through the air, and landed at her side. As if in a magic gesture, he flung open his arms, swaying on his legs now brought tightly together like the stalk of some plant. In subtle sweetness he contemplated the sleeping maiden. Then, to the calm almost recitational voice of Fokine, he rounded his arms above his head; his coarse, thick fingers suddenly seemed to be petals; and as the melody grew softer he began to whirl about, intoxicating his victim and luring her into a world of somnambulistic dreams.

Bakst was in a state of bliss. As always, he was smiling sideways

Michel Fokine. Detail of a drawing by Valentin Serov.

(*left*) The Théâtre de Monte-Carlo.

(*below*) An outing in Cannes. Left to right: Adolf Bolm, Ludmilla Schollar, Bronislava Nijinska. the ballet critic Valerian Svetlov, A. Botkina (a niece of Bakst), Ekaterina Oblokova.

into his red moustache. Not a single sketch had appeared on the white page of his album: he was loath to tear himself away from the magic power before him. In any case, he already knew how Nijinsky would be dressed.

By the end of the rehearsal the ballet was almost ready. Without touching his partner, the dancer lured her into the melodic flow of the waltz. His hands extended the motif, swirling and enveloping the movement like the fragrance of a flower. One moment she slowed her pace in order to catch the perfume wafting behind her, the next she knelt down and, whimsically, raised her slender hand to her face as she sought with her open but still sleeping eyes the phantom that was mocking her. Only before the final cadence of the music did Nijinsky put his arm around the waist of the weary and reclining Karsavina: the dream was about to become reality, but it would cease any moment. The final chords were sounding. Fokine raised himself from his seat and pronounced his last instruction in a clear whisper. Karsavina sank down into her chair and then seemed to wake up, opening her velvet eyes in astonishment. Nijijnsky flew back to the corner from which he had "appeared." He turned round and smiled, showing his uneven white teeth.

In March, Vaslav and Bronislava took a long farewell of their mother. They were going to Monte Carlo, the assembly point for the Diaghilev company. How strange it was to recall the snows of the St. Petersburg spring amid the decorations of Europe's gambling house. The Théâtre de Monte-Carlo was comfortable and, like every-thing else there, was controlled by the Casino. Built by Charles Garnier, the same architect who had designed the Paris Opéra, the Casino stood on a terrace above the sea. The smell of the sea wafted in through the open windows of the rehearsal halls; the sea itself was reflected in the glasses and decanters on restaurant tables, and at night it was full of moonlight.

On 6 April 1911, Diaghilev opened the tour with *Giselle*, danced by Karsavina and Nijinsky. He could have chosen a more exciting beginning, but he realized what this gesture meant to Nijinsky. This role, so recently dishonored, was to open the door to a future that, in Diaghilev's mind, would be a magnificent one. He was aware that many people regarded Nijinsky only as the ideal executor of other people's wishes. Perhaps Diaghilev himself was not sure of success, but he was ready to sacrifice his experience, his willpower, his gift of artistic insight in order to arouse the intuition of an original creator. He made grandiose plans. He carefully observed what was being done in art, what was attracting attention. One thing he was certain of: he would soon have to break with many of those comrades who were working with him, and he could see that Nijinsky would be the instrument of this rupture.

But for the moment, during the current season, Nijinsky should forget; his wounds must heal.

So *Giselle* opened the season, despite the obvious risk. The Monte Carlo audiences lacked the snobbish aestheticism of the Paris elite. Spectators of Paris debuts appraised them as works of art, but in Monte Carlo the center of attention was entertainment, roulette, and money. Diaghilev, trying to put his enterprise on a commercial footing, had come here for good reason. The aristocracy and plutocratic bourgeoisie led by the prince of Monaco now filled the auditorium, expecting to be entertained, hoping for intense emotions, even to be "knocked out of their seats."

Although *Giselle* did not fulfill their hopes of astonishment, it was nevertheless received with enthusiasm. Not just because Diaghilev had endeavored to stimulate interest in the rumors about the St. Petersburg scandal. Nijinsky's dancing conveyed something that appealed to any heart. Life itself had pierced the celestial dreams of his Albrecht and had broken through the barriers between reality and poetry. Albrecht shed bitter tears over Giselle's dead body, now comprehending his tragic guilt. The "illumination" of Act II was now perceived as the outcome of what had happened, as the result of purgation by suffering.

However, *Schéhérazade* and especially *Le Spectre de la Rose* scored the real successes.

A white and blue room with two huge windows opening on to a nocturnal garden. Like a poet's dream from the 1830s, Karsavina appeared in a white dress decorated with a wide flounce and in a white cape tied under her chin with ribbons. As she slumbered in her armchair, a magic creature appeared outside the window and soared above this expanse of virgin whiteness.

Bakst had, indeed, transformed the dancer into the soul of a flower. On the evening of the première the artist came into the dressing room and watched the pink and lilac petals being sewn onto Nijinsky's pink and lilac tights as he stood before the mirror. Bakst himself fitted a cap of the same petals on Nijinsky's head. Thick, drooping, they covered his hair. He did that before each performance, and rumor has it that Vasili did very well for himself selling off the crumpled and unwanted petals to the "admirers of talent."

Karsavina and Nijinsky danced as if they were improvising. *Le Spectre de la Rose,* one of Fokine's revelations, was created for them just as *The Dying Swan* had been for Anna Pavlova. While their dance was, technically speaking, not really very complex, it created the same kind of allusive, aerial perspective peculiar to Impressionist

The entrance of the Spirit of the Rose. Drawing by Ludwig Kainer.

Nijinsky and Karsavina in
Le Spectre de la Rose.

The photo above, taken
during a performance,
captures a momentary pause
in the ballet's swirling
waltzes. The demure dress
that Karsavina wore was
a far cry from the
sophisticated ballgown that
Bakst had originally
designed.

(*left*) Nijinsky as the Spirit of the Rose.

(*below*) Leon Bakst as the Spirit of the Rose. Caricature by Jean Cocteau. The French inscription says: "Because Vatza is in a bad mood, Bakst gets himself together and dances the Specter in his place. An enormous triumph makes Diaghilev decide to let him keep the role."

painting. This dreamy atmosphere evaporated with the final cadence only to be diffused again at the next performance. But only Karsavina and Nijinsky could create this illusion: she in the allusiveness of her pauses and poses, he in the delicate chiaroscuro of his movements, weightless, elusive, embodying the perfume possessed by the Spirit of the Rose.

Two months later, in Paris, Cocteau grasped the essence of this mystery when he remarked that Nijinsky seemed to convey the "unembodiable," the "sad but imperious advance of a perfume." He described how this fragrance, "proud in its crimson irrepressibility, circles in captivating whirlwinds, permeating the muslin of the curtains and enveloping the sleeping maiden in a viscous gauze." Cocteau got quite carried away and outdid everyone when he explained that "Nijinsky leaps through the window and disappears; and this leap is so pathetic, so inclined, so high, it so defies the laws of gravity that now, whenever I sense the soaring perfume of a rose, I shall always recall the indelible impression of this phantom."[2]

Le Spectre de la Rose was soon taken to Russia, but the performances there were copies. Although they were danced by conscientious and talented dancers and although they were sometimes helped along by Fokine, nevertheless, they did not convey the poetry of the original or of its imagery, at once diffuse and intense.

The Tcherepnin–Bakst ballet *Narcisse* was also tried out on the stage of the Monte Carlo theater.

"The same old story" is what Nijinsky probably thought when Fokine related to the company the myth of Narcisse, who scorned the love of the nymph Echo and who was transformed by the gods into a flower at Echo's wish. The dancer studied the role in great detail, but perhaps only Diaghilev guessed that Nijinsky didn't really like it. Diaghilev himself thought that Fokine was beginning to repeat himself. His subjects only seemed diverse; in fact, he just could not break loose from his favorite themes. He was treading water and in *Narcisse* was simply imitating Duncan's style. All these poses had long since begun to pall. Karsavina might be marvelous in the tragic dark violet veil of the nymph and Nijinsky (Narcisse) might be incomparable in his subtle "bestiality": that was all very well. Ultimately, another choreographer might perceive this immobility and "bestiality" in a very different manner. It was time to take a new step forward.

True to his own nature, Diaghilev was looking ahead. He had no need of the approbations of a public that had got what it wanted. An audience might be indignant, might feel shocked and abused, but sooner or later a chosen few would acknowledge his superiority, his boldness, and his ability to take risks.

It was evident that the audience was happy when it was presented with the sultry sky of Hellas, with rocks covered in lush green and a stream down in the meadow. Groups of maidens and youths had scared off some gamboling fauns and were now disporting themselves and lounging about. Diaghilev, in one of the boxes, frowned. He was irritated by the "erotically perfumed" allusions in all these jerks of the body, these embraces, these groups stretched out so bra-

Costume design for Nijinsky as Narcisse, by Leon Bakst.

zenly on the ground. "Fokine is not doing Bakst justice by populating his exquisite landscape with figures straight from Semiradsky," he thought sarcastically.

Narcisse ran in. He was dressed in a white tunic tied at one shoulder; his arms and legs were bare; his hair, combed out in ringlets on his forehead, was held by a ribbon. An ephebe, not yet aware of manhood, he took a childish delight in the games of the shepherdesses who had forsaken their shepherds for him. In the same mood he began to tease the nymph Echo, and she reiterated his movements and his poses as a kind of incantation.

The artistry of this duet in which Fokine had managed to impart contrasting feelings to synchronous gestures captivated even Diaghilev. Like a sorrowful shadow, Echo, smitten by love, reflected the sunlit movements of Narcisse. Graceful, unthinking, he mocked her until the merry band of shepherds carried him away. Echo turned her gaze heavenward, demanding revenge, and Narcisse returned, tortured by thirst. He bent down to the stream; he gazed in rapture and was still; he raised himself up still staring at the mirrorlike surface; slowly he threw his hands behind his head, smiling, perplexed by his reflection. Not heeding the cries of the frightened Echo, he fondly spread his arms above the stream, bowing lower and lower. An almost imperceptible twitch of his muscles, and Narcisse had disappeared into the stream—whence a white flower slowly unfolded.

As was his custom, Nijinsky listened to the compliments in silence. But a certain skepticism could be felt in this silence. Diaghilev bit his lips on hearing the words *as always* all around him: "as always, very poetic," "as always, exquisitely picturesque," "as always, it compels one to forget reality," and, finally, "as always, it's original." Diaghilev didn't like to be "original" "as always"—those words did not go together. His relationship with Fokine was now threatened.

Grigoriev first knew something was in the offing when Diaghilev announced that it was pointless for Fokine always to be rehearsing old ballets instead of putting on *Petrouchka*. Grigoriev made the diplomatic objection that Fokine had to do this because much of the company personnel was new and that many of the professional dancers were not very quick off the mark. They needed practice. "That's nothing to do with *me!*" Diaghilev interrupted angrily, "Fokine . . . must

find time now, even if he has to keep at it morning, noon, and night!" [3]
Grigoriev knew by experience that when Diaghilev was in that mood,
it was impossible to contradict him. He passed on the conversation
to Fokine who, understandably, was indignant. Meanwhile, time was
really at a premium. The whole of May was taken up with the Rome
tour and by the beginning of June they would be in Paris. Fokine
still had to prepare the Undersea Kingdom act from *Sadko* as well as
Petrouchka.

The ballet people scarcely saw Rome. They never left the Teatro
Costanzi, where they rehearsed both before and after the performances. Fokine had thrown *Sadko* together in haste, relying on Anisfeld's colorful decor for effect and also on the final dance, which was
simply a variation on the other corps de ballet bacchanalias (much to
Diaghilev's distaste). The choreographer dedicated all his ideas to
Petrouchka.

The corps de ballet took up a lot of time. Time and time again
Fokine went over the beat of the music with the participants in the
mass scenes, because the music was so unusual to the ear of a ballet
dancer. Sometimes he blew his top; he ranted and raved, complaining
of the "untalented supernumeraries who have been picked off the
street." [4] But the going was easy with the performers of the principal roles: Karsavina as the Ballerina, Cecchetti as the Magician,
the young dancer Alexander Orlov as the Moor, and Nijinsky as
Petrouchka were very quick on the uptake. But there were moments
when Fokine was so frantically busy that his creative imagination
deserted him. He was tortured the whole length of the rehearsal,
trying to find something that would keep the Moor busy while he
was idling away the time waiting for the Ballerina. Fokine was even
more put out by Benois' cautious suggestions and by the temporizing
silence of Stravinsky seated at the piano. Finally, he grabbed the score
from the music stand, flung it on the floor, and stormed out of the
hall. Much distressed, shaking his head, Grigoriev picked up the
music and declared the rehearsal over.

The next day, Fokine was more accommodating. During the
night he had thought of a bit of staging for the Moor. As the dumpy
Orlov lay on his back, Fokine brought him a rubber ball, representing
a coconut, and instructed him to throw it from his hands to his raised

feet, and back again. Orlov tried to keep in time with the music, tried not to drop the slippery ball, and earnestly gave himself to the task. Fokine and Benois were soon bursting with laughter, and a restrained smile even appeared on Stravinsky's face. After that it was plain sailing. By the beginning of June, when the Diaghilev company once again occupied the Théâtre du Châtelet, *Petrouchka* was going along very smoothly. It was ready.

Diaghilev rarely came to rehearsals. He was trying to tidy up the inside of the theater, which, as two years ago, had been severely neglected. He renewed useful acquaintances. He prepared the press releases and the advertisements. Cocteau's posters now multiplied on the streets of Paris, showing Karsavina or Nijinsky in various poses from *Le Spectre de la Rose.* Nijinsky was left to his own devices more than usual. Ever since Fokine had marked out his role as Petrouchka, he had become quite unsociable and withdrawn. Furthermore—and this was very unlike him—he now repulsed people if they interrupted his state of meditation too importunately. He wasn't writing anything and wasn't looking for reinforcement of his ideas in books, as he had done when he had been rehearsing *Giselle.* Something was developing within him, something that did not need external stimuli, something profound that compelled him to sit for long periods gazing fixedly but unseeingly at a point in space.

At rehearsal he turned into a mannequin, into a doll, sometimes a wooden doll, sometimes a rag doll stuffed with sawdust. His mechanical movements were terrifying in their verisimilitude. His head hung helplessly on its side, his arms swung loose, his feet were awkwardly turned in. And when this clumsy piece of equipment started up, it seemed to obey not a conscious rationality but some kind of foreign power that upset the coordination of all these loose parts. Each musical passage that Stravinsky played, each combination of movements that Fokine proposed seemed to contain this foreign power. Petrouchka obeyed these commands with a formless submissiveness. But as he fulfilled his assignments, he still gazed, bewitched, at something only he could see.

The season opened on 6 June. The program included something Parisians were already acquainted with, *Le Carnaval,* and the new ballets *Narcisse, Sadko,* and *Le Spectre de la Rose.* Diaghilev was apprehensive. When Grigoriev asked why, he countered with another question: Did Grigoriev remember Napoleon's words?—"It is not enough to take the Tuileries. The problem is to stay there." Diaghilev added that his situation was the same: this was the third and the most decisive Paris season.

Diaghilev held his Tuileries. At the première the triumph increased with each ballet: Nijinsky's final leap in *Le Spectre de la Rose* brought forth such an ovation that the orchestra was drowned.

Just one week was left before 13 June, the commencement of the second program. The playbill announced *Schéhérazade, Le Spectre de la Rose,* and *Petrouchka.* It was *Petrouchka* that was taking all the time and energy.

Pierre Monteux, the young conductor whom Diaghilev had just engaged, went over the score. He divided the orchestra into various groups of instruments in an attempt to gain some kind of inner harmony in the noise and bustle of the fairground. The parts of the fair itself were still piled up on the stage. The heads and hooves of the horses from the merry-go-round, which had yet to be erected, protruded from all manner of booths, boxes, and swings. Diaghilev and Benois set the lights up and tried out the scene changes. In the middle of all this, Fokine was trying to integrate the various separate episodes.

Diaghilev ordered a run-through with the orchestra and in costumes but without makeup. Stravinsky, Benois, and Fokine climbed down into the orchestra. There would now be a number of chaotic rehearsals that would seem to make no progress and that would threaten to end in complete disorder. But this one went very well, and Nijinsky created a Petrouchka beyond anything that Stravinsky, Benois, and Fokine had imagined.

Each of this trio was great in his own way. Each of them rather looked down on Nijinsky. Neither then nor later on were they able to reconcile their delight in the brilliant dancer with their scorn for the "young ignoramus." But whatever they may have said afterward, at these rehearsals Nijinsky astounded them all. He seemed to have comprehended, to have purified and universalized what had dwelt latently in their primary conception of the role, but what had lost its outline among a host of magnificent but secondary details.

The three Olympians (and, quite rightly, each of them considered himself as such) contemplated their design from the heights of Olympus. When he became insane, Nijinsky would later call himself a "god," but in no sense an Olympian. Now he sensed a very personal element in the image of Petrouchka, something that he had not encountered before and never would again. This personal element, which Nijinsky was only now perceiving as a tragedy, extended the boundaries of the ballet *Petrouchka* because it proved to be indissolubly linked to one of the eternal themes of Russian art. It was one of particular resonance now.

One could see at these rehearsals how the dancer carefully observed every detail of the dance text. But the image of the toy dancer "who had suddenly broken free from his chain," as Stravinsky said,[5] expressed its real meaning, its underlying sense, thanks only to the dancer himself. Petrouchka's puppetlike convulsions revealed his

Igor Stravinsky, composer of *Petrouchka* and *Le Sacre du Printemps*.

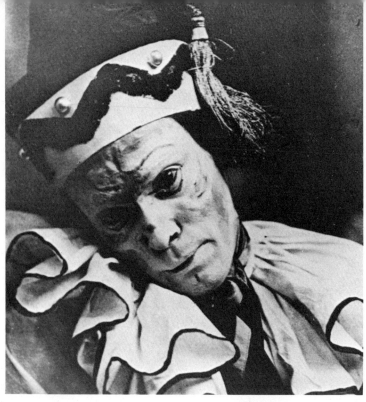

(*left*) Nijinsky as Petrouchka.

(*below*) Karsavina as the Ballerina and Nijinsky as Petrouchka, both in typical puppetlike poses.

soul's impetuous wish to escape; they expressed its tragic discord with life.

Only Diaghilev, who valued Nijinsky as a human being, could understand the prophetic meaning of this Petrouchka. But Diaghilev, the artistic egoist, did not value the spiritual reflection in this image; he did not hear the call for help transmitted so clearly. And perhaps he regretted not hearing it for the rest of his life. He should have seen beyond the mechanical movements, beyond the mask disguising not just the face but the whole body of Nijinsky's Petrouchka. He should have recognized a man gripped with pain, overtaken by grief and pitiful rage. He knew very well that Nijinsky's mechanical behavior in everyday life expressed his emotional constraint and that because of this the king of modern ballet seemed so awkward and clumsy off stage. Previously, the music, the footlights, the costumes of the stage had very often provided an escape into an illusory freedom. But now, this mechanical behavior, elevated into a grotesquerie and borne onto the stage, drew Nijinsky closer to the recesses of his own soul and to the edge of an abyss.

Many years later, when Diaghilev and Fokine had already passed away, when Nijinsky had found freedom in insanity, the elderly and wise Benois informed Françoise Reiss, who was collecting material for a book about the legendary dancer, that "he brought to life the sad, tragic puppet, without using any of the over-heavy present-day make-up. His innate taste enabled him to seize the subtle nuances. . . . He chiselled the role in an extraordinary way and in this sense can be called the author. Once he had entered into Petrouchka's skin he was able to express the inexpressible quality of the odd puppet with his primitive mechanism and at the same time to reveal the conscious and wretched being shaken by every sensation. His portrayal of this dual, simultaneous role was so felicitous. . . ." [6]

In this role, unknown to Nijinsky there suddenly loomed the shadows of many heroes from Russian art that took up their place behind Petrouchka. Invisible threads linked this character with the "little man" of Pushkin, of Gogol, and of Dostoevsky, and with many contemporary heroes: their organisms seeming to be so primitive, their forced affectations also disguised their souls stifled by fear and grief. With Nijinsky the role of Petrouchka became the role of his age, for he embodied therein both his own tragedy and the tragedy of his epoch. And when one looks back, one can see that this tragedy also affected the creators of the ballet: Fate swept them round and round in a carousel of events, forcing them to dance the parts she had assigned. But at the première of 13 June 1911, these three artists celebrated the success of *Petrouchka*. They went into raptures over Nijinsky, but were insensitive to the auguries of the image they had created.

That evening, the Parisians were offered the spectacle of a Russian fair framed by the spicy *Schéhérazade* and *Le Spectre de la Rose*, touched by the gentle decadence of Romanticism. It was a riot of aural and visual images: the hubbub of the crowd, the melodies and shouts of the touters, the roar of the bear dragged along by the gypsy, the doleful tunes of the barrel organ. The Admiralty was shrouded in February mist. But the square in front of it boasted merry-go-rounds, swings, and booths, and amid them all crowds of people scurried about celebrating the Shrovetide holiday. For the Russians this motley spectacle was part of everyday life; for the French it was an exotic fantasy.

The crowd had surrounded a magician, gray-bearded and wearing the tall hat and gown of an oriental sorcerer. He played a mysterious tune on his long pipe, and the curtains of the puppet theater parted. The puppets—the Ballerina, Petrouchka, and the Moor—bobbed up and down on their poles. The Magician set the mechanism in action: all together the puppets jerked their arms and legs, ran off into the crowd, did a funny little act, and then the owner chased them all back, as the hustle and bustle of the fair spread over the place where they had danced.

A room came into view, a complete contrast to the deafening noise of the fair. A portrait of the Magician on the wall looked down at the solitary Petrouchka. Someone had kicked him down and, crumpled, he was huddled up on the floor. His face, which could be seen under his ragged, tassled hat, seemed to stand out in relief against the dark blue wallpaper. His face seemed to be powdered with flour; his cheeks bore spots of rouge; and his eyes, beneath the precise angles of his painted eyebrows, were the eyes of a man horrified at the cruelty of the world, and lamenting it.

Petrouchka's monologue began with a groan that, now crescendo, now diminuendo, broke into a turbulent outburst of feeling. The clumsy gestures of this wild, convulsive figure hugging the ground contradicted the smoothness, the precision, the soaring movements for which the dancer Nijinsky was so famous. Petrouchka was exasperated by the fate that had treated him so diffidently. He stopped short, stiffly raised his arm and waved his fist at the portrait: the eternally tragic gesture, that eternal "Just you wait!" once again was being addressed to an incomprehensible power. To the disturbed mind of one man this power had once been embodied by the bronze statue of a horseman;[7] to another it was now the portrait of the fairground magician. The monument to Peter the Great was only a stone's throw from the booths on Admiralty Square. And beyond them loomed St. Petersburg, symbol of a dark and oppressive force.

Many people have compared Nijinsky with Petrouchka and Diaghilev with the Magician, especially after their rupture, inevitable but unforeseen, although only two years were now left until that moment. The analogy arose for good reason, although Diaghilev was just as guilty of Nijinsky's tragic fate as Nijinsky was of his own. Despite the differences in their characters, their aspirations, and their views, their fates crossed in a most curious manner. The genius of Diaghilev was nurtured on willpower and ideas, on the ability to anticipate his goal and to attain it. The genius of Nijinsky was based on his intuition, on his inborn and unfailing sense of the beautiful. Diaghilev consciously developed his taste, his unquestionable precision of judgment, in order to become the arbiter of artistic fashion. Nijinsky was not interested in fashion, even in the highest meaning of the word. His elemental talent, in all its versatility, simply encountered the trials and tribulations of his time. But the strong, arrogant, self-assured Diaghilev and the weak, pliant, terribly shy Nijinsky both proved to be insolvent at the hands of the Russian autocracy—although, in truth, the convenient phrase "at the hands of" is not very appropriate here. Until the end of his days, both before and after emigration, Prince Sergei Mikhailovich Volkonsky would spread his hands in perplexity, failing to understand why in 1901 such harsh measures had been taken against Diaghilev and why he had been refused a civil service career. Similarly, the Dowager Empress Marie Fedorovna,

Three scenes of *Petrouchka*.

(*left*) From Scene 2.

(*below*) From Scene 3.

(*right*) From Scene 4.

who also emigrated, would assert that in 1911 she had had no intention whatsoever of making a fuss about the Nijinsky costume in *Giselle*, and that if she had "found anything indecent, then she would have pretended not to have noticed to it." [8]

The manipulator of other people's destinies and the creator of his own, Diaghilev was, to some extent, the toy of Fate just as Nijinsky was. As Nijinsky came to rely more and more on Diaghilev, this became a burden to him. However much Diaghilev tried to gain Nijinsky's trust, he met only an alien submissiveness. With the stubbornness of a weak-willed man, Nijinsky refused to recognize Diaghilev as his friend, although, when the moment came, he saw him as his enemy. But at the première of *Petrouchka* these thoughts occurred neither to Diaghilev nor to Nijinsky. Only in his subconscious did

Nijinsky perhaps compare the Magician to the man who loved him so sincerely and egoistically.

For Petrouchka, the Magician was the source of all his troubles. The Magician's portrait seemed to watch Petrouchka's every step. The audience really began to think that this gaze took on a startled and suspicious expression when into Petrouchka's room flew the Ballerina, the delusive ideal of love and femininity. She spun about on her straight wooden legs and then disappeared, spurning the amorous confessions of her ugly admirer. And Petrouchka, tortured by jealousy, banged his fists on the wall, smashed through it, and hung above a void, as if broken in two.

The action moved to the Moor's room. He was content with his fate. He had an ottoman, and painted tigers gazed through the foliage on his walls. He was the owner and the servant of a very simple piece of property—a coconut, which he played with and which he prayed to, beating his forehead on the ground. He guarded his property against the Ballerina and, furiously but cautiously, watched her coquettish advances. Nevertheless, she fascinated the Moor, and whirled him around to the melody of a deliberate, barrel-organ waltz. Petrouchka burst in on this idyll. The Moor drew his scimitar and chased after the trespasser upon his cosy tête-à-tête.

The chase led all three of them into the fairground, now calm in the evening lassitude. Petrouchka ran like a man pursued by a recurrent nightmare—when his leaden body will not obey his desperate exertions and when his cry for help remains unheeded. Petrouchka stumbled under the lifted scimitar, and fell, staring wildly at the sneering Moor.

Bystanders idled about in the blue Petersburg twilight wondering whether this was a puppet or a man lying on the street. All in all, it resembled a broken puppet tossed aside by its owner. But the orchestra brought forth a groan that then increased to a howl of protest. The puppet stirred, leaned up on its elbow—and a man stretched out his hand, asking not for help but for sympathy.

The Magician pushed his way through the crowd. With an imperious smile he shook the rag body, and all the people went their separate ways, marveling at the hallucination they had had. The merry-go-round came to a halt; the booths emptied. It began to snow. The Magician set off for home, dragging the puppet behind him. But he became rooted to the spot when he suddenly heard a familiar groaning now mingled with derision. His expression of surprise gave way to one of terror: Petrouchka, alive, was poking out from above the roof of the booth and was threatening him with his unbending arms. The Magician wiped the sweat from his brow and touched his hat. The hat flopped down to the ground. He gave a start and then took to his heels. In the reflections of the whirling snow, above the silent fairground, the immortal Petrouchka issued his eternal challenge to Fate as the curtain came down very slowly.

Finale of *Petrouchka*.
Drawing by Alexandre
Benois.

In December 1928, a few months before his death, Diaghilev, already desperately ill, brought the hopelessly insane Nijinsky to the current performance of *Petrouchka*. Diaghilev, the magician of the Saisons Russes, hoped that the music and the action of the ballet would jog Nijinsky's memory, that they would provoke a response in his clouded mind. During the intermission before *Petrouchka*, Diaghilev took the pensive and submissive Nijinsky from his box, along the familiar corridors and staircases of the Opéra and on to the stage. Karsavina was waiting in the costume of the Ballerina together with a new dancer as the Moor, Serge Lifar. Grigoriev and Benois came up. Karsavina took her ex-partner by the arm. Diaghilev put his hands on their shoulders. The others joined the group. Nijinsky stood there, stiffly stretched his arms and smiled, staring in front of himself. The smile was more impenetrable than Petrouchka's makeup, and his answers in French given to the questions addressed him in Russian sounded strange indeed.

A photographer clicked his camera. Diaghilev led Nijinsky back and sat down next to him. His hopes had been in vain. The creator of the role of Petrouchka had not recognized his double on stage, just as he did not recognize now, at this last meeting, the man whose fate was so closely intertwined with his own.

The evening of the première of *Petrouchka*, Nijinsky locked himself in his dressing room to escape the adulations. He peeled layer after layer of white paste off his face and looked in the mirror, not at himself, but at Petrouchka's hat that Vasili had hung on the lampshade in the background. Vasili tried not to make a noise, realizing that Nijinsky, in a state of nervous tension, needed peace and quiet. Diaghilev had said that Nijinsky needed a break; they were going to have dinner in the Bois de Boulogne. So, Vasili dressed Nijinsky in his tuxedo, gave him his top hat and gloves, and off Nijinsky went to meet Diaghilev, Stravinsky, and Cocteau. The warm air, the lamps in the fresh green trees, the even murmur of the street, the rhythm of the carriage, its soft springs and comfortable cushions, and, above all, the silence of his companions also deserving a well-earned rest—all these things had a beneficial effect on Nijinsky.

At dinner Diaghilev mentioned an article that Cocteau had written the previous year with a passage concerning Nijinsky.

"Oh, yes, I can repeat it again here," Cocteau hastened to say. "Indeed, I am very grateful to you, M. Nijinsky, for showing me that Parisians still have enthusiasm—which I thought had long been extinguished by snobbery. Thanks to you I understood the simple reason why the Opéra is generally silent. You can laugh your beautiful oriental laugh when you leave us, and you leave us with memories, with dreams that people will not tell for fear of spoiling them or for fear of provoking distrustful smirks." [9]

Nijinsky raised his eyes from his plate and met Cocteau's gaze. He was silent for a second, thinking perhaps that his temperamental companion was free to nonchalantly condemn his own city without any risk of losing it. Then he smiled and, selecting the French words, said, "You love Paris a great deal. I also love her."

That summer Paris was truly beautiful. More than ever before she justified her reputation as the "capital of the world"; she welcomed and stimulated all that was talented and new. On the eve of the Great War, she hastened, as it were, to enjoy the blessings of life and the revelations of art. "In Paris I felt free," recalled Picasso, who was then also a young man, adding, "If Cézanne had lived in Spain, he would probably have been shot." [10]

But Diaghilev knew that he must not overstay this welcome. A week later his company traveled across to London, where a great deal seemed very strange, especially after Paris. Frenchmen did not stay at home, but sauntered in the gardens or along the boulevards in droves. Even the cafés crawled out into the streets, scattering their tables all along the sidewalks. But the English liked to shut everything in. There were many gardens in the block near the British Museum where the company was staying, but it was prohibited to walk in them because they were kept locked and the keys were with the owners.

London was preparing herself for a majestic occasion—the coronation of George V. The streets were decked out in flags and lights, although this did not disturb the decorum of the city. On 21 June, coronation eve, the Diaghilev company was to make its debut with *Armide*. The Russians were amazed that the Royal Opera of Covent Garden stood in the middle of a fruit and vegetable market and that to reach it you had to make your way through piles of potatoes, carrots, and cabbages. But the theater itself was clean and comfortable—except that the boards of the stage were abnormally flat and did not slope toward the footlights as the Russian dancers were used to.

At the Coronation Gala on 26 June, *Le Pavillon d'Armide* was the only ballet on the program. There were, in addition, the second acts from the operas *Aïda* and *Romeo and Juliet* as well as the third act from *The Barber of Seville*. When the curtain rose on the ballet, last on the program, the Russian "Gardens of Versailles" were filled with a fragrance coming from the auditorium. More than 100,000 roses had been used to form the crown above the royal box and the Order of the Garter just below it. All along the gallery leading from the box medallions of roses bore the names of the British Dominions: Canada, Australia, New Zealand, South Africa. The flowers were rivaled by the precious jewels of the elite audience, an audience that looked with a reserved benevolence at the stage.

But success was assured, and audiences at other performances applauded enthusiastically, although it turned out that certain elderly ladies were rather shocked by the *Polovtsian Dances,* and one or two people were put out by the relationship between the white women and the black slaves in *Schéhérazade.* Ironically, Diaghilev calculated that the vegetarian ambience of Covent Garden ought to be applied to the repertoire too. So he cut performances of *Cléopâtre* and *Schéhérazade,* and focused attention on the Romantic *Les Sylphides, Le Carnaval, Le Spectre de la Rose,* and *Le Pavillon d'Armide.* When the Covent Garden directors suggested a fall season, Diaghilev came up with a counter proposal: he would show Londoners two famous St. Petersburg ballets—*Swan Lake* with Kschessinska and *Giselle* with Pavlova. Nijinsky would be the partner in both.

Diaghilev thought out his plans like a general. Kschessinska would amaze the public by her technique. Pavlova was already well known and liked in London from her appearances at the Alhambra Theatre with Mordkin. And now she was about to appear in one of her finest roles, Giselle, unfamiliar to the British public. This would not hurt Karsavina: she was going back to St. Petersburg for the beginning of the season there because she did not wish to break with the Mariinsky.

The Diaghilev season was to open in October. For the moment

Members of the Diaghilev company photographed near London:
Left to right: Leonid Leontiev, George Rosai, Alexander Orlov, Alexis Kozlov.

the company split up and its members went on holiday. Diaghilev was worried by Nijinsky's melancholy. After some hesitation, he told Nijinsky, as they sat in Venice, that he planned a surprise that would happen very soon: he intended to present a season in St. Petersburg. Thanks to Kschessinska, he had been promised the People's House on the Petrograd Side.[11] That had a first-rate stage and a huge auditorium. He, Diaghilev, would show Teliakovsky what the members

187

of the Imperial Theaters could really do, including, above all, those members who had had to quit. So it was not worth going back to Russia right now. They should have a good rest.

Nijinsky felt that Pavlova would not really relish seeing him again.

For the fanatical and divine egoist, Pavlova, the model partner was her teacher Gerdt. *He* knew how to place his merits at the feet of ballerinas. Quite unlike Mordkin, with whom she had recently had a terrible row and with whom she had parted—not wishing to share the laurels. And quite unlike Nijinsky, whose success in *Armide* she could never forgive. Nijinsky knew this. Furthermore, he understood full well that he did not meet Pavlova's idea of masculine beauty for the part of the ballet cavalier. He had heard too that, ever since Pavlova had left the Imperial Theaters and had founded her own company, her willfulness knew no limits.

Nevertheless, Nijinsky did want to partner Pavlova in *Giselle*.

They met on tour at one of the rehearsals. Pavlova was in a bad mood and slighted her partner. She made it understood that his reputation as a world celebrity was all the same to her. Silently he endured her capricious gibes.

On the evening of the performance, Pavlova appeared on stage after the short overture had begun. She stood on the stage side of Giselle's dilapidated house. As always, she was nervous as she waited impatiently for her entrance into her favorite role. In the distance, she could hear the applause. That was for Albrecht, but she now no longer cared which Albrecht. Silence, and then her heart beat faster as she heard the knocking on the shaky door. Giselle, and no longer Pavlova, caught her breath and flew into the bright morning. Pavlova, in fact, perceived the new round of applause with a kind of "second sight," as Giselle skipped about the stage, effusing her sudden joy in light waves of movement.

Pavlova's Giselle did not possess the subdued and modest charm of Karsavina's interpretation. This young child of nature, dressed in the muslin attire of a ballet peasant girl, danced spontaneously, as if her movements were dictated by nature, by her awakening of first love. Summoned by Albrecht's long-awaited signal but not noticing her beloved in his hiding place, she immediately forgot about him.

She found consolation, amusement, and delight in her dancing—a passion so natural, yet so pernicious in its innocence.

At last Giselle paused and became pensive, she grew sad, turned toward the house—and met Albrecht.

True, this young boy, smiling at her in such confusion, was not exactly imposing. But everything in Giselle responded to his eyes, to the reverential gesture of his hands, outstretched but untouching. The poet now playing out a love affair of which he had so often dreamed led her through a series of lovers' games and dances. He delighted in her, he bowed before her, guarding the harmony of this fragile moment of reality while knowing that it was doomed to destruction.

That melancholy sense of resignation with which Nijinsky's Albrecht observed Giselle's insanity and death did not hinder Pavlova as it had Karsavina. He did not dispute the judgment of destiny, he did not repent, but waited for the denouement, following the poetic logic and destruction of a romance that did not come true.

What had to happen happened, and carried the heroes into perfect tranquility, into the unalterable harmonies of Act II. In the Kingdom of the Wilis nothing divided them. As intended, the wand of the queen of the pitiless maidens broke in two before the innocent embrace of Giselle and Albrecht. Pavlova and Nijinsky responded with the serenity of their duet. Giselle's smile was reflected in Albrecht's face, and his winged flight intrepidly followed the lure of her dance.

And, even if the phantom of Giselle vanished with the dawn, even if Albrecht's earthly bride, Bathilde, took him back into life, still, he returned there as a poet, as the knight of the Beautiful Lady, of the dream Giselle.

St. Petersburg would never see such a *Giselle* as this, with Pavlova and Nijinsky as partners, and perhaps, of all pearls of the Ballets Russes that it lost, this was the most precious. They danced *Giselle* several times in London, and it became one of the starting points for the founders of the British ballet theater. But this was the last time that the dancers of the primary roles partnered each other. Pavlova the dancer and Pavlova the human being contradicted each other. The day after their last appearance together, Pavlova, the elegant and languid prima ballerina, coldly gave her hand to Nijinsky, who imprinted a kiss of farewell upon it.

Meanwhile, Diaghilev had decided to shorten *Swan Lake* to two acts. He was afraid of wearying his unaccustomed audience with what he considered to be superfluous detail. Kschessinska's dances, especially as Odile, now became the center of the piece. Nijinsky's part as Prince Siegfried—which, in accordance with the Gerdt tradition, he did not dance—was merely a way of attracting attention to Kschessinska.

Not in vain did one anonymous French critic write of Nijinsky: "This young Russian does not dance his ballets, he acts them, he lives in them. If it is correct to say that he dances, then we should say that he dances as well with his face, his hands, his entire body as he does with his legs. Without uttering a single word, he still compels us to comprehend him, and this is very moving." [12] The theme of Albrecht could be recognized, albeit in a different key, in the enforced "silence" of Prince Siegfried. Siegfried's birthday celebration was not included in this production. The Prince appeared straightway at the edge of the lake in the mourning clothes of a poet. His black jacket and black cap with its long feather underlined the paleness of his face; his slanting eyes were shining. All signs indicated that this man had been here before many times and that he was possessed of an eternal dream. "As he walked near the lake, peering up at the treetops or gazing towards the placid water, he made you aware of the presence of mist by the contraction and dilation of his nostrils, and by an almost imperceptible groping movement of his hands, as though he were brushing the mist aside." [13] Thus wrote the English critic Cyril Beaumont many years later, and confessed that, apart from Nijinsky, he could remember nothing else in the *Swan Lake* of the Diaghilev tours.

Act II. The Prince sat before the guests dancing in his honor in his castle. But he gazed into the distance, to the phantom of the Swan Queen that only he could see. He was deceived by the resemblance of Odile to Odette and was happy that the vision had come alive, had entered from the mist of the lake into the brilliant and crowded ballroom. At this juncture Siegfried became like Albrecht when the latter was astounded by his meeting with the spirit of Giselle. But the theme now took the opposite course. The mystery that had seemed to be reality now abandoned the poet and betrayed him: Odile had vanished. It was impossible to return to Odette. Thickening mist enveloped the lake. There was no way back into the illusion of the dream.

Nijinsky waited impatiently for the end of the tour. He himself had not realized how attached he was to the city where he had gone to school and where he had made his debut on stage. Far from expansive, and quite unsociable, Nijinsky was as happy as a clam when Leontiev arrived. Leontiev was to replace him as Harlequin. After sitting through *Petrouchka,* Leontiev, a talented and very professional dancer, expressed more in his terse sentences than all the loquacious tirades of the phrasemongers and rhetoricians.

After the last performance was over, Nijinsky took his leave of Kschessinska, saying, in a curiously vivacious manner, that he hoped to see her soon in St. Petersburg. The company was due to go there from Paris, where Diaghilev had already gone in advance.

Nijinsky did not find Diaghilev at the station among the welcoming crowd, and for the first time he felt sad about this. He set off with Grigoriev for the hotel. When they entered Diaghilev's room, Diaghilev rose wearily to greet them and handed Grigoriev a telegram. Grigoriev slowly read out: "People's House burned to the ground this morning."

A silence ensued. Diaghilev watched Nijinsky out of the corner of his eye, watched him press his lips to stop himself crying like a little boy. Then he looked at Grigoriev, sighed, and mumbled almost to himself: "Well, it seems I was not destined to show my ballets in Russia now, which is a great pity. For I've a presentiment that after this I shall never be able to show them there at all." [14]

Grigoriev objected, saying that, of course, it only seemed so because Diaghilev was so upset. Diaghilev did not reply. Silence once again descended except for the dull noise of Paris outside the window. The three men, each in his own way, peered at the mirage of their homeland that had enticed them and received them. Mother or stepmother, whatever Russia was, she held the ends of those invisible threads that stretched from childhood on: from the first, indelible impressions of nature; from the people, the customs, the conventions (perhaps stern and cold, but one's own); from one's home, even if it represented only a stopping place, a temporary refuge for the restless soul.

At last Diaghilev straightened himself and said that St. Petersburg had been meant to provide them with an engagement until their return to Monte Carlo, and that they must think of some way out. [15]

It was not long before something else was found: the Opéra proposed a winter season, and in January Diaghilev's company would visit Berlin, Vienna, and Budapest.

They greeted the New Year, 1912, in Paris. That evening Nijinsky and Karsavina danced *Le Spectre de la Rose* at a gala performance at the Opéra in honor of French aviation. Afterward, in a restaurant, amid excited but alien chatter, to the music of a fashionable tango, Diaghilev and Nijinsky clinked their glasses in a toast to the flowering of Russian art. The time had come to show that the Russians were capable of revealing to other nations their own cultural treasures. Diaghilev thought that Nijinsky might try himself out as a choreographer precisely in that context, and he even knew how to begin. He had in mind Debussy's symphonic *Prélude à l'Après-Midi d'un Faune*, based on a poem by Mallarmé.

Nijinsky listened carefully and, suddenly, as was his wont, fixed his gaze on something remote and absent. Somewhere, he could see a ballet studio with sets of double barres (only recently he had held the lower one); one set ran along the middle wall toward the stove, the other down toward the piano. Nijinsky, the schoolboy, got the right tempo, leaped from the corner, squatted on one leg, entwined it about the other, and began to play his imaginary pipe.

Nijinsky roused himself, looked at Diaghilev, and said that *L'Après-Midi* should be produced by Fokine, since it was exactly his cup of tea. But Diaghilev replied with a phrase that he had already used several times, that is, that Fokine was repeating himself, and that it was easy to imagine the kind of *L'Après-Midi* he would create: there wouldn't be much of Debussy or Mallarmè in it. No, this ballet would have to be "anti-Fokine"; it would have to run without bacchanales, without picturesque embraces and poses. "It must be . . . a search," Diaghilev said slowly, "a search for new trends in movement, but one that will circumvent Isadora Duncan, who doesn't appear to be old-fashioned simply because her talent is so forceful." That's where the conversation broke off.

In Berlin, where the old repertoire was presented, Fokine began to rehearse Reynaldo Hahn's one-act ballet called *Le Dieu Bleu*. Cocteau had devised an exotic plot that combined various motifs from the Saisons Russes and that would have done Théophile Gautier for a

Nijinsky in *Le Dieu Bleu*.

good three acts. The ballet started with an initiation ritual: a young boy was entering service in an Indian temple. His bride implored him to return, just as Ta-hor had beseeched Amoun to reject Cleopatra. The troublemaker was incarcerated in a dungeon where beasts of prey and grandiose, "unbelievable" (Bakstian!) serpents threatened to kill her. But a lotus emerged from a pool and from the flower came a goddess, who summoned the Blue God from heaven. He, like the Firebird, cast a spell on the beasts and serpents. He then commanded the priests to unite the lovers and, in picturesque fashion, ascended the stairway leading to his heavenly chambers.

Obviously, Diaghilev was not interested in this piece. And when Fokine demanded real lambs for his second production, Ravel's *Daphnis et Chloë*, Diaghilev became angry. But Nijinsky learned from the parts of the Blue God and Daphnis in the same way that he had learned from dancing Vayu in *Le Talisman* in St. Petersburg. His absolute intuition told him that, however short Fokine's ballets, their epoch and style had already been exploited to the full, just like those of the nineteenth-century academic ballet.

On the way from Berlin to Vienna, the Diaghilev company gave a few performances in Dresden. The audience that filled the beautiful Baroque theater was, for the most part, seeing ballet for the first time, and their reception of this kind of entertainment was cool. Some members of the company said that it was pointless to come here, but, of course, this was said behind Diaghilev's back. Actually, Diaghilev very rarely visited the company. Every day when rehearsals were in full swing, he would come for Nijinsky and go off with him some place, returning two hours before the performance. Even the omnipresent Grigoriev did not know that they were visiting Hellerau, where the Dalcroze eurhythmics school was located. That was why the trip to Dresden had been organized.

At first Nijinsky did not respond to the exercises being done by the pupils of Emile Jaques-Dalcroze, exercises that were supposed to transmit the design of a musical accompaniment to plastic movement. But, little by little, he began to respond to the instructions by just moving his fingers and his head.

Once, after he had returned to Dresden from Hellerau, he asked for Debussy's prelude to be played. Pierre Monteux took his seat at the piano in one of the small theater sitting rooms. Waves of noon sunlight floated from beneath his fingers. Monteux repeated the prelude twice. Nijinsky asked him to play it once more. He half-closed his eyes and advanced into the narrow space between the piano and the chair in which Diaghilev was sitting. He swayed slowly, trying to recall forgotten memories and to revive that feeling of oneness with nature that he had experienced as a child: somehow, this erased the memory of the jumps and poses of Fokine's faun.

Cautiously, the dancer turned his head into profile and then turned his hand palm outward, bending his arm at the elbow and lowering his wrist. His figure lost its dimensional quality and appeared flat, rough, like the figures in Gauguin's paintings, pressed against the background and at the same time suggesting the volume of space around them.

Diaghilev stirred in his chair. He cocked an eyebrow.

The melodies of the music, of this trembling mirage, evoked many feelings. Contemplative, indistinct, they accumulated and then melted away in the pale and sultry sky. It was impossible for the dance to follow the fragile structure of the score, for it presupposed no action and diffused at the very moment of its apprehension. The dance was too material to convey such a capricious melodic structure. Diaghilev realized that Nijinsky did not intend to dance in the conventional meaning of the word. The potential choreographer kept his pose for a few bars and then responded to a new musical phrase. Elastically he pulled himself up and stood in profile and then stretched his hands out in front of him, paused once more, and then sat down on one leg. His figure seemed to be part of a square delineated by the back position of his elbow and the forward position of his knee. Again a sonorous pause. He gathered his body into a tight, angular polygon, stretched himself pliantly, and leaned back. In a semi-supine position, Nijinsky leaned on his arm, stretched one leg forward, and bent the other out flat. Diaghilev noticed one thing: as the dancer went through these designs, developing a kind of plastic frieze, he did preserve one position, he pulled in his chin and stuck out his forehead as if about to butt.

Nijinsky sat out the rest of the music on the floor. He did not move, but listened in meditation.

Diaghilev looked at him, marveling at the intuition that had prompted this incarnation of Debussy's *L'Après-Midi d'un Faune:* this laconic stylization, this series of static and intentional, angular poses that so characterized the inner world of the music, its elemental force now harmonized within its rhythm. To Diaghilev, this demonstrated not the timid experiment of a novice but the bold conception and firm hand of the master. There was no doubt that this was a leap forward after the Fokine ballets. It was all so strict, so severe. One could see that it would be a problem trying to adjust the public to

(*left*) Pierre Monteux, conductor for the Diaghilev company from 1911 to 1918. He led the world premières of Stravinsky's *Petrouchka, Le Sacre du Printemps,* and *Le Rossignol,* Ravel's *Daphnis et Chloë,* and Debussy's *Jeux.*

(*below*) Claude Debussy, composer of *Prélude à l'Après-Midi d'un Faune* and *Jeux.*

Nijinsky the choreographer. And enemy number one would be Nijinsky the dancer: his flight in *Le Spectre de la Rose,* his Harlequin, the lusty sensuality of his Golden Slave.

The Parisians were notoriously blasé. But were they really? Was it not in Paris that men of genius were "discovered" only after their funerals? How much were Gauguin's pictures going for now? And not so long ago he had died in poverty. But a choreographer's endeavors just disappear and cannot provide a posthumous visa to immortality. So wouldn't he, Diaghilev, be sacrificing Nijinsky by delighting in the dancer's artistic prophecies rather than by discouraging him? But Nijinsky right now was happy in his new discovery, and Diaghilev really wasn't very concerned with how the public would react. One thing was clear: by rejecting simple illustrativeness, Nijinsky was restoring the ballet's organic connection with music; he was restoring its own particular convention that would explain this connection in a new way. Some day, this would receive recognition.

Meanwhile, the final phrase of the music had died away. Nijinsky cast an inquisitive eye up at Diaghilev, sprawled in his armchair. Diaghilev nodded approval. Nijinsky said that he would like to have some experienced dancers for the nymphs. But for the moment he needed just Bronislava. She understood everything and he would test out everything with her.

Unlike Dresden, Vienna had age-old musical traditions. But Diaghilev was troubled by the very stability of these traditions. He was not going to risk putting on Stravinsky here, and he even had qualms about *Schéhérazade.* But even minus these pieces, the repertoire was big enough to guarantee the success of the tour. The newspapers wrote of the worldwide fame of the company and, as if to confirm this, Diaghilev was invited to make a trip to South America the following year.

Diaghilev was delayed in Vienna by his negotiations with the American impresario, and the company went on to Budapest without him. The Hungarian capital welcomed its guests warmly, but poor Grigoriev got into an awful scrape, at the very moment when he was first carrying full responsibility for the company.

The theater people greeted him with the news that all tickets had been sold and that, moreover, their auditorium was a very large one. So it was. But the stage was quite out of proportion to the auditorium.

It was so narrow and inconvenient that there seemed no way in which it could accommodate the decors for the ballets.

Grigoriev had just managed to sort this out when he was informed that Nijinsky was ill. Kschessinska came to the rescue. She had joined the tour as a substitute for Karsavina, who had managed to get away from St. Petersburg only for a short while and had now gone back. Mathilde Felixovna took charge. She brought her own samovar to Nijinsky's room and set to work to cure her partner of his terrible cold "by home remedies."

As always, the crème de la crème filled the auditorium on the evening of the première. One of the boxes was graced by the celebrated Hungarian actress Emilia Markus. Next to her was her daughter Romola de Pulszky, just turned twenty-one. Romola became so enthusiastic over the Ballets Russes that she attended every single performance. Toward the end of the tour, she fell in love with Nijinsky, who so captivated her romantic imagination with his mysterious mask, the "iron strength and resilience" of his Harlequin. Three months later, Romola became a daily visitor to the current season in Paris, where she was taking drama lessons from Gabrielle Réjane. This wayward young girl, who possessed remarkable willpower and tenacity, announced to her mother that she was giving up her drama studies. When the Russians returned to Budapest at the end of 1912, she became acquainted with many members of the company. She made friends with Adolf Bolm and won the sympathy of Cecchetti, who had a particular weakness for flattery and who liked receiving presents. This was the "knight's move": the maestro allowed his young admirer to visit his classes and indicated that he would be willing to let her study with him. There remained just one more obstacle, and the most terrifying one: Diaghilev.

Ludwig Karpath, the Hungarian critic, helped Romola as a token of his gratitude for a certain favor she had rendered him. In Marienbad one summer, still a little girl, she had accompanied him one evening to his hotel through the woods, for the venerable Karpath was afraid of the dark! He now asked Diaghilev for an "audience" and took Romola with him.

Many years later she described this visit in her book *Nijinsky:* "Apparently a young society girl had come to the great artistic organiser with a request. In reality, two powerful enemies had crossed swords for the first time." [16]

Well, the young lady had an advantage in that Diaghilev did not suspect any dirty tricks. With unusual attention he went into the details of the matter. He said that it would be ideal if she could join the Imperial Theater School, but, of course, they wouldn't take her. First, Mademoiselle was not Russian, and second, she had long passed the required age. Then he advised her to take private classes with Fokine in St. Petersburg, but at last decided: "I will talk to Maestro Cecchetti. He has taught all our greatest artists. I am sure he will take you as a special, private pupil. This way you will have not only a marvelous teacher, but also the possibility of traveling with us and closely studying our work." [17]

And so it happened that Diaghilev himself allowed into his domain a woman who was destined to deal him a cruel blow. For the moment, Nijinsky's future wife, guarded by her devoted maid, followed the Diaghilev company everywhere, and she was most annoyed that, however many times she was introduced to Nijinsky, he looked at her as if he was seeing her for the first time.

In the spring of 1912, after their first tour in Budapest, the company appeared in Monte Carlo. Immediately, Fokine began to work on Balakirev's *Thamar*, but it just wouldn't come off. The main reason for this seemed to be *L'Après-Midi*. No longer was it possible to hide the rehearsals of Nijinsky's ballet from Fokine. Until now the permanent choreographer of the Saisons Russes, Fokine became terribly jealous.

Diaghilev couldn't have cared less. He was quite convinced that any art form that could see nothing beyond its own established norms was doomed. He now had no doubts that Fokine's various themes had already reached the limit of their potential. His own reputation as a man of faultless artistic intuition and good taste was dearer to him than any feelings or relationships. He became cruel, and discounted Fokine and everyone else. Even Benois, his bosom friend—more, his first mentor in art—now irritated Diaghilev more and more by his devotion to the beauty of bygone epochs in the theater. Indeed, it was precisely this kind of beauty that was being renounced or, rather, derided everywhere. New views on poetry, painting, and art in general were being advanced. Diaghilev followed with interest the development of a movement that was calling itself Futurism. Both in the West and in Russia new artists and poets were emerging whose strange art contained the idea of displacement in man's consciousness, of a lost harmony—perhaps, indeed, a prophetic idea. As much as possible, Diaghilev read the poetry and manifestoes of the poets, and he took note of the new artists. He was especially interested in two of them: Natalia Goncharova and Mikhail Larionov.

Diaghilev remarked to himself that in *Thamar* Fokine was chewing over the same old confection of bacchanalian feasts filled with fatal passion. As of old, as in *Cléopâtre* or in *Schéhérazade,* the servants of the Tsarina Thamar (who, of course, would turn out beautifully with Karsavina) would dance against the background of Bakstian luxury and would intoxicate the Traveler, the handsome and showy Adolf Bolm. And, as of old, the cunning temptress would order the hero to be killed at the end of this amorous episode. The same with Ravel's *Daphnis et Chloë.* The music was beautiful, of course, but once again the fields of Hellas would unfold and Karsavina and Nijinsky would play out Longus' idyllic romance. As for *Le Dieu Bleu,* Nijinsky would appear as an exquisite being; Bakst intended to cover his face and body in blue and to paint his nails and lips silver. Each of these ballets was bound to be successful. But this would be a success anticipated by the audience and, consequently, would hold nothing out of the ordinary. It would be a serene success, and serenity was contrary to Diaghilev's nature. Among his colleagues, those who did not promise tranquility were Stravinsky (and Diaghilev put great hopes on him) and Nijinsky. Diaghilev continued to visit Nijinsky's rehearsals and time after time was confirmed in his initial impression.

All this was torture for Fokine. Egocentric, proud, he suspected intrigues against him at every step. At first he shared his sorrows with Grigoriev, but soon he quarreled with him. Diaghilev insisted on daily rehearsals of *L'Après-Midi,* but Fokine, who required the same dancers as Nijinsky, suspected Grigoriev of playing into the hands of the "enemies" by not sending the dancers to his rehearsals. Only Nijinsky managed to avoid war with Fokine. Always very correct at rehearsals, Nijinsky was now particularly attentive and did not take offense at anything.

Eleonora Nikolaevna came to Monte Carlo. She had missed her children a great deal, and they now devoted all their spare time to her. But her son had very little free time. Every morning he studied with Cecchetti, noticing very occasionally the new Hungarian pupil. She would install herself on the side somewhere and would follow his every movement. She didn't take her eyes off him, as if she were hypnotized. Then followed rehearsals with Fokine and his own rehearsals for *L'Après-Midi*. Unless there was a performance, rehearsals took up the evening as well. Nevertheless, in his free moments, Nijinsky would go some place with his mother. Once he took her to Nice. Like an adult who has organized a day out for a child, he took her around to the stores, and he shared her delight as she, who had been poor her whole life, bought herself things both necessary and frivolous. They finished their excursion by dining in a smart restaurant and returned to Monte Carlo late at night, weighed down with bundles, and very happy.

The relaxation was beneficial to Nijinsky. The most difficult and the most creative period in his life was beginning. For the first time, he felt he was not an instrument that subtly responded to the will of other artists (however great they might be), but an independent artist and the executor of his own designs. These designs came fast and furious, sometimes as clear images, sometimes as obscure ones. It seemed to him that he could not control these fantasies, that they were bursting upon him and that they were leading him by some unknown path to imminent discovery.

One thing Nijinsky was sure of: his *L'Après-Midi* would differ in every way from the Fokine ballets. Even though he could picture the end result only in very unclear terms, he could sense the proximity of his endeavors to the painting and sculpture of artists who held no attraction whatsoever for Fokine. Diaghilev eagerly bought him reproductions of Rodin, Matisse, and Gauguin. The very orderly Vasili constantly cleared up the books and albums lying on all the tables, the chairs, and windowsills of the hotel room. Grumbling that it was a waste of money buying all this stuff, he remembered "pockmarked Egorka" back in his village who could paint better than all these daubers and whose trees were the color they should be. Vasili was certain of the infallibility of his beliefs and took affront when Vaslav

Fomich, amazingly sociable and jovial, teased him by declaring that Egorka's real name was actually Henri Rousseau.

Nijinsky asked his sister to drop by his hotel room to try out the meeting between the Faun and one of the nymphs. Bronislava opened the door, passed around the row of chairs that Nijinsky used to delinate the long, narrow space of his imaginary stage, and sat down on the divan. Folding her legs, she opened her large mouth and followed her brother with her eyes, slanted just like his. He moved about in the defined space, on straight feet, step by step, trying out first one pose, then another. Then he suddenly stopped and began to talk about that summer long ago when, still children, they had stayed with their mother in a *dacha* near St. Petersburg. A landscape gradually emerged from details that only brother and sister could remember and that in themselves had little significance. But he could feel at one with this remembered landscape, an experience which occurs only in childhood.

Nijinsky explained that the Faun should be half-child–half-beast, but that his "beastness" would have none of the sensuality that was central to the Golden Slave in *Schéhérazade* or that was supposed to be germane to Cleopatra's Slave or to the Moor in *Petrouchka*. However strange it might seem, the Faun was closer to Petrouchka himself, or even to Albrecht. He is pure. He sees the nymph and feels desire. But it is the instinctive, natural, and confused desire that a normal, healthy boy experiences.

He went on to say that it would probably be difficult to teach the female dancers the movements. It was more than a matter of the plastic design. It would simply be a case of becoming accustomed . . . or, rather, becoming unaccustomed. The dancers would have to forget the "turned-out" classical positions and the "natural" compositions of Fokine's dances. They would have to get used to the convention of angular positions of the body, just like on ancient bas reliefs. What would be most difficult would be adapting this plastic movement to the music of the prelude. The dancers would have to perceive the music as a whole; they'd have to keep it in their minds. *And,* they'd have to move between beats and sense the rhythm of the dance *after* the rhythm of the conductor's baton. Nature is music, but man exists in accordance both with the laws of nature and with his own.

Nijinsky in rehearsal. Drawing by Leon
Bakst. The pose suggests that Nijinsky was
working on *L'Après-Midi d'un Faune*, done
in 1912, but this drawing is sometimes
identified as the Sportsman in *Jeux*,
created a year later.

Bronislava, who did not know then that she would later join the constellation of the Diaghilev choreographers, was enraptured by these ideas. Unusually musical, she knew Debussy's prelude by heart already and quite understood what her brother was trying to attain. When he demonstrated the steps for the nymph, using his heels and straight legs, she at once grasped the image of a young girl, graceful yet awkward. She also understood that divine sense of unison that distinguished the dances of the corps de ballet in *Swan Lake, The Sleeping Beauty,* and *La Bayadère* but that had been rejected by Fokine.

When Diaghilev dropped by to see Nijinsky, he was met by a curious sight. Bronislava was frozen in a pose. Her legs were in profile, one in advance of the other, with the knees slightly bent; her body faced front, but she had turned her head in profile to look backward, in the direction opposite to that indicated by her legs, petrified in their running position. The bent elbow of one raised arm pointed in the direction she wished to run; the other arm made a backward gesture of aversion. Both raised arms were bent at the elbows; both hands were turned palm outward. And these broad palms, these fingers so widely spread, were the exact replica of Vaslav's hands. Diaghilev recognized this spontaneously, and was amazed at the expressivity of this immobile pose embodying the girl's frightened and impulsive run. Nijinsky stood three paces behind his sister. In profile, standing upright, and with his legs close together, he was holding in his chin and had cast his eyes down. He had let his hands fall, with straight fingers pressed tightly together, and merely pointed his wrists in the direction of the fleeing nymph. Diaghilev saw the slanting line of the wrists as a delicate brushstroke. In contrast to the fleeing nymph, the Faun hesitated from an unfamiliar feeling of embarrassment, from a timidity born by the feelings she had aroused in him.

Working with the other dancers was not so easy as working with Bronislava. For a long time they could not grasp the angular plastic movement needed for the sister nymphs. They were supposed to appear as if they had been taken from the ornamental border of a vase and stretched out in a straight line. They just could not grasp the rhythm and became confused as soon as Nijinsky stopped beating time. Patiently, calmly, he demonstrated and repeated the movements; he counted out loud, convinced that mechanical repetition would eventually make them remember the movements in their intricate dependence on the music. The eight-minute ballet required as many rehearsals as all three of Fokine's ballets together. As was to be expected, a lot of spiteful things were said about all this. But who could contradict Diaghilev? Diaghilev had decided that "the game is worth the candle," and he was not mistaken.

On 13 May the fourth season opened in Paris, again on the stage of the Théâtre du Châtelet.

As Diaghilev had predicted, *Le Dieu Bleu* and *Thamar* had what the French call diplomatically "un succès d'estime" (the word *estime* replacing *médiocrité*).

Fokine blamed this on Diaghilev's "intrigues" and on the fact that Diaghilev (so he thought) had to prepare the audience for *L'Après-Midi d'un Faune*. He felt insulted, and the rumor gained ground in the company that Fokine, once he had terminated his contract in June, would not renew it. Diaghilev remained unperturbed by the rumor. He was indeed preparing the public and the press for the première of *L'Après-Midi* and he deferred *Daphnis et Chloë* to the very end of the tour.

After several performances of *Le Dieu Bleu* and *Thamar*, the moment of the première arrived: 29 May 1912 was to be one of the most memorable nights in the history of the Diaghilev company.

5

Sitting in front of the mirror in his dressing room, Nijinsky tried to concentrate. His head was in a whirl. The calm that he so desired, the calm that heralded artistic inspiration and freedom, the calm that usually came upon him during the last minutes before his entrance on stage, this time would not come. He kept remembering all the things he had to say, do, and clarify, and these troubled him. He felt truly awful.

Sighing, he took a dab of sallow, yellow paint and put it on his face. After shading in his high cheekbones, he continued the line of his eyebrows up to his temple and extended the slanting line of his eyes, using a fine brush. Then he delineated his slightly swollen mouth with dark brown paint. Kneading a pellet of plasticine, he used it to lengthen the tips of his ears, so that they became sharp like a foal's. This method of makeup, which he had so carefully thought out, did not alter his face, it simply exaggerated its natural characteristics. He pulled on the tight-fitting wig, interwoven with golden threads, and then mounted his horns on top, with their sinuous forms beginning at his forehead and protruding slightly in back. He looked in the mirror. Something between a man and a beast looked back at him—drowsy, languorous, intelligent.

Nijinsky sighed again, but this time with less constraint. He got up, threw off his dressing gown, and allowed Vasili to cover his body with the same sallow, yellow color and to paint his forearms and elbows with uneven, dark brown spots.

Vasili did not allow himself to sneer, but simply gave him his costume. There certainly were grounds for sneering. Fifty years later people would still be sneering at ballet characters costumed only in tights and no more. The Faun opened up the "era of tights" in the twentieth century. His tights, duplicating the color of his hands and face, were also painted in big, uneven spots, resembling kidskin. A bunch of grapes encircled the base of his long, thick neck, and a similar bunch encircled his loins, ending in a short tail. He wore golden sandles made of rubber.

Nijinsky threw on his dressing gown and went on stage. The ramp had already been put up. A low hill rose in the shallow space between the proscenium and Bakst's decor of a lake surrounded by purple plane trees and silver willows.

Nijinsky did several quick pliés; bent right, left, back; then more pliés and some grands battements to limber up his legs.

"Come on, come on," said Diaghilev impatiently.

Nijinsky took a short reed pipe from the prop man, ran up the hill, and lay there comfortably as if he were lying in the grass. The feeling of freedom that he had so desired had come at last. It possessed him just as the curtain rose and the orchestra evoked the first languorous waves of the sultry midday heat.

Claude Debussy had not ventured to familiarize himself with the spectacle that, apparently, was going to "materialize" his prelude. Egocentric and very scrupulous, he now hid himself deep in his box and nervously picked at his beard. He cursed himself for having yielded to Diaghilev and for having let these ballet people ruin his music. He wished to close his eyes and listen, to immerse himself in the obscure "desires and dreams" of the faun as they soared on high, for they were the fruit of his own moods nourished by the verses of Mallarmé.

Nijinsky as the Faun.

The creature visible on the low hill seemed a rather fantastic one. Well, as long as this faun lies there just extracting those long drawn-out sounds from his pipe, everything will be all right.

The Faun moved, stretched, changed his position. The dancer's movement expressed the feeling of heat, of still air. An idle somnolence enveloped the Faun; he basked in the sun, flexing his muscles, taking a spontaneous delight in the tranquility. He seemed to superimpose his intermittent, angular, and strangely harmonic movements on to the smooth sections of sound. The composer suddenly grasped the logic of this harmony: without following the beat, Nijinsky was nevertheless carefully following the rhythm, the melodic design of the music, and was expressing its important ascensions and cadences.

Following, but not blindly; expressing, but in his own way. The Faun was subordinating his movements to the angular, flattened stylization of an ancient bas relief.

The nymphs also subordinated their movements to this angular stylization as they advanced across the flattened space of the stage toward the puzzled, bemused Faun.

Not in vain had Nijinsky repeated at rehearsals that the formal pattern of his ballet must not be disturbed even for one second, that although the ballet was short, it was difficult in that no one could relax on stage after she had danced her bit. Prince Sergei Mikhailovich Volkonsky, a one-time enemy of Diaghilev who had now made peace with him, was enraptured by this convention. As an ardent supporter of Dalcroze, he said: "From the moment the curtain rose to the cadence of the rhythm, the element of chance was entirely absent on stage; what in military instruction is called 'at ease' and 'fall out' was missing. All the time they were at arms and under orders." [1]

As befitted mythological deities, the nymphs came on "under orders" of the musical and plastic design, and they did bear an outward resemblance to such deities. Bakst had made up each of them with his own hands and had circled their eyes with a white and pink border, making them look like those of doves. The soles of their bare feet and their toenails were also touched up with the same pink. The long curls of their wigs, made from golden thread, fell down over their transparent, pleated costumes, which were cream-colored and decorated either in pale blue or in pale green. The nymphs placed their feet in profile, heel to toe, stretching the line of their walk parallel to the footlights. Each one crossed her breast (held en face) with one arm so as to touch her other shoulder, the other she held loosely by her side. The head was held in sharp profile. The nymphs, equally tall and slender, moved as if they were floating along, commencing each step from the heel, using the whole foot. At first, three of them appeared and paused to contemplate the foliage and the water. Then two more. Then one by herself (Nijinska). Finally, there appeared the tallest nymph (Lydia Nelidova), who intended to go bathing. The others surrounded her, guarding her with their dance and raising their hands to their shoulders, palms opened outward.

The Faun came out of his trance. Induced by the instinct of a young beast, he crept toward them. The nymphs saw him and took to flight, and as they "ran" they shortened the intervals between the interchange of positions within the plastic cipher of their movement. The bather and the Faun were left alone. She now attempted to save herself; he attempted to catch her, in that same convention of fluent movement. Each step and pose lent the Faun new signs of consciousness. The human element now arose in the beast bringing with it a new feeling, countering the peace and serenity of nature with an inexplicable unrest. At length, he approached her. She sank to one knee, covered her breast with her folded arm, and, raising her other arm above her head, stared at him through the fingers of her outstretched hand. Entwining his hand with hers, the Faun seemed to awaken in surprise and, eyes wide open, stared at the fugitive.

The nymphs appeared and bore away their sister. The Faun took up the veil she had left behind and returned to his lair on the hill. He sank to one knee, unfolded the veil and raised it to his quivering nostrils. Then he stretched out one leg behind him, threw back his head, opened his mouth in a silent laugh, and, spreading out the veil, lay down upon it, deep in thought. A momentary effusion of dreams—and then back to the placidity of contemplation.

The curtain came down. The venerable audience was silent. And then something strange occurred. A rumble came from the auditorium, loud applause mingled with loud protests. Diaghilev had suspected that the response would be an unusual one, but even so he couldn't believe his ears for the first few seconds. Until this performance, the

L'Après-Midi d'un Faune, 1912.

(*left*) Nijinska as the sixth nymph and Nijinsky as the Faun.

(*below*) Nijinsky as the Faun and Lydia Nelidova as the principal nymph.

(*right*) Costume design for the principal nymph, by Leon Bakst.

criterion for judging whether a piece had been accepted or not had been the greater or lesser amount of praise and delight displayed by the audience. He raced backstage. Grigoriev noticed in his confusion that Diaghilev's face, normally pale, had turned purple. Diaghilev went over to Nijinsky standing in the middle of the stage. Nijinsky turned to him and, as if they had suddenly exchanged roles, smiled reassuringly, even derisively. Behind the curtain could be heard "Encore! Encore!" sounding above the shouts of indignation. Diaghilev also smiled, turned pale, and asked abruptly whether a repeat was possible. Nijinsky nodded his head.

Once again the orchestra evoked the mirage of a sultry midday sun, the Faun played his pipe pensively and languidly, the nymphs expressed the rhythm of a Grecian bas relief. . . .

After the performance was over, the mood backstage was not the usual one of triumph and celebration. Dissent could be felt, not so plainly as in the audience, but nevertheless it was there.

Few members of the company realized that with his *L'Après-Midi* Nijinsky had forestalled future currents in the ballet world. Almost

(*left*) Nijinsky as the Faun stares curiously at the veil left behind by the nymph.

(*right*) Nijinsky in the final pose of the Faun.

everyone in the company regarded Fokine as the apostle of the new credo and found his pictorial "naturalness" to be quite comprehensible. The lifelike, pantomimic gestures and dances (dance being the culmination of feeling) in his productions gave dancers scope for demonstrating properties that were scenic and purely balletic. But Nijinsky had swept all this aside and had changed the performer into an instrument obedient to the "whim" of the choreographer. True, members of the company were wary of manifesting their discontent and whispered among themselves in corners, but, essentially, they sympathized with Fokine. As he was leaving the company, Fokine said exactly what he thought. In his own way he was objective; he understood the merits of *L'Après-Midi* and even acknowledged some of them publicly. He liked the profile, the foreshortened perspective. He said that "the groups are at times very beautiful and exactly reproduce bas reliefs and painting on vases." He approved of the economy of expression for he also "tried to express the essence of the moment with a minimum of movement." He acknowledged the comparative immobility of the performers vis-à-vis the uninterrupted flow of the music. He had always considered the need to move with every beat as "rhythmomania," and he openly approved of Nijinsky's restrained poses.

But all this was ruined by the "unnaturalness" of the movements, by what he considered the absurd device of stepping from the heel on to the whole foot: this was particularly absurd during the run because any normal person "coming down with our full weight" would obviously touch the ground with his toes and not with his heels.[2]

Fokine argued as a professional. Still, he was wrong to attack the finale of *L'Après-Midi*. Only recently he had been annoyed by the English ladies who had been shocked by the sensuality of his bacchanalias. Only recently he had parodied the fools who had climbed up into the fly gallery with the titillating aim of peering behind the screens that hid the couch of Cleopatra and Amoun. And then, just before the première, he had declared the Faun's final gesture to be indecent—and in a ballet that was about to be "demonstrated . . . in front of thousands of people among whom will be young girls."[3] As if his experience had not told him that young girls will see impropriety precisely where they are told it is. So it transpired that Fokine the iconoclast of taboos went even further than the Paris philistines.

Several newspapers anathematized Nijinsky's production, and at the same time attacked Debussy, the composer of "all this subtle game given out to be a masterpiece." [4]

The correspondent from *Le Temps* rushed to the defense of Mallarmé's "intangible vision." He could scarcely have read the eclogue in which the poet describes, in very tangible and racy terms, the love frolic between the faun and two of the nymphs. [5]

Gaston Calmette, editor of *Le Figaro*, confessed frankly: "Our readers will not locate in its usual place on the theater page an article by my esteemed colleague Robert Brussel of the first performance of *L'Après-Midi d'un Faune*—a choreographic scene by Nijinsky produced and danced by that amazing artiste. They won't find it because I have destroyed it." And then, contradicting his own words about the "amazing artiste," Calmette described how "justified booing greeted the all too explicit miming of this misshapen animal body, repellent when seen en face and even more loathsome in profile." He predicted that "our public will never accept such bestial realism." [6]

"Depends what kind of public, of course," observed Diaghilev coolly. "Rodin was among the public at the première."

That was a wonderful trump card. The grand old man had sat through *L'Après-Midi*, had solemnly proceeded backstage, had indicated his delight to Nijinsky, and had asked him to pose for him. On the pages of *Le Matin*, in an article entitled "La Renaissance de la Danse" he explained why Nijinsky in *L'Après-Midi* "had never been so remarkable." He was enraptured by the "harmony of mime and movement," by the fact that the artist "expresses with his body what his spirit desires," and he described him as the "ideal model" for artists and sculptors. [7]

Indeed, Rodin soon began to sculpt Nijinsky—which, in turn, gave rise to yet another legend. Many people have tried to divine why nothing came of these sessions in Rodin's studio. Some say that the sculptor could not fathom the essential character of his model and refused the work. Others think that someone stole the preparatory sketches that must have existed. Yet others prefer Romola Nijinsky's version—the eternal complaint about Diaghilev's jealous despotism, that Diaghilev forbade Nijinsky to visit the seventy-year-old sculptor.

This is very hard to believe. Diaghilev loved publicity, and the

Two action drawings of Nijinsky as Daphnis,
by Valentine Gross.

story of a new Rodin sculpture would surely have been a good piece of
publicity. Just then, after the scandal of the première, Diaghilev was
in dire need of favorable publicity. But he could not postpone the
company's imminent departure for London, where the next season was
to begin on 12 June, and, meanwhile, the première of *Daphnis et
Chloë* was set for 8 June at the Châtelet. Those hours that Nijinsky
might have spent in Rodin's studio were now taken up with rehearsals
for *Daphnis.*

Nijinsky's Daphnis pleased both Fokine and the general public.
The innocent shepherd rejected the seductive advances of Lykanion
and incarnated the Fokine ideal of the antique dance in his duets with
Chloë (Karsavina).

The ballet *Daphnis et Chloë* was the apotheosis of that ideal and at the same time served as a serene requiem to it. However, Fokine did not realize that his time had come. Even many years later he still prized his production and still expressed his annoyance at Diaghilev and Nijinsky. He recalled how, as soon as the curtain went up, both his friends and his "enemies" set to with equal dedication: "A whole herd of sheep walked across the stage. They were tended by shepherds and shepherdesses. The prayers, the offerings of flowers and wreaths as gifts to the nymphs, apotheotic dances, pastoral peace, harmony . . . how far off this was from the belligerent atmosphere and the narrowly averted riot just a few seconds before on the very same stage!" [8]

Yes, quite distant. . . .

Nijinsky felt sorry for Fokine. Dispassionately, Diaghilev wound up the first period of the Saisons Russes. It had brought him fame. He knew that he was taking a risk by putting his stakes on Nijinsky the choreographer, whose first creation had been born in an atmosphere of aesthetic conflict. But Diaghilev understood artistic creativity to be one continuous risk. Diaghilev would not have been Diaghilev if he had not realized that, by smashing the established conceptions of beauty, he was being truly contemporary; that, in being in advance of his time, he was laying the foundations of the new art.

In London Diaghilev received the Russian newspapers and magazines with their reactions to *L'Après-Midi d'un Faune.*

The reporters discussed every aspect of the scandal that Rodin's fellow countrymen had made for him. The defenders of bourgeois morality even reproached the government for granting Rodin the use of the Palais Biron, city property and previously a chapel of the Sacré-Coeur.

Diaghilev and Nijinsky knew all that. They were more interested in serious articles.

The poet Minsky declared: "The *L'Après-Midi* production points to the possibility of a new structure in art." When Nijinsky saw these words, he read on. He learned that ancient bas relief had helped him embody an "issue of almost topical relevance" containing more of Wedekind's *Frühlings Erwachen* than of Mallarmé's poem. This surprised Nijinsky—he had never read Wedekind. He found out that this was a fashionable German dramatist who discussed the problems of free love. But everything else in the article seemed quite justified. "Nijinsky's Faun," Minsky wrote, "is closer to the hero of the ballet *Petrouchka* than to the exultant god of Mallarmé's poem. He is a timid, innocent boy wounded by the sting of passion newly aroused, a boy who sees Woman for the first time and who rushes toward Her; silent, his heart on fire, he has not yet learned the rhetoric of love; he is still dumb, neither beast nor yet Apollo." [9]

Somehow this seemed to hit the nail on the head. Minsky's complex and diffuse words expressed Nijinsky's secret: "I am the Faun" was one of the laconic statements that later appeared among the chaotic thoughts of his diaries.

Nijinsky praised Minsky's article when he next spoke to Diaghilev. Diaghilev agreed that it was written very well. He added that Minsky was well known—somewhere between Nadson and the Symbolists. But who was this Lunacharsky? He was supposed to be a political émigré who had been living outside Russia for several years, but who published in Kugel's St. Petersburg journal *The Theater and Art*. He wrote sensibly; take this, for example: "What should I call the two camps who are clashing swords over Nijinsky's risqué dances and extraordinary inventions? I would say that one camp, represented by a world celebrity, Auguste Rodin, is the one that supports free beauty, free aesthetics; the other camp, whose paladin, Calmette, the influential editor-in-chief of *Le Figaro*, has come upon the scene with an almost indecent fervency, might be called the camp of philistine morality, the savior of the pure ethics of the real petit bourgeoisie." The author went on to remark quite accurately that "when the Russian spectacle was condemned as indecent and morally dangerous, the philistines responded by cramming the Châtelet full. 'What? Something indecent? Go and get a ticket immediately' said the average lady to the average cavalier." [10]

"Well, what do you expect? The petit bourgeoisie is the same everywhere" was Diaghilev's ironic judgment as he put the journal aside. "On the other hand, *L'Après-Midi* is not the innocent pantaloons of *Giselle*. If we were to present it in St. Petersburg, we'd be hauled off at once to the Nikolai the Miracle-worker Lunatic Asylum, or we'd be sent to Siberia for our hooliganism."

The events section of the journal *The Footlights and Life* soon confirmed what Diaghilev had said. It reported that the director of the Theater Office in Moscow had asked Teliakovsky whether he would object if negotiations were started with Nijinsky with a view to hiring him for the Bolshoi. Teliakovsky had replied that, in principle, he did not object. But after the Paris scandal over *L'Après-Midi*, Teliakovsky telegraphed Obukhov telling him to break off any negotiations with Mr. Nijinsky at once.[11]

This remark might have been apocryphal. Nobody had started any negotiations whatsoever with Nijinsky, so there was none to break off. Still, once again, the mirage of returning home to Russia came and went.

Actually, in what capacity could Nijinsky have returned to Russia? As premier danseur of the Bolshoi? Hardly. Moscow considered the methods of St. Petersburg dancers to be far too refined and prized the masculinity and temperament of her own men—Vasili Dmitrievich Tikhomirov and Mikhail Mordkin. Nijinsky the dancer just would not be suited, let alone Nijinsky the choreographer. Alexander Alexeevich Gorsky had been producing ballets at the Bolshoi for nearly twenty years. Teliakovsky was his patron and certainly would not have permitted the creator of *L'Après-Midi* to try out his ultramodern experiments there. And he would have been absolutely right. Such experiments needed conditions that could not be established on the Imperial stage. Even if they could have been, the audience would probably have just whistled and booed.

Nijinsky sensed more and more clearly how firmly Diaghilev had attached him to his endeavor, and Nijinsky himself no longer yearned for freedom. As soon as he recovered his energy after the exhausting première of *L'Après-Midi*, Nijinsky again experienced the creative urge. At first he had no definite plan; only fragmentary ideas and obscure images crowded into his mind. But they could be materialized with Diaghilev's help. Diaghilev said nothing specific, although he did hint that *L'Après-Midi* was just a beginning and that new experiments lay ahead.

Before leaving Paris, Diaghilev invited a few friends to the Bois de Boulogne.

From the terrace of the restaurant they could see the spring foliage, the avenues strewn with sand now empty at this noon hour

Nijinsky, 1912.

on a weekday. Nijinsky leaned back in his chair and gazed out at all
this. He relaxed his muscles, rested, and listened lazily to the table
talk. Bakst, Debussy, Reynaldo Hahn, Robert Brussel, Cocteau, the
artist Jacques-Emile Blanche, and the newspaper correspondent Hector
Cahusac were discussing ballet affairs.

Bakst, who obviously disapproved of the break between Diaghilev
and Fokine, suggested that Diaghilev turn once more to history as
a source of inspiration. History contained plots, themes, and images
that could nourish the imagination. Modern man was tired, Bakst said,
and therefore thirsted for oblivion. We could provide this oblivion,
we could resurrect the past in any shape or form, from bloody orgies
of the Orient to Romantic elegies.

They listened to him attentively. But Diaghilev objected, saying
that elegies and orgies had begun to pall and that, anyway, the other
arts were looking in other directions as well as backward. Brussel

took up the conversation: perhaps the magic charm of ballet lay precisely in its old-fashionedness. Anyway, how, for example, could the dance be adapted to the modern ideas of painting? The Cubists fragment the world into elements, but the choreographer has at his disposal a human body, not paint and canvas, and the human body has only limited possibilities.

"Not so," pronounced Nijinsky quietly but distinctly. Everyone turned to him in surprise. He blushed and stopped short, but then started to speak, not noticing that Cahusac had taken out his notebook, had placed it on his knees, and was taking notes.

"The kind of man whom I see on stage"—Nijinsky seemed to be meditating out loud as Diaghilev translated almost inaudibly—"is first and foremost a contemporary man. My dream is to create costumes, plastic movements that would be characteristic of our time. Undoubtedly, a man's body contains elements that denote the era that he himself represents. If we watch our contemporary walking down the street, reading a newspaper, or dancing the tango, we won't find anything in common between his gestures and those, let's say, of a stroller in Louis XV's time or of a monk deciphering manuscripts in the thirteenth century."

Nobody interrupted him. He became still bolder:

"I've been giving a great deal of attention to polo, golf, tennis, etc., and I am convinced that these games are not simply healthy pastimes, but they also form a plastic beauty. Studying them has given me the hope that in the future our own time will be characterized by a style just as expressive as those antique styles that we admire so much at present."

"Allow me to mention," interrupted Reynaldo Hahn, "that if you do compose a modern theme, you will inevitably run up against the need for appropriate music. And that will be a problem."

"There's no need to compose a theme," replied Nijinsky. "A ballet theme should either be universally known or it just shouldn't be. As a ballet progresses one shouldn't have to think any more profoundly than when one is looking at a painting or listening to a symphony. . . ."

He stood up. Intrigued, everyone turned toward him. Several waiters looked out when they heard the chairs move back.

Nijinsky softly paced back and forth in the space they had made. He felt at ease, as if Bronislava were sitting in front of him and not all these important aesthetes and arbiters of art. Nijinsky started to illustrate his word with movement. He said: "I wish to compose a score of movements in which everything would be defined by the bend of a finger, by the modulation of a muscle, and not by leaps and pirouettes; it will be a score that will reveal boundless possibilities for the human body. . . ." [12]

Nijinsky placed his legs firmly on the floor; he bent his arm and clenched his fist; his bicep swelled beneath the fabric of his summer suit. He raised his other arm as if holding a tennis racket. Without moving from the spot, he released an electric current from his flexed muscles through his entire body. He did, indeed, "fragment into elements" this ultimate outburst of energy by concentrating in his strained neck the fixed, mad dash of the tennis player who deflects the approaching ball. He retained his position, but threw back his head, turned it from view, and pretended to follow the slow flight of an airplane.

"Childish," Bakst muttered.

He was angry with Nijinsky. Although Diaghilev had approved of the decor for *L'Après-Midi,* Nijinsky had disagreed and had ventured to tell Bakst, albeit rather indecisively, that he imagined a different kind of setting; something along the lines of the "displaced planes" of Cézanne and Matisse in which the human figure becomes the focus of the general ornamentation, which is, in turn, extended into flat surfaces. Bakst was angry, although deep down he recognized that his three-dimensional decor was not really suited to dance extended, as it were, along a flat surface. Then he had read in Lunacharsky's article that for Nijinsky's choreography what was needed was "not a landscape, but a carpet" and that the artist should have consciously "destroyed perspective." This, so to say, added insult to injury and made Bakst furious.

Bakst expressed a malicious interest in the kind of costumes that this ballet on the theme of the plastic beauty of sport would require.

Nijinsky replied that the costumes would be tennis clothes, although, of course, these would be made lighter for the stage.

Then Jacques-Emile Blanche mentioned diplomatically in support of his colleague that this kind of H. G. Wells vision was scarcely feasible: tennis costumes as they would be in 1920, airplanes flying over the stage. . . .

Nijinsky seemed to wilt. He went back to the table. Diaghilev, who hated Nijinsky's way of suddenly retreating into his shell, said abruptly that in art one should not follow only the feasible and well-worn paths. He turned to Debussy and proposed that he compose the music for a ballet dealing with a flirtation on a tennis court. Nijinsky started at the word "flirtation," but he again fell silent.

In 1924 Jean Cocteau, who had forgotten the lunch and arguments in the Bois de Boulogne of twelve years before, composed the scenario for the ballet *Le Train Bleu*. Diaghilev commissioned Darius Milhaud to write the music. Bronislava Nijinska realized the choreography, which proved to be remarkably close to her brother's fantastic visions. Some young people in swimming costumes and tennis clothes were flirting on the beach. As the action proceeded, the participants looked up and watched the flight of an imaginary airplane.

Nijinsky did not wish his ballet to include a flirtation. Diaghilev foisted it upon him. That's why Nijinsky wrote in his diary just after "I am the Faun": "*Jeux* is the life of which Diaghilev dreamed." [13]

Dream or no dream, Nijinsky heeded the command—at least, apparently—and it percolated through his own consciousness. The flirtation turned out to be a game played by children, who were, in fact, apprehensive of the whole idea.

Debussy agreed to write the music for what Nijinsky called *Jeux*. Meanwhile, Stravinsky, somewhere in the Russian countryside, was writing the music for another ballet based on pagan rites of spring. The young composer was distressed at being parted from Fokine. He wrote to Roerich, the scenarist and artist of *Le Sacre du Printemps*, complaining of Diaghilev's tactlessness: Diaghilev "wasn't even interested in finding out whether we would like to work with someone else." [14]

After parting with Fokine, Diaghilev thought of Gorsky as a possible choreographer for Stravinsky's ballet. He probably would have invited him, even though Stravinsky obstinately declared that "Gorsky might be a genius," but he still preferred Fokine. After the lunch in the Bois de Boulogne, Diaghilev changed his mind and decided that Nijinsky would choreograph the two ballets for the fifth Paris season. He marveled at how the seeds from all those "lessons" in picture galleries and concert halls had fallen on fertile ground. The "teacher" now behaved with more caution, remembering the lesson that his "pupil" had taught him unintentionally in the Bois de Boulogne. Intuition was advancing this "dimwit," which many people still thought him to be, to the vanguard of artistic thought.

Diaghilev was pleased that his hunch had turned out to be correct. So he brought Nijinsky a photograph of a painting by the young artist Alexandra Exter.[15] The picture was called *The Hunt:* against a background of a conglomeration of cubes three women, a man, and their dogs were chasing an invisible animal.

"Painted recently," said Diaghilev. He pointed out the male figure. His stance—with legs planted firmly on the ground and head turned sharply away from his shoulders, positioned en face—focused attention on the tense muscles of his neck: all the force of his imminent dash forward was concentrated there.

Diaghilev screwed up his eyes as he appraised the photograph. He mentioned that Russian Futurism, apparently, promised rather more than its Italian counterpart. Come what may, art was making an about-face. Retrospectivism was being replaced by forecasts of the future. Diaghilev smiled—his severance with Fokine had come just at the right time. Nijinsky's new ballet would announce the turning of the tide.

With his thumbnail, Diaghilev sketched the contour of a figure in the air. It was a figure that bore a remarkable resemblance to the one Nijinsky had demonstrated on the restaurant terrace. He put the photograph aside, was silent for a moment, and then ended by saying, "We'll date this ballet 1930 in our programs." [16]

Just before the departure for London, Bronislava Nijinska visited her brother in his hotel. She paced up and down the room, leafed through some books and then suddenly said that Kochetovsky, a dancer in the company, had proposed to her and so she was getting married.

Vaslav fell silent. He was not gladdened by the news, for he felt that he was losing his sister, a close friend. Then, noticing how distressed Bronislava was, he hastened to congratulate her. The wedding ceremony was conducted in London, in a Russian church. The young couple intended to go on their honeymoon, but Diaghilev disappointed them (and, indeed, the whole company, which was about to go on holiday) by announcing an August engagement in Deauville.

The resort on the coast of Normandy had only just been opened. A modest theater had been built next to the splendid Casino, and its tiny stage could accommodate only the simplest decors. Hence the Ballet Russe could put on only *Les Sylphides, Le Carnaval,* and the *Polovtsian Dances,* and actually there was hardly enough room for the Polovtsian romp. But the directors had invited a constellation of celebrities to the first Deauville season, and Diaghilev considered it to his advantage to accept the engagement. He did not regret it. The crème de la crème was coming to Deauville, and Diaghilev never missed the chance to make new acquaintances and to strengthen old ones. Among the latter was Gabriel Astruc, director of the Société Musicale in Paris, who had been in charge of the Grands Saisons d'Eté for about eight years. He was now preparing to open the Théâtre des Champs-Elysées and offered Diaghilev a contract. Astruc named a huge sum of money in order to entice the Ballet Russe away from the clutches of the Opéra.

The company recessed for two months. Before departing for St. Petersburg, Diaghilev asked Bronislava Nijinska to stay a while in Monte Carlo to rehearse *Jeux.* Vaslav was silent, but Bronislava knew how important her support was for him at this busy period (two ballets were being produced simultaneously) and she agreed at once. In Monte Carlo she soon sensed the gratitude of her brother, normally so reserved. He expressed his joy on meeting her and her husband and he proposed, diplomatically, that he see them more often, as long as they did not mind.

Nijinsky explained to his sister that Tamara Karsavina, the third participant in *Jeux,* was being temporarily replaced by Alexandra Vasilievskaya and that they would begin rehearsals the very next day. Debussy had actually written only part of the music, which he had played for Nijinsky in Paris, but, anyway, the important thing was to get going.

The next day, the two women appeared at the theater at the appointed time and discovered to their amazement that Nijinsky had

Nijinsky and Gabriel Astruc. Caricature by Sem.

not turned up yet. He arrived some time later, disconcerted and very distressed. The entire Casino orchestra had gone off somewhere, including its pianist. If Diaghilev had been there, he would have found a way out of the situation; he would have dug one up or hired one from some place. But Nijinsky was incapable of such exploits.

After several days of racing around the deserted resort, they managed to find a certain music teacher. She listened to their requests in great confusion and then confessed that Debussy was just not her cup of tea. Bronislava looked at her silent and despondent brother and decided not to give up. After a good deal of persuasion, the music teacher agreed to give the music a try and took the manuscript score with her for two or three days.

But nothing came of this. Four days later the embarrassed lady came to the rehearsal and played something that was obviously a long way from the refined music of the famous composer. Nijinsky listened, chewing on his thumb, and then deliberately stopped her. He looked over the pianist's shoulder at the music, closed his eyes, and tried to recall how Debussy had played the beginning of *Jeux*. He looked again, turned to the two dancers, and said that he would demonstrate the entrance and the groupings.

He led them downstage, to the sides. "We moved towards each other on our toes in a dainty pas de bourrée," wrote Bronislava Fominichna Nijinska in a letter sent from her California home in the summer of 1971. "We kept walking on our toes and, in coming together, slightly bent our knees, just inclining our bodies towards each other."

Nijinsky went to the upstage corner on the left. He took out a tennis ball from his pocket, threw it up, took a run, jumped after it, and appeared in the center of the stage. He stopped, his right hand up as if he had just hit the ball with his racket.

He asked the dancers to turn their backs on the audience so that they could see their partner, and as soon as he touched the ground, they were to run off to the sides.

That's how they worked, without a pianist, trying out the groupings and transitions of the three participants in *Jeux*. Nijinsky saw that a good deal would have to be changed, and he awaited Diaghilev's arrival with impatience. But, as if on purpose, Diaghilev was delayed.

That winter, there were to be tours in German and Austrian cities and, in the spring, in Paris and London. Diaghilev was very busy. While in Paris he had concocted a mixed season. The opera repertoire was now to include *Boris Godunov*, *Ivan the Terrible* (*Pskovitianka*), and *Khovanshchina*. Apart from Debussy's *Jeux* and Stravinsky's *Le Sacre du Printemps*, he wanted to put on a third new ballet—Florent Schmitt's *La Tragédie de Salomé*. Boris Romanov, a young dancer from the Mariinsky and a disciple of Fokine, was to choreograph it.

Diaghilev's enterprise was now in its fifth year. A great deal had changed since that group of supporters of Russian art had organized the first season. Of the committee that used to meet at the tea table in Diaghilev's apartment, hardly any of the leaders now remained.

General Bezobrazov had died. Benois and Fokine had left in a huff. Diaghilev, who had become used to doing things himself, often repeated a favorite joke: that in his ballet company there was only one head to which he attached any weight—his own.

Still, there was one kind of support that he was always in need of—money. Not that he was attracted to money for its own sake. On the contrary, he scarcely knew its value, whether his own money or anyone else's. Money, fantastic sums of money, were needed for new productions, for paying composers, artists, ballet masters, for maintaining the company. Diaghilev knew how to secure this kind of money by drawing up advantageous contracts and by resorting to the financial support of patrons and friends. He simply despised the idea of making a profit and did not trouble about lining his own pocket. Hence he regarded it as quite natural that Nijinsky should have every comfort, that he would be satisfied with the money given him for everyday expenses, and that he would require no contract either as a dancer or as a choreographer.

Nijinsky, indeed, did not find his voluntary captivity to be a burden. He was refused nothing, whether he wanted to send his mother some money or to buy himself something, from diamond cuff links to rare books. He did not need much in this constant move from country to country, city to city, hotel to hotel. Moreover, he was as dependent as a child. Between his school life, when everything had been taken care of, and his meeting with Diaghilev, there had been only a few months during which he had been obliged to fend for himself and his family, and he had almost forgotten that time.

Nijinsky did not give any thought to his curious position. On the one hand, he was always occupied with his classes, with rehearsals and performances, and now his own productions were taking up all his thoughts and energies. On the other hand, he steered clear of people as always and avoided all their futile cares and worries. He did not look to the future and he did not make any plans. So what did he need money for?

In October 1912 there arrived in the company a certain man who was not directly connected with art. Baron Dmitri Nikolaevich Gunsbourg belonged to one of the most powerful banking families of St. Petersburg, and he was prepared to buy his membership in the

Diaghilev enterprise. Behind his snobbish façade and passion for ultra-smart clothes, he possessed a lighthearted, easygoing character. He liked to encourage romantic love affairs and, what was most important, was not averse to lending money. True, he might sometimes refuse if a request coincided with the day a painting or rare statue was coming up for sale. But if and when he had money, the baron would hand it over to Diaghilev, noting the four- or five-figure sum on his starched shirt cuff. The shirt would go off to the laundry, but the lender and debtor contented themselves with an approximate restoration of the sum recorded on the lost "document."

Even so, Diaghilev was always in need of cash, and he was forever borrowing or trying to find new sources for loans. One had truly to be a man of iron will, one had really to believe in one's mission as the apostle of modern art to renounce the proven, to take bold risks, and to advance along an unfamiliar path.

Berlin and Budapest were the last engagements for 1912.

At the Kroll Theater in Berlin, Diaghilev attempted to present *L'Après-Midi d'un Faune* with the old favorites—*Les Sylphides, Le Spectre de la Rose, Cléopâtre,* and the *Polovtsian Dances.* But, as he expected, the ballet did not win the public's sympathy. Among the few who delighted in the ballet was Hugo von Hofmannsthal. He suggested to Diaghilev that he, Hofmannsthal, compose a scenario for Nijinsky on the theme of Joseph and the wife of Potiphar; Richard Strauss would write the music, and Diaghilev would meet him in Vienna during the January tour. The meeting with Hofmannsthal consoled Diaghilev: it was worth showing *L'Après-Midi* to the uninitiated to win the sympathy of a single poet.

When he was in Budapest, Diaghilev reached a final agreement with a South American impresario concerning the summer tour. He told Grigoriev that Baron Gunsbourg would be in charge of the company then. Grigoriev was curious to know why Diaghilev was not going himself. In response Diaghilev said, "Well, you know, I can't stand the sea." Diaghilev, master of many fates, feared his own and never forgot that a gypsy had once foretold that he would die on the water.

1913. The last year of the European peace and for Nijinsky the moment of his zenith—and of a tragic turning point in his life.

Nijinsky had climbed to the pinnacle of his art, in pain and torment he had conquered the steep slopes, little knowing that on the other side was an abyss. He did not complain. Diaghilev measured everything by his own endurance. He remembered how Fokine had so easily composed several ballets all at once, and he did not notice that excessive work was leaving its mark on Nijinsky's psyche. He did know, of course, that Fokine and Nijinsky were very different people.

Fokine had already found his own aesthetic criterion and believed in its perfection.

Least of all, Nijinsky imagined himself to be the creator of definitive aesthetic laws. He viewed himself as the interpreter, not the creator, of something that needed immediate embodiment. "Viewed himself" is correct, probably, because intuition meant a great deal to him. His intuition was bounteous, mysterious, capricious. Each time, he started from the beginning.

Fokine was able to work only on the production of ballets. As premier danseur of the Mariinsky, he did not dance for Diaghilev. This was in his contract.

Nijinsky, the premier danseur of the Diaghilev company, composed ballets and at the same time supported the kind of repertoire that no Imperial dancer would have ever dreamed of.

During the two weeks spent in Vienna after the New Year, the ballet master Nijinsky and Stravinsky worked on *Le Sacre du Printemps*. But it was also during this time that the dancer Nijinsky fell into a lot of hot water.

The Viennese had been brought up on the classical musical theater and prized its traditions. Consequently, they rejected *L'Après-Midi* out of hand. Unlike the zealous Parisians, they did not make a scene, but just maintained a cool silence. Still, the first rehearsal of *Petrouchka* did turn into a kind of scandal. Stravinsky's presence notwithstanding, the members of the orchestra declared his music to be "impure" and refused to perform it within the sacred walls of the Vienna Staatsoper. Immediately, rumors began to go around the city, which did not contribute to success of the ballet. At both performances of *Petrouchka*, the orchestra attempted to sabotage it.

On the other hand, an "old faithful," billed variously as *The Golden Bird, The Bluebird,* or *The Enchanted Princess,* had an uncommon success, even in the experienced opinion of the Diaghilev people. This classic piece of ballet theater—choreographed by Petipa to Tchaikovsky's music and performed by Nijinsky, the leading dancer in the whole world—satisfied the tastes of unsophisticated audiences as well as the demands of blasé snobs.

Nijinsky himself now had a different attitude toward this classical piece, the only classic in his repertoire—different, that is, from when he had believed absolutely in the Fokine reform. From time to time he discovered a perfect beauty in it, one that was capable of surviving whims of fashion. A divinely simple, divinely pure harmony was expressed in the transparent phrases of this pas de deux, in the intermingling echoes of its voices. The classical dance, which Fokine had rejected and which found no place in Nijinsky's *L'Après-Midi* or his other ballets, now reappeared as an intact and timeless work of art. Just as classical music could not die, so the classical dance would not either. Nijinsky recalled other examples of the classical ballet in all its wealth and abundance of adagios, variations, ensembles, and he pondered over the organic connection between music and the dance. It occurred to him that by turning to the great classics of music (but not à la Fokine, that is, not illustrating, but exposing the central idea, an exception being *Chopiniana*), one might open up new horizons for the kind of dance that is conventionally called "classical."

These thoughts came to him rather unexpectedly during the intervals between the performances of the current repertoire and his meetings with Stravinsky. The latter was busy with *Le Sacre du Printemps*. He tried to explain the complicated rhythms of his music while Nijinsky listened carefully: the rude ancestors of man appeared to him as a confused, frenzied, and exultant mob. Without knowing it, he was about to discover the concept of a new classicism. But as far as the Diaghilev company was concerned, "neoclassicism" would be fully realized only some years later, by Stravinsky and a youthful disciple of the Russian school of ballet, George Balanchine.

There was something else Nijinsky did not know: that it would be Stravinsky, who adored Tchaikovsky, to whom he would relate his strange vision and from whom, perhaps, he would receive an enthusiastic response. He imagined Stravinsky to be alien to such ideas. To unburden himself of these importunate thoughts, Nijinsky communicated them to Diaghilev, and Diaghilev, who could always listen to and understand Nijinsky's often incoherent speech, suddenly voiced his approval, asked him which composer he had in mind, and did not object when Nijinsky said Bach. Diaghilev was silent for a moment and then said that they'd have to try it out, but only after the Stravinsky and Debussy ballets had been staged in the forthcoming season.

Meanwhile the work with Stravinsky was going slowly.

Nijinsky was frightened by the music of *Le Sacre du Printemps.* Not by the difficulty of interpretation (that was something that came of its own accord), but by its primitive and coarse strength, by its deliberate lack of psychologism. The music renounced all the usual methods; it contradicted all the conventions with which Nijinsky the dancer had operated, from the instrumental arabesques of the academic system to Fokine's pictorial figurativeness. The music demanded the same effect from the dance, the same hypnotic sense of continuum.

Nijinsky saw this music as some kind of monster, breathing evenly as it got nearer and nearer, a monster with many hands, many legs, many eyes. But it was also something that attracted, that seemed at times inexplicably beautiful in its rejection of the conventional ideas of beauty.

Nijinsky thought even that in some way the music had deceived the composer. Stravinsky, in fact, had agreed to write it for Roerich, who had thought up the theme immediately after the success of the *Polovtsian Dances.* At that time (1910) Roerich had told a correspondent from the *St. Petersburg Gazette:* "The new ballet will present a number of scenes from a ritualistic night in the time of the ancient Slavs. . . . The action begins on a summer's night and finishes just before sunrise when the first rays are appearing. Strictly speaking, the choreographic section consists of ritualistic dances. This piece will be the first attempt to present a reincarnation of antiquity, that is, without a specific plot." [17]

Nijinsky knew and appreciated the severe colors of Roerich, the scale of his compositions, their majestic calm even when they depicted the gloomy and menacing forces of nature. Roerich probably envisioned this balletic "scene from pagan Russia" as a version of the *Polovtsian Dances.* That's how Stravinsky and Fokine, the other two

Nicolas Roerich, scenarist and designer of sets and costumes for *Le Sacre du Printemps*. Portrait by Alexander Golovin.

creators, had first seen it after they had eagerly responded to Roerich's idea. As the artist said, all three "became equally fired with this picture and decided to work together on it." [18]

But during the three years that had passed since then, a lot of water had flowed under the bridge. Stravinsky had written music that could not be reconciled with the pictorial inclinations of Fokine's imagination and that could hardly be united with Roerich's epic, contemplative mood.

A savage nature reigned over the sharp, tense rhythms and their frenzied repetitions. That savage nature was being seen, as it were, through the eyes of primeval man, man who was still part of it, still subordinate to it. Seized by an elemental fear of the Earth's power, intoxicated by its vernal flowering, the human mass muttered magic

235

incantations. Stravinsky could hardly have known then that, in renouncing old methods and conventions, he had something in common with Velemir Khlebnikov. Khlebnikov, the clairvoyant tramp, the "president of the earthly globe," the wanderer through the towns and villages of the Russian Empire, was destroying the rules of meter in his "pagan" verse. His poems carried titles similar to Stravinsky's ballet, such as *Maiden's God* and *We Are Weary of Roaring at the Stars*. Nijinsky could make out the heavy stamp of pagans carrying out a mass ritual, and he would have found confirmation of his own plastic movements in the words of Khlebnikov's incantation:

> To you we sing, O maker!
> To you we sing, O exister!
> To you we sing, O delighter!
> To you we sing, O enchanter!
> To you we sing, O grayheader!
> To you we sing, O owner!
> To you we sing, O sorcerer!

Khlebnikov was searching for the "roots of words" and not in vain did Nijinsky also set himself the mad aim of revealing the "roots of movements." [19]

He worked out the beat of the music, analyzing it with the care and patience of a jeweler who has come into possession of a valuable piece of metal. Stravinsky observed with delight how the images of his ballet gradually assumed tangible form. After one of their joint rehearsals, Stravinsky wrote to Roerich: "Heavens! Just so long as Nijinsky manages to put on *Le Sacre;* it's so complicated. Everything indicates that this piece is going to 'come out' uncommonly well!" [20] But Stravinsky was unable to go along with the company, and so Diaghilev asked Dalcroze to provide one of his pupils to help Nijinsky.

Dalcroze sent a girl pupil. Her name was Miriam Ramberg (later changed to Marie Rambert). Of Polish extraction, she spoke both Polish and Russian and she was a year older than Nijinsky. She got completely carried away by his production.

Working together, they overcame the intricate rhythms of the music, and Ramberg went over the sections prepared by Nijinsky with the dancers. Later on she would be destined to play an important role in the evolution of the new British ballet. Fifty years later she recalled her days as assistant to Nijinsky and still delighted in the plastic simplicity of the "prehistoric" formations "hardly resembling man." "We walked, we ran, we stamped our feet, we jumped, jumped on both feet or on one foot. . . . And he permeated our movements with such fury that an entire people seemed to be dancing, summoning the fertility of the earth." [21]

Nijinsky never stipulated any conditions; he was never capricious, even when the number of his performances was astronomically high. But now he suddenly declared that he could not continue with *Le Sacre* if he had to keep moving around. He demanded that he be allowed to stop in one place for a while.

Standing idle meant losing money. But Diaghilev refused a number of profitable offers. The company installed itself in London six weeks before the beginning of the next tour and commenced daily rehearsals.

Le Sacre du Printemps did not really have a plot. But its inner action developed, reached its climax, and then broke off abruptly in the finale. As the pagan ritual proceeded, the elders of the tribe selected a victim to sacrifice to the earth so as to ensure good harvests in the future. The one female protagonist in the ballet was supposed to express the sacred joy and terror of the Chosen Virgin whose dance of ecstasy was interrupted by death.

Bronislava, of course, was to be the Chosen Virgin. Nijinsky did not rush to demonstrate her part to her. He was working with the corps de ballet divided into groups of elders, young men, and girls.

He realized from the very start that the company was hostile both to the music and to the dancing. The ceaseless pulsation of the musical rhythms and the plastic image—a stamping, jumping, convulsive mob—seemed exhausting and very ugly to the dancers. The pigeon-toed gait provoked ribald jokes among them—and ballet people are experts in cracking jokes. Things went very badly when the choreographer made them jump on straight legs. By tacit agreement, the male section of the company, wishing to create dissent, made as much noise as they could as they did these jumps. Then followed all manner of complaints about body pains and headaches: landing from these jumps with straight legs was having a pernicious effect on the brain. This was not just a captious objection. Nijinsky, who was constantly jumping in front of each group or with it, felt a leaden weight in his head after the rehearsals. But he persisted in jumping higher and longer than anyone else, and always demanded repeats.

To have heeded these complaints, however justified they might have been, would have been to give in. In all this jolting up and down, which was sheer agony, in all these jumps, Nijinsky perceived the rhythmical foundation of his image: cells of a breathing organism— moving, trembling. The people were not trying to break away from the earth; they wished to grow *into* the earth, to loosen its soil, to bring forth its nutritive juices.

The dancers were divided up into what at first glance seemed to be shapeless groups but what were, in fact, based on precise calculations. They seemed to stand apart from each other, but in fact they touched each other with their elbows. Consciously or unconsciously, they began to establish the plastic motif and to repeat it in monotone. It rose and fell clumsily; it rocked ponderously. Gradually, the discipline gave results. The dancers' bodies, so accustomed to a harmonic movement, began to submit to the music and to the beat that "Mimi" Ramberg was clapping out. Nijinsky began to work on the other dancers and then, at long last, switched to the girls' dance.

He put great store by Bronislava. He asked her to come to the rehearsal and made her listen to the music of the long dance several times. He explained that the Chosen Virgin was communicating with the heavens, that she was entreating them to appease their anger, to retract their threat to the earth and to all who inhabited it.

Nijinsky demonstrated how the maidens would force the Chosen Virgin out of their dance.[22]

As if some invisible hand had pushed him, Nijinsky froze in a strangely expressive pose; he shrank into himself, turned his feet and knees inward, clenched his fists convulsively. Without altering his position, he informed Bronislava that all the elders, the maidens, in fact, everyone was honoring the victim in this section of the music. Then he told her that her dance was about to begin.

Suddenly, spontaneously, Nijinsky jumped. It was an awkward

238

jump, as if he were a wounded bird, one leg folded beneath him. He raised a clenched fist to the sky and held the other to his body. Then he squatted down, touched the ground with one hand, and began to stamp, beating his hands against his bended knees. Now he resembled a bird busily building its nest. Still in his squatting position, he took long paces off to the side and then covered his head with his arm. As if in a low arabesque, he stretched out his leg, stuck out his arms and banged them against the floor—as if they were wings.

He had not been mistaken. Bronislava had understood everything. She had listened keenly to the music, and now repeated the demonstration. She had assimilated both the movements and their inner meaning. Landing from jumps on straight legs, even on both knees, did not worry her. She at once demonstrated that vertical position that Nijinsky had been vaguely thinking of for several days. She raised her arm as she jumped, made a lightning zigzag in the air with her fist, and then fell to her knees. Ecstatically she bowed, touching the ground with her forehead and banging it with her fists.

Demonstration. Repeat. Demonstration again. They went over it together, extending the chain of incantational movements. They bore a curious resemblance to dervishes gripped by the accelerating impulse of their dance. They both opened one leg wide in a jump, then, falling, squatted down, bent low, and, gripping this leg—wooden, outstretched toes pointing up—raised and lowered it at the same time as the body, knocking the heel against the ground as if digging with a hoe.

For the first time since starting *Le Sacre*, Nijinsky felt that he was working to good purpose. By the third rehearsal the Dance of the Chosen Virgin was almost ready. Bronislava was late for this one, and arrived without having changed.

Frightened, but looking him straight in the eyes, she confessed that she was pregnant. Vaslav, always so even-tempered, flew into a rage. When they were children, their father used to have such fearful outbursts. Nijinsky almost accused his sister of malicious intent, and refused to listen to her confused arguments that this kind of thing might easily happen to a married woman.

Cooling down, Nijinsky went off to see Diaghilev. Diaghilev shook his head and thought a while. Finally he said that a substitute

(*left*) Bronislava Nijinska, 1913.

(*below*) Maria Piltz, 1913.

could be found for *Jeux*, but that for *Le Sacre* a young dancer would be needed, raw material that could be molded for the part. Reflecting further, he suggested Maria Piltz. She had not been in the company very long. She would be happy to receive a primary role. And, besides, she had a fine figure.

Nothing better. Nevertheless, the rehearsals proved to be absolute torture. Piltz had been classically trained and, moreover, responded to music in a superficial manner. She did not have the ear of Bronislava and for a long time could not master either the style or the rhythm of the Dance of the Chosen Virgin. Nijinsky shut himself up alone with her and the pianist in the rehearsal hall. They practiced and practiced so that the dancer would master each beat, each note, with her conscious mind as well as perceive them with her ear. Standing in front of the mirror, he patiently went through the rhythms of the musical sections with her. Again, and again, and again.

Only when everything seemed to be going all right did rehearsals, in the full sense of the word, begin. Nijinsky continued to struggle with his "material," which was still not pliant enough. The young dancer's body had been drilled in the rules of the academic school and was certainly manageable, but her regimentation kept bringing her back to the usual open positions and to rounded fluency of movement. Piltz was disgusted by the sharpness, the angularity, the deliberate constraint in the incomprehensible plastic movements of the Chosen Virgin. While the gestures and poses might be perfected and polished one by one, they did not gell when put together, and they lost their intended expressivity when used in transitions.

Once Diaghilev brought a noble guest to Nijinsky's rehearsal. The visitor gave the impression of pampered elegance, from his silken beard and white fingers with their almond nails to his soft voice and impeccable manners. Diaghilev introduced him as Prince Sergei Mikhailovich Volkonsky, a specialist in the Dalcroze system. Nijinsky vaguely remembered that Volkonsky, as director of the Imperial Theaters, had once signed an order for Diaghilev's dismissal, and he bowed stiffly. But Diaghilev chatted affably with his guest, took him over to the chairs in front of the mirror, and asked Nijinsky whether they might watch the rehearsal.

Nijinsky soon ceased to be embarrassed by the presence of this modest dandy. But Piltz, the slender, green-eyed blonde, was scared stiff. She was frightened of Diaghilev, who was examining her so closely. Everything she had learned fell to pieces. She was on the verge of tears and wanted to run off. Nijinsky, however, ignored, as if on purpose, the things she already knew and began to study the difficult movement with the "leg-hoe" loosening and kneading the earth. He probably understood what the young, inexperienced dancer was going through, and he remained unusually calm and quiet. Gradually, Piltz forgot about the unnerving visitors.

After the movement with the "leg-hoe," Nijinsky demonstrated the leaps from side to side, with legs bunched and turned in, while accompanying each ponderous flight with a sideways throw of the arms. Tours en l'air, whirling, twisting, gave way to new leaps from side to side, but this time more like classical jetés, except that his arms flailed above his head. Allowing Piltz to catch her breath, he explained to her, just as if there was no one else present, that almost all the movements of her dance derived essentially from classical ballet, that the very roots of this dance were classical movements, except that they were to be felt and seen in a different way.

Half an hour, one hour, one and a half hours: at last Nijinsky stopped and thanked the pianist. Nijinsky smiled as he told Piltz, in an affectionate tone of voice (not at all the sharp, curt tone that he had used to count time in), that today had been much better. Tomorrow they'd have to go through it from the beginning. Covered with sweat, the girl wiped her hand across her forehead, sighed as if waking up, and went out, making a ridiculous schoolgirl curtsey to Diaghilev.

Volkonsky stood up and gave an inspired speech. He said that only with Dalcroze had he seen such a close, "organically close" integration of music and movement, that he would like to see the rehearsals with the corps de ballet, because in *L'Après-Midi* (he had recently seen it for the first time in Vienna) he had been struck by how the individual figure had been "absorbed into the totality of the choreographic design." He explained: "Only natural phenomena can provide such examples of self-negation, as when the totality of moving drops of water creates a wave or when the totality of falling drops creates a downpour." He added that only with Dalcroze had he seen such "human necklaces joined by the thread of rhythm." [23]

Nijinsky was standing in a normal pose for dancers: legs in third position, hands hanging loosely at the sides, the body slightly drawn up. He was wearing his usual rehearsal clothes: black trousers fastened from the knee down by four buttons and clasping the calves tightly, a crêpe de chine shirt whose color might vary from pale green to blue and white, and chamois ballet shoes. He politely thanked the guest, smiled wearily, and then asked, suddenly, why "only with Dalcroze"? In ballet, rows and groups of human figures are always moving in total unity. Take *Giselle*, for example, or *La Bayadère*, or Tchaikovsky's ballets. The whole of Petipa's work for the corps de ballet is like that.

Then Nijinsky thought for a moment and added that, however strange it might be, it was precisely his collaboration with Stravinsky and their work on this ballet—

Volkonsky interrupted, exclaiming (but diplomatically) that *Le Sacre du Printemps,* evidently, was "not a ballet, thank heavens. It is a ritual, it is an ancient rite. Nothing could worse prepare the prospective audience of this spectacle than the word *ballet* and all the associations that it brings with it." [24]

"On this ballet," repeated Nijinsky, obstinately, and retired into himself. All the ensembles of swans, the shadows, the wilis—weren't they all part of a ritual? Working on Stravinsky's ballet (he tried to conclude his chain of thoughts quickly) was actually making him think more and more about classical dance, about its inner connection with music, a connection that still had to be understood and revealed, and about the possibilities that this union contained.

Diaghilev recalled his recent conversation with Nijinsky on the same topic. He wondered how Nijinsky could be so enthusiastic, so ardent when normally he was so retiring, and how could Nijinsky still remain unaware of the extent to which he was reliant on him, Diaghilev.

Volkonsky steered the conversation toward compliments. With the same diplomacy, he affirmed that he had no desire to "belittle the merits" of the talented dancer, the pupil who danced for Nijinsky today, but he couldn't help noticing the difference between what Nijinsky demonstrated and what she actually did. Of course, one should not forget that this was all new and unnatural to her. But, after all, what a difference there was between a movement that was conscious right down to its last detail and a movement that was left to itself. He said that right now, this evening, he had understood the "difference between flexibility of limb and limpness of limb, between holding the fist tight and letting it hang loose." [25]

Nijinsky came down from the clouds. He sighed as he mentioned that the role of the Chosen Virgin was to have been taken by his sister, but she had fallen sick. All her movements were more conscious and, consequently, more expressive. But Piltz was gifted and she was doing her best. She would make out all right.

Le Sacre du Printemps was almost ready when its rehearsals were interrupted by a short, two-week season in London. Diaghilev had decided to show the British *Petrouchka* and *L'Après-Midi d'un Faune*. He asserted that he wished to get the public used to Stravinsky's music and to Nijinsky's choreography, so that he could show them *Jeux* and *Le Sacre* in the summer season.

The London tour was not accompanied by particular pomp. The aristocratic ladies and the colonels home from India did not grace it with their presence. On the other hand, it became known that a circle of fervent admirers of the Diaghilev ballet had existed in London for three years now. As a result, neither *Petrouchka* nor *L'Après-Midi* provoked anyone's indignation. On the contrary, both pieces were accepted and appreciated, albeit less ardently than other ballets in Paris had been. As the proverb says, "One man's meat is another man's poison." It was not in the English character to race backstage and personally express one's delight to the performers. Obviously, the much respected and self-respecting John Galsworthy would never have done that. But no doubt the writer long remembered *L'Après-Midi*. Many years later he made one of his characters, the artist Aubrey Green, say, after resolving to paint a picture called *L'Après-Midi d'une Dryade*, "Shades of Nijinsky, I see the whole thing!" [26]

Nijinsky now needed success. Like medicine. He was terribly tired, but he still had to finish *Jeux* and *Le Sacre*. There was little more than a month before the Paris premières.

Diaghilev left London for Russia. In St. Petersburg he tried to get leave for Ludmilla Schollar and Boris Romanov. Schollar was supposed to be dancing with Karsavina and Nijinsky in *Jeux*, and Romanov

244

Nijinsky in rehearsal clothes.
Drawing by Maxime Dethomas.

was to stage *La Tragédie de Salomé*. In Moscow Diaghilev signed a contract with Gorsky for a production of Tcherepnin's ballet *The Red Mask*. Diaghilev had realized at long last that Nijinsky was not Fokine and that he could not carry the repertoire for a whole season.

The company departed for Monte Carlo, where Nijinsky finished *Le Sacre*. He at last had a pianist to work with on *Jeux* and was looking forward to the arrival of Karsavina and Schollar.

Diaghilev arrived for the opening of the season in Monte Carlo. Grigoriev informed him that he had had a terrible time trying to maintain some kind of tolerable relationship between Nijinsky and the male corps de ballet in *Le Sacre*. The dancers referred to the rehearsals as mathematics lessons because there was no melody and they had to beat time continuously. In addition, they were annoyed by the ceaseless, rhythmical stamping that they were forced to do without any other kind of movement. Rehearsing the Fokine ballets was, in comparison, a kind of relaxation.

Grigoriev's statement produced an effect contrary to the one he expected. Diaghilev said that the fact that *Le Sacre* was so unpopular was an excellent sign. It meant that the ballet was original.

By the time Karsavina and Schollar arrived, there was not much time left for staging *Jeux*. They could have rebelled at the very first rehearsal, no less violently than the corps de ballet in *Le Sacre*. In its own way Debussy's music was no less difficult than Stravinsky's. It flowed forth in a continuous, radiant stream, and it seemed impossible to catch the "sparks and flashes" of its sonorities. It was just as difficult to master the staccato choreography for *Jeux*. But Karsavina was already agreeable to anything that Diaghilev sanctioned, and Schollar was very flattered to be appearing in a ballet with two celebrated dancers. So neither Karsavina nor Schollar had any intention of rebelling.

The choreographer explained the situation of *Jeux* to his partners. It was as simple as *Le Sacre*, although not so dramatic. Strictly speaking, it was not a ballet, but a dance poem, and it dealt with a modern theme. But this was not the only way in which it differed from Fokine's intricate pictures. It did not contain any distinctive conflict—something that was indispensable for Fokine. On the contrary, it was supposed to embody the moods of the moment, moods that burst forth in the same will-o'-the-wisp lightness and with the same fluency as the music. True, its only action was the game—or, rather, an unexpected break in the game, when time was stopped, allowing the players to examine their feelings and to look deep into the recesses of their consciousness. It was like an Impressionist painting: the painter reveals on the canvas some inward property of his model, something that she was quite unaware of. Only the plastic movements must not be impressionistic, but angular and tense. The time of Impressionism had passed. Even children could now feel the anxious and uneven pulse of life.

Nijinsky went into the center of the hall. He glanced at Karsavina's and Schollar's dancing shoes, which had blocked points to support the toes. He then said that they would not be dancing on their toes; they should put on soft shoes, like his, and all three of them would dance on demi-point.

He raised himself on demi-point, placed his feet in second position, although not turned out, and looked in the mirror. He raised his arms to his shoulders, bending them slightly at the elbows, and half clenched his fists.

This, he said, was the key position: frontal on demi-point, with bent wrists, creating angular and broken lines. He looked at himself once more and asked the two dancers not to smile or flirt in the dance, but to keep their faces motionless. Expression was to come from the plastic movement of the body.

Karsavina and Schollar caught on to everything at once with the adroitness of professionals. But Nijinsky himself was having a hard time. He was worn out by the rehearsals of *Le Sacre* and was at the end of his strength.

He did not want to get up in the mornings and to face the prospect of a long day at the theater. He and Diaghilev were installed in the luxury hotel Riviera Palace, which had just been built on the top of a hill. The dancers in the company immediately nicknamed their residence "Olympus." The bus took almost half an hour to get from this Olympus. Still, there was a fantastic view of the beach and the sea, and most important, it was more secluded than down below. More than ever before, Nijinsky fought shy of noisy crowds of people.

But Nijinsky was glad when Chaliapin came to Monte Carlo. This giant of a man, so strong, so free and easy, brought with him the best of old Russia, and Nijinsky liked it when Chaliapin affectionately called him "Vatsa." Diaghilev, who fussed over Nijinsky as if he were his nurse, used to take them for dinner on the terrace of the large Hôtel de Paris after each performance.

Cecchetti's Hungarian dance student, always accompanied by Adolf Bolm, also used to sit on the restaurant terrace at one of the free tables. Nijinsky vaguely remembered that he had been introduced several times to her, but he could never remember her name. When this girl had been first brought to see him in Budapest, he had taken her to be a local ballerina. Rumor had it that she was rather fond of Bolm. But each time Nijinsky met her, which was far too often now, he noticed how she pursued him with her eyes. And now, when he was so busy with finishing the two ballets and when anything irrelevant just got in the way, Nijinsky found her persistence most annoying.

Time flew, and the days before the opening of the Paris season grew even fewer. The program (the cover was decorated with one of the Bakst designs for *L'Après-Midi*) carried a photograph of the Théâtre des Champs-Elysées, which was situated on the Avenue Montaigne, in one of the most fashionable districts of Paris. The description said that Gabriel Astruc, founder of the theater, had taken the combination of "English comfort, German technology, and French taste" as his ideal. The Russian dancers, beginning the season with the première of *Jeux*, were the first to savor this ideal.

But *Jeux* was still not ready when, on 8 May, one week before the performance, the company arrived in Paris.

Nijinsky felt that he would never be able to carry through his responsibility. He was irritated by everything, and especially by Debussy, who obviously regarded Nijinsky's already finished fragments of the ballet only as preparatory designs. A feeling of panic slowed his thoughts, confused his intentions.

At one of the rehearsals Diaghilev came in unexpectedly and said that they couldn't wait any more. Nijinsky seemed to fall into a trance. Standing in the middle of the hall, he stared straight ahead, a distracted smile playing about his lips.

Grigoriev came to the rescue by loudly suggesting that they go through the ballet from the beginning. This helped Nijinsky to get his thoughts together, to recapture the thread. Unexpectedly, he went on to the finale, telling Grigoriev that the tennis ball would have to fly once more past the "group sitting over there."

Le Sacre was going ahead without any setbacks, and, most important, Stravinsky liked it. He said that the choreography was "superb"—adding, "I am confident in what we have done." [27]

6

On 15 May 1913 a very smart audience crowded the very smart foyers of the Théâtre des Champs-Elysées. It was the intermission before *Jeux*. The new ballet had already prompted a lot of interest.

The day before, Hector Cahusac had published in *Le Figaro* his notes of Nijinsky's "monologue," the speech that Nijinsky had given at that lunch in the Bois de Boulogne. This day, the day of the spectacle, Debussy had confessed to his involvement in the adventure. He had embarked upon this enterprise "so fraught with consequences" simply because "one has to eat lunch," and once he had been "lunching with Diaghilev, a man both terrifying and enchanting, a man who could make the stones dance." He added, not without coquetry, that he was awaiting the "performance of *Jeux* like a well-behaved child who has been promised an outing to the theater." [1]

Everybody knew that the ballet involved only three people— Karsavina, Schollar, and Nijinsky—and that the action took place in a park, and they all expected the usual triangular love affair, although cloaked in an alluring manner. In the various sections of the audience could

be heard various comments: "A modern ballet" . . . " A ballet about tennis" . . . "A cinematographic ballet in which movements are broken down into their component parts and which are not normally visible to the eye" . . . "Bakst did the decors, but, apparently, the costumes are not his—they are the latest designs from Paquin" . . . "It will be curious to see Karsavina and Nijinsky probably without makeup and dressed like sportsmen" . . .

The last bell. The lights went down. Pierre Monteux took his place at the conductor's stand. The sophisticated public soon recognized Debussy's signature in the weblike patterns of the music.

The stage really did depict a park: thick branches of trees and bushes, round flower beds distributed as if on a chessboard. Two storys of a house, flat like a cigarette pack, could be seen behind the foliage in the light of the moon and an electric lamp.

A white ball flew out from behind the trees, bounced over the flower beds and disappeared in the bushes. A young man raced after it. He jumped over a fence, but, as he leaped, he froze for an instant, preserving the tension of his impulses. Yes, this was a sportsman. But it was a sportsman of the future. To that audience enjoying the last summer of peace, he was the herald of generations to come, generations who would pass through two world wars.

His costume looked strange. Was it this, perhaps, that distinguished him from his contemporaries? He wore a white shirt with sleeves rolled up, a red tie under a turned-down collar, and white flannel trousers, a copy of the black trousers in which Nijinsky always rehearsed. The trousers did not quite reach the ankles, but they gripped the calves tightly, delineating their contours by a pattern of tiny side buttons up to the knee. The trousers were loose above the knee and were fastened at the waist by a buckle. On his feet, Nijinsky wore white suede shoes.

No, it was not the costume that made him so distinctive, although Nijinsky the choreographer had given a lot of attention to the costume of Nijinsky the dancer. The entire physiognomy of this strange young man differed from the typical manner of the sportsman of the 1910s. His light and tensile body, in which each muscle obeyed instantly each command of the will, in which a graceful strength involuntarily reminded one of the ideals of antiquity, had surely been developed by

253

Nijinsky in *Jeux*.

sport, sport as a system of education, as a profession, and *not* as an amusement or pastime. An athlete of future competitions, of great endurance, trained for battle, stood in a classical position. He had thrown the weight of his body on to one foot, while stepping back with the other; he had raised his arm, bent at the elbow, and had clenched his fist, holding it facing the audience; he had inclined his head toward his shoulder, displaying his neck, strong and well proportioned.

But there was something strange. Although the position was common both to the athlete of antiquity and to the sportsman of the "real, not the calendrical, twentieth century," [2] it manifested two essentially different moods. The vertical of the arm raised in a defensive gesture, the other arm bent and held closely to the body, the slightly displaced lines of the entire figure denoting a centripetal rather than a centrifugal force, betrayed suspiciousness, nervous introspection, and not a proud serenity. The hero of *Jeux*, nurtured by modern civilization, contrasted his own complex worldview with the spiritual harmony of the ancient Greek. He appeared as an enigma from the future, and one that it proved to be more difficult to decipher than to materialize the visions of H. G. Wells.

He appeared—and vanished immediately. Two girls made their way into the garden. They wore socks and white skirts with the hemline just below the knee; they had identical, wavy hairdos. They were dressed according to a fashion that had yet to be born. Their plastic movements, so angular and awkward, were those of teenagers. They approached one another and then, as Nijinsky had stipulated in Monte Carlo, moved away in parallel lines. But now they moved on demi-point as they brought their legs together in the intended pas de bourrée or put them apart in a turned-in second position. That is exactly how little girls play hopscotch in the sand. Serious and unsmiling, they moved, paused, moved again, as if, willy-nilly, they were jointly involved in a game that had united them and had subjected them to its own mechanical rhythms. That is how children compete with one another, consciously ignore each other, and at the same time are slightly jealous of each other.

The choreographer of *Jeux* did not copy any masters of the contiguous arts, and he was not inspired directly by anyone else's themes or "style." Nijinsky returned to a primitive conception not because Gauguin had sought inspiration in the customs of the Polynesians or because Picasso had created his first Cubist painting under the influence of African sculpture. Nijinsky himself perceived the concerns of his own time, its nostalgia for a lost purity. There is no doubt that he was being original in his endeavor to embody the atavism of certain children's games in the methods of ballet movements. Enveloped by the music of a moonlit night, but moving according to their own, independent beat, two young girls dressed in Paquin outfits were carrying out an unconscious ritual. Their friend returned and, moving with an awkward grace, went through a series of repeats, pauses, and cadences.

He took part in their game but did not attempt to follow their beat. On the contrary, he seemed to break the established rhythm. The stylized movements conveyed the motif of skipping. It was conveyed by the position of the two girls who stood erect, their legs closed and their heads inclined toward their shoulders, holding the ends of imaginary skipping-ropes whirling through the air. They stood close to each other at arm's length, their fists clenched tightly, indicating continuous skipping. The figure of the dancer darted between the two partners as if he cut through their childlike ritual with his elbows and his chest.

Motifs of rivalry now permeated the stylized image of the game. Jealousy seemed about to disrupt the synchrony of the girls' ritual, to lead them almost to the verge of a flirtation. One of the girls tucked her feet under and suddenly sat down on the ground. She leaned to the side, put her head on her shoulder, dropped one hand to her knee in a gesture of annoyance, and placed the other on her breast. As before, the clenched fingers imparted a childish and pitiful expression to the figure. The second girl, erect, turned stiffly toward the first and stretched out her fists in a gesture of reconciliation. The young man stood a short way off and, half turning, watched the course of the girls' quarrel. The girl who had been angered soon stood up and, still sulking, allowed her friend to embrace her. And she was embraced with that same awkward solicitude with which a little girl embraces her doll.

The male partner again entered the game. He stood erect and,

Jeux, 1913.

(*left*) Ludmilla Schollar and Tamara Karsavina.

(*below*) Schollar, Nijinsky, and Karsavina.

(*right*) Karsavina, Schollar, and Nijinsky.

looking straight ahead, put his arms on the girl's shoulders and brought them close. Each in turn entwined one arm around his head and joined the other with her partner's in front of his torso. Their fists were still clenched. The final pose retained the same awkward grace. The dancer sank to the ground, putting his arms around his knees. The two girls positioned themselves on either side of him, also putting their arms around their knees, throwing back their heads, and leaning with their backs toward him. The music enveloped this symmetrical group in a mist of moonlit dust.

The flight of a tennis ball interrupted the pause. Thrown by one knew not whom, the alarming white sphere shattered this idyll of 1913. The curtain came down on the empty garden, lit, as at the beginning, by the moon and the electric lamp.

The applause was thin as the house lights came up. One would think that the ballet would have met the expectations of the audience: the time and place of the action, the movements fragmented into elements, the ultramodern costume, Karsavina and Nijinsky behaving almost as if in real life. But, actually, there did not seem to be any action whatsoever, and the dance movements somehow were disappointing: more than that, they were an insult. Many people tried to take their cue from the members of the elite, but they did not seem to be acting either for or against.

Debussy resolved the question. He shoved back his chair, stood up, and walked out of his box.

As if in response, the audience suddenly came alive, began to move about and file out. The philistines were delighted; they were overjoyed, and their tongues began to wag. They made allusions to the effect that the modern Vestris was becoming too lazy to dance, otherwise why would he have neglected his trump card—his leap? They said that it was easy to reject what was good and what had received public acclaim, but it was much harder to make the public accept what had been proposed in its place as being better. In all this the philistines saw a deliberate and pretentious endeavor to be original, from the fractured, impressionistic music to the offensive and quite inappropriate costumes, looking as if they'd been rented from a music hall. For the moment they gossiped in a restrained manner so that they could let fly when the chance presented itself.

258

Karsavina, Nijinsky, and Schollar in *Jeux*.

In their own way, the Parisians were right. Nijinsky had been free to break with the Fokine tradition, to destroy his ballet style, one that had received the approval of connoisseurs and had already become a convention for them. Even the most benevolent of these snobs would have needed a time machine to transport him forty or fifty years ahead so that he could have seen himself at a ballet première of the future. At first, he would have seen himself as part of the audience, among ladies in trousers and men in brocade caftans and lace jabots—an audience that had rejected out of hand the ethical norms of his own very proper era. He would then have recognized Nijinsky's far-sighted, scandalous innovations in the even more shocking ones of Roland Petit and Maurice Béjart. He would have recognized the same treatment of the music as an equal member of the ensemble. One moment the rhythms of the music and the choreography were joined indissolubly, the next they were at variance with each other. He would have recognized the disharmony of the movements, the gestures and the poses, making up the uneasy harmonies of the whole. Perhaps, ultimately, he would have fathomed that enigmatic choreographer who had outstripped his own time, who had expressed plastically, and not illustrated, the ethos of his contemporary world.

Historically, the problem—and the greatness—of the choreographer Nijinsky is that he was born before his time. He was not understood by those who savored provocative flirtations. Neither was he understood by those of a more refined sensibility. Several years later, André Levinson still persisted in saying that *Jeux* was a failure, although he did confess that "a genuine novelty of conception, one perhaps not altogether fruitless, was to be seen in this ballet, in its harsh, its meager and very deliberate form." [3]

Indeed, not altogether. The conception of *Jeux* is still operative in our own time. But in 1913 it was not Nijinsky who realized this, but Diaghilev, and Diaghilev had no intention of retreating from his position. Diaghilev was convinced that he had transcended an important boundary. He knew that his new experiments would force him to break with his old associates, and that the Fokine ballets could be restored only as moneymakers. On the other hand, he could foresee that some associates who had only recently been persuaded to join him would now take to their heels. He did not doubt, for example, that Debussy would henceforth fear the ballet like the plague. That's how it turned out. When he had recovered from his shock at the première, the composer wrote in a letter to a friend that "the perverted genius of Nijinsky had excelled" in the so-called "stylization of gesture" accompanied by his music—music that, added Debussy, "you can be sure, no one is going to defend. . . ." [4]

But Diaghilev had no time for diplomacy. He was preparing for battle, a battle before which the risks of the early seasons and even the daring of *L'Après-Midi* and *Jeux* simply paled. He was quite aware of the fact that the spectacle he had prepared would strike at all conceptions of the meaning, the object, and the aim of the ballet. It could ricochet and destroy everything he had created with such effort. But the awareness of risk only encouraged this indomitable innovator. He even increased the danger by billing the new ballet between two Fokine masterpieces at the première: *Les Sylphides* and *Schéhérazade*. He sensed that the time would come when 29 May 1913, the date of the première of *Le Sacre du Printemps*, would be acknowledged as a turning point in the history of the ballet.

A general before the attack, surrounded by his staff, issuing orders, checking that his troops were ready for action—such was Diaghilev during the last moments before the première of *Le Sacre du Printemps*. The staff would have been a good subject for a group portrait. Stravinsky, in his dress coat, with his impeccable, straight-parted hair, maintained an outward calm as he discussed a point in the score with Pierre Monteux, wide-shouldered and a head taller than Stravinsky. Roerich, who had pushed up his wedgelike beard, stared with his unbearably penetrating eyes at the backdrop that had just been lowered. Nijinsky, still in his rehearsal costume, was pale and very calm. He held Maria Piltz's hand in both of his, as if trying to extract the nervous tremble that went through her body. Grigoriev anxiously looked about and, glancing sideways at Diaghilev, waited for the signal to begin.

Diaghilev turned around and nodded. The group broke up. Stravinsky and Roerich went off to their seats, Monteux proceeded into the orchestra pit, and Nijinsky went behind the first wing, motioning away the chair someone had offered him.

The auditorium, where, as the saying goes, "you couldn't swing a cat," also seemed to be ready to do battle. The people, chatting away, exchanging signs, had divided into groups obviously hostile to each other. Valerian Yakovlevich Svetlov informed Levinson, next to him, that "certain people who knew their audience well" had told him the day before, after the closed dress rehearsal, "At first they'll laugh, at the end they'll be outraged." [5]

The reed pipe sounded sharp and savage, and brought forth an avalanche of tumbling sounds from the orchestra. People began to giggle at once (too early to denote genuine response) and were then silent when the curtain rose. The scene revealed green hills upon which lay bodies prostrate in prayer, looking like white specks. They stirred, stood up, and, seized by the harsh rhythm, they pulled and dragged themselves in fits and spurts along their beaten path. The women wore long dresses or skirts and loose overblouses; the men wore similar garb—loose tunics, knee-length trousers, and pointed felt

Roerich's set design for *Le Sacre du Printemps*, Scene 1.

hats. All wore *onuchas* (leg bindings) and bast shoes. This mass of people, an organism composed of undivided cells, breathed regularly as it submitted to the repeated sounds of the music. The Maidens took up a ritualistic stamp. In their red dresses, loosely draped as in ancient icons, they descended from the hill like a frightened flock of birds. An old hag darted between the dancers and began to lead the rhythm.

For a few minutes the auditorium was silent, in a state of shock. Suddenly, people began to giggle again, loudly and maliciously. And then, as if on a signal, the whole hall exploded in shouts, whistles, banging of fists on the backs of chairs, drowning the orchestra. One moment from the orchestra level, the next from the boxes, then from the balcony could be heard the words "Get the hell out of here! . . . Go back to your Moscow!" Because the Maidens had held their hands against their cheeks, there were shouts of "Is there a dentist in the house? They've all got toothache!" . . . answered by "Quiet! . . . Shut up!" . . . and applause drowning the boos.

Roerich's set design for *Le Sacre du Printemps*, Scene 2.

Le Sacre du Printemps, 1913. (*above*) Tribesmen. (*above, right*) One of the Elders. (*below*) Maidens.

Stravinsky was not looking at the stage. He concentrated his gaze on Monteux's back and seemed to be repeating to himself, "Don't give up, don't give up," in time to the conductor's movements. Monteux did not seem to notice or hear what was going on behind him. Then Stravinsky quickly left his seat and rushed backstage.

Diaghilev observed everything from his box, an arrogant smile on his lips. The scandal threatened to drown out the music, and it was only this that made him get up slowly, advance to the edge of the box and, in a tone of command, not of supplication, to pronounce very distinctly, "Laissez achever le spectacle!"

The effect was like oil on stormy waters. For a few seconds the music and the heavy tread of the dancers could be heard. Then the audience again started to bellow, and it seemed twice as loud.

Diaghilev went on stage and ordered the lights to be put on in the auditorium. The chandeliers illuminated an unprecedented scene. The pagan festival, although rejected by the public, had actually unleashed people's primordial instincts. The swell dandies and refined ladies were not merely protesting. They had separated into camps, and they were really going for each other, without sparing slaps in the face.

Nijinsky was startled and shaken by the very first sounds of the scandal. Then he froze, motionless. The waves of noise would drown the music any moment and the dancers might diverge from the inaudible orchestra. Not taking his eyes off the stage, not noticing that Stravinsky was standing behind him, Nijinsky groped for the chair, pulled it toward him, jumped up on it and began loudly to count time, snapping his fingers to the rhythm.

The spectacle proceeded. The young girls did their dance and mingled with the men in the martial Games of the Rival Tribes. The Elders led out the Wise Man, who went through the ritual Adoration of the Earth. Suddenly the participants in the ritual stopped and froze in sacred terror. Only a tremble ran through their petrified limbs. And then they renewed their tramping Dance of the Earth until the curtain came down.

A full intermission had been scheduled to take place between the two scenes of *Le Sacre*. But Diaghilev ordered the lights to go on and to have the rowdiest brawlers thrown out. That did not help. The second scene provoked a new outburst, although not immediately.

265

The audience grew quiet when the Maidens appeared in the valley and against the background of stony hills, beneath the ominous low clouds and amidst staves crowned with the skulls of men and horses. The fearful intonations of the music, depicting the secret games of the Maidens, fused with the theme of nature's deep and boundless flowering, with the nocturnal fermentation of her vernal juices. Nature and Man seemed one, united in an elemental thirst for eternal youth.

Stravinsky's lyrical intermezzo had provided Nijinsky with much food for thought. He now stood in the wings and waited, perplexed, for the savage horde on the other side of the footlights to trample on this, his favorite section of the ballet, the one that he had perfected with such difficulty. The composer called it the Dance of the Mystic Circles. This name, so evocative of the music, had transported the choreographer back into the intended anachronism. Diaghilev had taught Nijinsky to appreciate the Russian icon. And the mysterious round dance of the Maidens now appeared as an example of the northern spring as seen through the eyes of an icon painter and stylized in the manner of an ancient primitive. The nocturnal gloom dimmed and deepened the red of the Maidens' dresses with their long, pronounced folds. The circle of the dance gradually closed and the dancers turned to face outward. Each leaned her head on her right hand and placed her elbow on her left hand. With their feet turned inward, they wove an angular but exquisite pattern. The Maidens' dance circled toward the right while maintaining the stance of affectedly despondent figures. Suddenly, as if obedient to the same impulse, the Maidens raised themselves on demi-point, dropped their right arms to their sides, and sharply threw back their heads to the left. They regained their primary position and continued their monotonous advance. They did this once more, and the line of the dance again twisted and turned. It had now come full circle, and every second Maiden sprang forward, quickly returned to her place, and the smooth circular movement crept forward again.

A whole night seemed to have been given to this magical dance. The tribe was on the track of the Maidens and approached stealthily, watching and waiting. Suddenly, instead of repeating their spring forward, the Maidens pushed out one of their number.

The Chosen Virgin was petrified. Her body convulsed. The Elders in their bearskins began to dance a frenzied dance around her. As if by some reflex action, the audience reacted to their stamping.

The public did not quieten down even when the Chosen Virgin began her sacrificial dance. Only very gradually did the magic of her extraordinary movements overcome the laughter, the shouts, and the boos. The elemental dance, organized so deliberately and so strictly, reached its climax—and was victorious. The image of a prehistoric bird was conjured up by the force of the music and by the mad scramble of jumps, but it was a bird whose wings were attempting to raise its clumsy body still not ready for flight. At last the whirlwind of the stamping movements took the dancer and twisted her around and around into a vortex, then raised her into the air and crashed her down on the ground again and again. There was total silence in the auditorium—there did not seem to be a soul there. The Chosen Virgin came to a halt. Sticking out her elbows, clasping her fists to her breast, bowing her head, she shook with her whole body and beat her elbows against her ribs. Suddenly, some kind of mysterious force seized her from the Earth, and the Elders, who had been guarding the victim, caught her lifeless body in their arms, raised it on their outstretched arms and then rushed off as the final, cadential chord sounded.

The audience could not forgive this "psychological attack" and took its revenge. On stage, Diaghilev surveyed the faces—frightened, confused, and deceptively complacent. He ordered the curtain to be raised, and, turning to Piltz, told her to take a bow.

Piltz backed to the wings. Furiously, Diaghilev strode after her and pushed her out onto the stage. Nijinsky winced as if in pain. The modern Pygmalion, leaning on the back of a Viennese chair, stared sullenly at his rejected Galatea. Piltz mechanically assumed her pose of the victim ready for sacrifice, and stood amidst the thunder of applause and shouts of protest descending upon her from the auditorium. She did not move, standing just like an idol hewn from wood. Except that tears flowed, making furrows in the greasepaint on her face.

Fifty years later in Leningrad, in a room on Ligovsky Prospect, which looked out on to a rather gloomy courtyard, an old lady stricken with paralysis maintained a long and persistent silence, until she pronounced: "Sergei Pavlovich pushed me out onto the stage. I stood there in the middle and just howled."

The past now opened up before her, it broke loose and slithered into the distance. Her bony hands, with their swollen veins, beat down on the divan like the wings of a bird floundering in the nest. She could sense the invisible figures of the Elders as the music for the Dance of the Chosen Virgin came back to her inaudibly. Their one-time victim confessed, "I was afraid, I was truly afraid of the Elders."

Then she recalled other events and characters from the recesses of her memory. At length she remembered one person in particular and her eyes, which had seemed colorless, now took on a bright green hue. This brought out the noble features of her cheeks, her mouth and nose.

"Vatsa! He was so nice! But he was strange. . . . He used to joke around with me. Once I asked him, 'What do you love best in the world?' He laughed and replied, 'Insects and parrots.' I think he liked me. Once he asked me to go for a ride with him in Paris. But when I was getting into the carriage, somebody pulled me from behind." Maria Yulievna smiled and gripped her dressing gown. "I looked round. It was Sergei Pavlovich. He said, 'Get out. You're not going anywhere with him.' " [6]

And, of course, she didn't.

As always, Nijinsky submitted, suppressing his interest in the innocent and unsophisticated female dancer to whom he had given the the baptism of fame. A difficult and terrifying baptism, but the only one that she cherished her whole life long.

A great despondency settled on Nijinsky after the première of *Le Sacre*. He was terribly tired.

Diaghilev took him and Stravinsky to a restaurant after the performance, but he could not touch anything, remembering with disgust how those who defended *Le Sacre* overpowered the opposition when Stravinsky, Roerich, and he (at Diaghilev's bidding) went on stage.

Diaghilev and Stravinsky dined as if nothing had happened. Diaghilev said curtly and haughtily, "What took place was exactly what I wanted." [7] The usually silent Stravinsky suddenly became loquacious. He talked about *Le Sacre* using the pronoun *we* and was quite indifferent to the fact that "they" had just been booed. Like Diaghilev, he thought that this indicated a token of future appreciation. He repeated, "I am confident in what we have done." He assured Nijinsky that the choreography was fantastic. A young man, Stravinsky had now had a foretaste of a boundless future, and he was not troubled by the fact that "we still have to wait a long time before the public grows accustomed to our language."

Stravinsky really did regard *Le Sacre du Printemps* as the indissoluble union of his own music with Nijinsky's choreography. He was being as sincere then as he had been a few hours earlier when he had told a reporter, "I am happy that I have found a perfect dance associate in Nijinsky." [8] Just as sincere as a few days later when he informed a reporter from *Gil Blas* in his impeccable French: "Nijinsky is a delightful artist. He is capable of renewing the art of the ballet. Not for one second have we encountered discord in our designs. You will see what he will attain. He is not only a wonderful dancer, but he is also able to create, to supply a new vitality. Working with him on *Le Sacre du Printemps* was productive. We just have to educate the public to understand this kind of thing." [9]

Years later Stravinsky betrayed Nijinsky with the same Olympian nonchalance with which he had once observed their common enemies. And he was just as sincere. He managed to forget the choreography of *Le Sacre* (performed only six times) so that in his memory the "back of Monteux was more alive than what was going on on stage." He remembered Nijinsky as the executor of Diaghilev's will, as a dependent and timid little boy who lacked conviction in his own strength. The conclusion easily gained ground that Diaghilev had vainly put his hopes on the fact that the "qualities which seemed lacking in Nijinsky would one day or another suddenly manifest themselves." [10] Actually, there were other circumstances that can explain the aberration, if not the callousness of Stravinsky's memory (Stravinsky wrote those cruel words in his *Chronicle of My Life*.) By then, in the 1930s, Stravinsky had found a "perfect dance associate" in George Balanchine, and both of them were trying to orient ballet audiences to the freedom of the neoclassical dance.

In any case, the plastic movements demonstrated by *Le Sacre* did not pass in vain. They gave results, even if choreographers did not realize that the roots of their art were in the fertile soil of Nijinsky's *Le Sacre*. Fokine recognized the vitality of what Nijinsky had discovered in *Le Sacre* and declared war on it from a position quite contrary to Stravinsky's. In 1931 Fokine wrote an article called "A

Melancholy Art" [11] in which he condemned Martha Graham's plastic expressionism: dancing on flat feet with toes turned in, arms held loosely at the side or raised up with the elbows sticking out, clenched fists, the chest hollow or protruding. Fokine presented evidence from which it was easy to track down the real "criminal." The investigation led to 1913, to Nijinsky's *Jeux* and *Le Sacre*, so all that was left was to collate the "documents of the trial." How contradictory would have been the testimonies submitted by all those implicated in that distant litigation!

The French reporters behaved like children who demand their favorite toys when they do not feel like reading. *Gil Blas* and *Echo de Paris* asserted, on behalf of Parisians, that the Ballet Russe owed all its greatness to Fokine, and that Stravinsky and Nijinsky were destroying the natural grace of the art. *Le Figaro* expressed an ironic regret, as it had after the première of *L'Après-Midi*, that Nijinsky's belief in what he had done was ample proof of his lack of talent. It also affected a defense of Stravinsky, expressing surprise that such a musician "could allow himself to catch the infection and introduce the dancer's aesthetics into his own art." [12] Pierre Lalo expressed his indignation on the pages of *Le Temps:* "In the entire ballet there is not one movement, not one line that bore the imprint of grace, lightness, nobility, eloquence, and expressivity." [13]

Diaghilev could anticipate the unexpected turns of art; he knew what to reject and what to cultivate, whatever public opinion might say. But he could not read men's souls, perhaps because he did not really try to. Still, among the few people whom he did value, Nijinsky occupied a foremost place. This accomplisher of destinies, the destinies of many different artists, would no doubt have given much to find the path to a heart so inaccessible to him. He could see that Nijinsky was indifferent to the insults of the French pen-pushers. But he also noticed that unlike the previous year, after the première of *L'Après-Midi*, Nijinsky was now apathetic even toward his supporters.

He remained apathetic as he read the successful passages (heavily underlined) of Minsky's article in *Morning of Russia*. This poet, who wrote rather old-fashioned poetry, clearly distinguished the innovatory conception of rhythm in Nijinsky's ballet. The choreographer had "by means of rhythm" transformed the simplest tangible movements into

270

Drawings of the Dance of the Chosen
Virgin by Valentine Hugo (née Gross).

an object of art. Minsky emphasized that "it is all a matter of the quality, the nature of this rhythm. And if we can define the essence of this rhythm, then we will not only comprehend Nijinsky, but we will illuminate in full this entire complex artistic event." [14]

Nijinsky did not get to the end of the long article and, drowsily, he handed it back. He also remained untouched by the praises of Kostylev, critic for the *Russian Report*. Kostylev affirmed that the value of *Jeux* had been revealed "with particular clarity when the second innovation, *Le Sacre du Printemps*, was presented." Kostylev wrote that in this the producer had not bowed before any of the taboos of the established ballet aesthetic. [15] Neither Volkonsky's compliments nor the rapture of the young artist Valentine Gross lightened Nijinsky's despondency.

Valentine Gross attended all the performances and managed to make sketches of the group poses in *Jeux* and the movements in *Le Sacre*. She preserved the spirit of the original in the former but decorated the latter with the elegance of a vignette. However, these sketches and a few photographs are all we have of original documents. There are so few because Diaghilev, in his anger, was soon to drop the Nijinsky ballets from the repertoire and to recast *Le Sacre* in the production of Leonide Massine, his new ballet master. Sketches and photographs cannot rival manuscripts that, in the words of Bulgakov's hero, "do not burn," [16] or written music that awaits its second and authentic interpretation. Still, together with eyewitness accounts [17] such as Maria Piltz's story, with the recordings of those who took part, with the detailed, consistent restoration of the Chosen Virgin's dance that Bronislava Nijinska made, with the fragmentary references in the memoirs of Tamara Karsavina and the English dancer Lydia Sokolova, these sketches do help us to resurrect something lost. Ultimately, the true criterion emerges. Sometimes the most unexpected evidence is brought to bear: the composer Francis Poulenc recalled as an elderly man that Nijinsky's choreography had struck him as more revolutionary than the music when he saw the ballet in his teens. Sometimes pangs of conscience among former collaborators also help to restore, paradoxically, this criterion. Four years before his death and at a very venerable age, Stravinsky told the ballet master Yuri Grigorovitch, whom he regarded as the representative of the Russian ballet in the

United States, "Of all the interpretations I've seen, I consider Nijinsky's production to be the finest embodiment of *Le Sacre*." [18]

In May 1913 no one could have foreseen the imminent rupture between Nijinsky and Diaghilev. They least of all. For a long time Diaghilev, with his inexhaustible energy, could not understand that Nijinsky's apathy was caused by a terrible exhaustion and that his attempts to distract and entertain Nijinsky were only annoying him. Still, Diaghilev did not try to do this too often, since he had very little time for leisure.

The 1913 season proved to be perhaps the richest and fullest of all. At the twilight of Imperial Russia, Diaghilev gave Paris a last dress parade of her theatrical armies. Once again he brought *Boris Godunov* to them and, for the first time, presented *Khovanshchina* (production by Sanin, decor by Fedorovsky) under the baton of Emile Cooper. Chaliapin led the brilliant cast of singers. In addition to the best Fokine productions and the Nijinsky ballets, he also showed *La Tragédie de Salomé*, a test piece by the young choreographer Boris Romanov. This student of Fokine followed in his master's footsteps, and displayed distinct talent. But neither the fatal temptations of Salomé (Karsavina) nor the exotic splendor of Sudeikine's decors and costumes enjoyed even a fraction of the success that *Cléopâtre* and *Schéhérazade* had had. Diaghilev even took heart at this. He rejoiced in the same way a tutor does when his wards renounce their old amusements, still not suspecting that they themselves have grown out of them.

On 17 June the Diaghilev company took its leave of Paris, and the whole cumbersome enterprise moved on to London. The English were discussing the forthcoming tour sometimes so earnestly that it was quite funny. Diaghilev roared with laughter when he came across a supplement to *Sketch* magazine that contained photographs of *Jeux* surrounded by photographs of sportswomen of all nationalities playing lawn tennis. He was especially delighted by a certain stout German Frau wielding her racket with the fervor of a Valkyrie. Even so, the English, while laying no claim to fame as arbiters of artistic taste, showed much more tolerance toward Nijinsky's two new ballets, and at the third performance of *Le Sacre* they interrupted Piltz's long dance with applause several times.

25 June marked the final performance of the season and the one-hundredth performance by the Diaghilev company in London. The program was *Schéhérazade, La Tragédie de Salomé, Jeux,* and *Le Spectre de la Rose.* For Nijinsky, who danced in three ballets, it was his last appearance in the Diaghilev company on the European stage.

He assumed that he would be moving from country to country in the same old monotonous way for a long time to come. Vasili would pack the bags in one hotel and open them in another. After the usual class with Cecchetti, he would have to rehearse his own and others' ballets. In the evenings he would go on stage, dance, change costume and makeup in the intermissions. This was not tedious, but his dependence on Diaghilev was. He wished more and more to free himself from this tutelage, to be free like Chaliapin or Stravinsky. He rejoiced when Diaghilev announced that he would not be going to South America. The question "How come?" flashed through his mind, but he did not voice it.

Diaghilev mentioned something about urgent business in Europe, but people in the company gossiped about how their formidable boss feared the water and how he was frightened of traveling across the ocean. There was truth in both reasons, probably, but was there not also a third reason? Did not Diaghilev himself wish to give Nijinsky the semblance of freedom for a brief moment while ensuring, so he thought, reliable surveillance?

Baron Gunsbourg was very pleased that he was to officially represent Diaghilev during the trip and he promised to look after every want of the premier danseur. The very proper, obsequious Drobetsky, Diaghilev's personal secretary, affirmed that he would send a written report at every available occasion. Diaghilev also counted on Grigoriev, although he knew that the latter did not like to go outside the bounds of his duties as artistic director. Vasili listened to the last instructions and muttered in vexation: there was no need for the *barin* to trouble himself; he knew what he had to do, and had known for a long time.

Diaghilev set about preparing the tour. There was more than enough to do. A new conductor, Rhené-Baton, was contracted instead of Pierre Monteux. But the main problem was that many members of the company refused to embark on the ocean voyage. It was not at all easy to find replacements for them. Cecchetti, who was just leaving for Milan, advised Diaghilev to hire the English dancers Hilda Munnings (who later graced the company under the name of Lydia Sokolova) and Hilda Bewicke. He also recommended his Hungarian pupil Romola de Pulszky. Diaghilev decided to hire Romola after her mother had journeyed to London especially to ask him this favor. Emilia Markus, it would seem, already saw her daughter as the prima ballerina of the famous company. Moreover, she did not insist on a salary and she reserved a first-class cabin for Romola and a second-class cabin for the maid Anna. Like many grand people, Diaghilev liked to economize on small things.

On 15 August 1913 the S.S. *Avon* left Southampton. Karsavina was not on board, since she was coming on another ship, but Nijinsky was not on board either and his name was on the passenger list.

After a few hours, the *Avon* dropped anchor at Cherbourg. A motor launch left the jetty and approached the liner. The passengers soon made out the figure of Nijinsky among a group of Frenchmen. He was as cheerful as a cricket and was saying something to Vasili, morosely looking out from over his shoulder. Nijinsky, the first to grab hold of the gangway lowered from the *Avon*, dashed up on deck. In response to the greetings, he pulled off his round traveling hat, bowed, and immediately disappeared.

The voyage would last three weeks.

This was actually the most fascinating holiday Nijinsky ever had. The huge, majestic *Avon* cut through the waves. Day in, day out, it reflected the sun on the metallic parts of its gleaming white decks. Occasionally, it would stop at various ports, which, after Lisbon (the last European stop), became more and more picturesque.

Every morning Vasili obediently woke up the dancer early. Nijinsky would go through his indispensable class in a roped-off section of the deck while the sun was still cool and the breeze was still fresh. His allegiance to Cecchetti's principles did not stop him from inventing new movements and unprecedented combinations that probably would have enraged his old teacher. A crowd of inquisitive people, mostly English, would gather on the other side of the rope. They cut short their own constitutionals so as to take a look at Nijinsky and, with a purely sportive zeal, discussed Nijinsky's methods and the discipline of his light but strong body. Two men always observed this

Nijinsky (center) en route to South America, on board the S.S. *Avon*.

morning ritual as if they were part of it, but although they stood side by side, they never talked to each other. Vasili was angry that Nijinsky did not chase anybody away and just smiled at the spectators, but he stood silently by, ready with the watering can, the jar of rosin, the towel, and the dancer's green dressing gown. In contrast, Mr. Williams, Nijinsky's masseur, encouraged his fellow Englishmen. He answered their questions curtly but sensibly and sometimes even gave short speeches, saying, for example, that it was easier to massage any boxer for hours on end than it was this dancer even for half an hour, because his muscles were tougher than cast iron.

During the day Nijinsky appeared on deck in white trousers and a dark blue jacket. He lolled in a deckchair reading or leafing through albums of reproductions. Sometimes he would insert his finger in the pages and stare after the seagulls or the waves racing toward the horizon. At such moments he recalled the freedom of a summer holiday in his childhood. Gradually, his feverish tension of the past few months eased. The rhythms of nature, its infinite serenity, pacified him, enticed him. In response to these pleasant promptings, the figures of a dance arose in his mind, a dance very different from anything created before. This dance was also serene in the perfection of its severe and pristine forms, in the constancy of its fluent lines. For dances like this, Debussy's music seemed too mannered, Stravinsky's too cruel. What were needed were graceful consonances, harmonies placidly clear, musical patterns serenely ordered. Nijinsky wanted so much to hear such music, to discover such music. He was soon to have the chance.

At their first meeting, Rhené-Baton, the new conductor for the company, confessed that he adored Nijinsky's art. The unsociable dancer felt he could trust this big, fat, bearded man, so good of heart. Baton and his affable but ever-twittering wife shared a nearby table in the dining room, and, speaking in Nijinsky's broken French, they did their best to gain his good will. Once Baton asked Nijinsky about his plans. He replied that Diaghilev had designated Richard Strauss's ballet *La Légende de Joseph* as being the next production in which he would be taking the principal role. Nijinsky did not mention his own attitude to the Hugo von Hofmannsthal plot—what he considered to be a rehash of the same old Fokine theme of fatal temptations. Baton voiced his approval and, without replying to this, Nijinsky suddenly asked whether he would play some Bach for him.

They installed themselves in the little salon where the piano stood. A witness of this and subsequent meetings was . . . Romola de Pulszky.

Nijinsky knew that this girl was after him and that she had begun to appear everywhere that the company went. During the very busy period of *Le Sacre* and *Jeux* he had been annoyed whenever he encountered her in the most unexpected places. He even devised a malicious kind of game in which one moment he would indicate his recognition of this, his relentless shadow, and the next would look through her. After the scandal at the Théâtre des Champs-Elysées, he had been worn out and was already repelled by the idea of the forthcoming London season. When he had boarded the Paris–Calais train with Nouvel, she had suddenly appeared in the corridor opposite the open door of their compartment. He had gone out and talked to her, if one can call a pantomime mixed with fragments of French phrases talking. Later, on the voyage from Calais to Dover when she had managed to overcome her seasickness and had found him on deck, he had also been amiable in a tedious sort of way. But at the first rehearsal in London he had looked through her.

The patient submissiveness of his victim now aroused something within him. For the first time Nijinsky saw that the girl, whose name he could not remember, was still very young and pretty, and he decided to stop his heartless game once and for all. The more persistently, the more desperately she sought to meet him, the less he noticed her, and the more often he caught himself thinking about her.

It was the same here on the ship. He raised his head as if hearing a voice, encountered her gaze, and promptly fixed his eyes on the music. She installed herself on the top step of the stairs that led to the first-class restaurant. Baton, who had followed these interchanges, went up a few steps and politely asked the girl to leave. She stood up obediently, but Nijinsky, irritated by his own instability, motioned Baton not to chase her out.

Every day, as soon as Nijinsky and Baton went down to their refuge, Romola de Pulszky settled in her usual place. Day after day she watched the mysterious act of artistic creation: "Baton played on the piano and Nijinsky stood beside him. Sometimes he closed his eyes and gave the impression that he did it to concentrate more on a whole choreographic theme. Or with his fingers he danced a full variation, which he composed while Baton played the piece; or he stopped him suddenly, made him play the same bar several times. All the time, as he stood there, one could feel that he was dancing constantly the steps he invented. . . . Occasionally, he searched with Baton for hours a suitable chaconne or prelude. He stopped Baton often, saying, 'Crois, plus vite'; and Baton laughed. 'How true. I made a mistake. It is supposed to be faster.' . . . Baton told me Nijinsky was composing a new ballet on the music of Bach, to be as pure dancing as his music is pure sound. He wanted to lay down the harmony and the fundamental truth of the movement." [19]

Who knows how Nijinsky's experiment would have turned out if he had been able to follow it through. Perhaps it would have proved to be as premature as the productions of his other three ballets. Perhaps the choreographer Nijinsky, who initiated the age of neoclassical choreography fifteen years before Stravinsky and Balanchine did, would have drawn on the help of the dancer Nijinsky and would have proclaimed a new aesthetic canon, a new style for modern ballet.

The plan was never realized, and the reason for this was his three weeks of freedom. It was, as always, an illusory freedom, and, as always, he had to pay dearly for it.

For the first time, Nijinsky was left to his own devices. He was surrounded by people now living without a care in the world and who, in their enforced idleness, were eager for entertainment and amusement. Nijinsky suddenly acquired a taste for life, a life that would, it seemed, last forever. He was young, full of strength, and, after a good rest, he managed to forget all that had been. He was shy as usual, but he did not avoid groups of merrymakers, although he did prefer to observe them rather than to participate. He attended Gunsbourg's masked ball, even though he did turn up in his tuxedo, and noted that his Hungarian admirer was also one of those who had not worn a costume.

He smiled as he underwent the symbolic baptism by champagne when the *Avon* crossed the equator. For some reason he frowned when he saw pretty Mademoiselle de Pulszky deliberately flirting with one of the ship's officers. He frowned, but he would scarcely have been able to explain that this girl was breaking the "rules of the game," which she herself had established and which he had almost accepted.

The days flew past. Nijinsky became more and more convinced that Romola did not demand his submission, but was willing to submit to him, to acknowledge his will, his authority, and to consent to any kind of subordination. The fewer the number of days before the end of the journey, the more feverishly Romola sought to meet him. Sometimes she happened to make mistakes, but she recoiled only to make a new attack. The instinctive wisdom of love guided her in her subterfuges.

At one of the balls someone brought her to meet him once again and introduced them—once again. Nijinsky stood on deck, leaning on the railing. It was stuffy. The Southern Cross blazed in the black sky, a fabulous sight for a person from the north. Nijinsky looked sidelong at the girl beside him who was showering French words at him in desperate excitement. Dressed in a dinner jacket and holding a black lacquer fan decorated with a golden rose, he half closed his eyes, knowing that that made them still more "oriental." He listened to the words that, spoken at such a furious pace, he could not understand, and was silent.

The next day Nijinsky went down into the third class to watch the Italian and Spanish peasant emigrants dance the tarantella, the fandango, and the real tango, not the salon variety. Romola appeared by his side, and together they made their way back. She began to speak slowly, and he understood that a year ago he had left a cushion, a small pillow given him by his mother, in one of the hotels and that she had come across it. Romola proposed to return this precious memento. But Nijinsky turned to his friend, the dancer Kovalevska, and said in Polish that the pillow might as well remain with its new owner.

The next day they were scheduled to call at Rio de Janeiro, and in five days' time they would reach Buenos Aires, their final destination. Nijinsky locked himself in his cabin—he was contemplating something—and then had a confidential talk with Gunsbourg. After that, Gunsbourg went off to look for Romola and found her sitting in the bar with Josefina Kovalevska and the Baton couple. Taking her aside, he conveyed Nijinsky's proposal of marriage to her.

That evening, in a corner of the empty deck, Nijinsky pronounced in his broken French, "Mademoiselle, voulez-vous, vous et moi?" These words Romola never forgot. And, following a convention of nineteenth-century ballet mime, Nijinsky pointed to the fourth finger of his left hand, where one wears the engagement ring.

On 10 September 1913 Vaslav Nijinsky and Romola de Pulszky were married, first in the town hall of the Argentine capital and then in the Catholic Church of San Miguel.

Nijinsky escaped with his devoted Romola, escaped so as to save himself from his customary submission to Diaghilev. He imagined that he had ensured his future freedom. But he had yet to learn (and to pay dearly for this knowledge) that submission to Diaghilev was submission to his own art. For all her genuine love of Nijinsky, the solicitous Romola became a hindrance to his art.

This did not become immediately apparent. At first Romola Nijinsky endured a number of disappointments. The day after their wedding Vasili, not without delight, barred her way into her husband's dressing room: Diaghilev's faithful lackey hated this woman who had

(*above*) The wedding of
Romola de Pulszky and
Vaslav Nijinsky, Buenos
Aires, 10 September 1913.

(*left*) Romola and Vaslav
Nijinsky after their
wedding.

managed to outdo his master. But Romola Karlovna, as the Russian dancers in the company now called her, was mistaken in thinking that Vasili was acting on his own initiative. She stood in the corridor waiting for Nijinsky in order to complain to him. But he just walked past her, did not even turn toward her, did not even recognize her. This was the actor about to become a character on stage. Later he explained that the incident had nothing to do with Vasili: during a performance he had to have complete solitude.

But soon, too soon, Romola found out something else. Outside work, Nijinsky was compliant, like an obedient child. She realized this and began to exploit it, but carelessly. Now that she had captured Nijinsky from Diaghilev, she became jealous of her powerful rival, and, blinded by this jealousy, she gave her enemy a trump card. Romola constantly prevailed upon her husband to somehow show his independence. Once, in the middle of the Rio de Janeiro tour, she did persuade Nijinsky to refuse to appear in *Le Carnaval*. By playing on her husband's more urgent wish for independence, by encouraging him in this, Romola rejoiced at the opportunity of *showing* Diaghilev that Nijinsky was not subordinate to him. But such politics were shortsighted. A naïve wish to establish his independence in mere trifles impeded the dancer's ability to serve his art freely and selflessly. Nijinsky heeded his wife's advice, and it was in vain that Grigoriev and Gunsbourg reminded him that missing a performance without a doctor's certificate could have grave consequences. Nijinsky did not go to the theater that evening and his part as Harlequin was taken by the dancer Alexander Gavrilov.

At the end of the tour, Nijinsky said goodbye to his partners, little knowing that he would never see many of them again and that he would see some of them only in later years and in very different circumstances.

The Nijinskys set off for Paris. From there they intended to go on to St. Petersburg, paying a short visit to Romola's mother and stepfather in Budapest on the way. But at this juncture Diaghilev nullified Nijinsky's last practical endeavor to return home.

In December 1913 a small section of the Diaghilev company had returned to St. Petersburg. A biting wind had been blowing across the station square. Passersby had turned to look at all these suntanned people. Sergei Leonidovich Grigoriev and his beautiful wife, the dancer Liubov Pavlovna Tchernicheva, had set off at once for their apartment.

They were still unpacking their bags when they received a note from Diaghilev. He invited Grigoriev to visit him the next day.

Vasili Zuikov opened the door to Diaghilev's apartment. In answer to Grigoriev's "How is Sergei Pavlovich?" he muttered "You'll see for yourself."

Diaghilev looked ill. But Grigoriev restrained from commenting when he heard the metallic sound of his voice. They got down to business at once. Diaghilev handed Grigoriev a telegram he had received the day before: Nijinsky was asking when preparations for the season would begin, whether they would soon commence work on the new ballet, and he also requested that the company not be required to work on any other ballets when they rehearsed with him. Diaghilev took back the telegram, put it on the table, and covered it with the palm of his hand. He looked askance at Grigoriev, gave an angry smirk, and said that as artistic director he, Grigoriev, would have to sign the reply.

He took a telegram form from his desk, screwed his monocle into his eye socket, and, biting his tongue (Grigoriev knew that sign of controlled fury very well), wrote, not overconcisely: "In reply to your telegram to Monsieur Diaghilev I wish to inform you of the following. Monsieur Diaghilev considers that by missing a performance at Rio and refusing to dance in the ballet *Carnaval* you broke your contract. He will not, therefore, require your further services. Serge Grigoriev, Régisseur of the Diaghilev Company."

As Grigoriev read it through, his boss coldly observed the expression of his face. Taking the telegram from the astounded régisseur, he turned to Vasili standing in the doorway. "This is what it means in Russian," said Diaghilev slowly and proceeded to translate the French text. The servant stood upright and made it understood from his expression that it was dangerous to joke around with his *barin*, that this was an old story, and that there was nothing to be surprised at.

As he helped Grigoriev with his coat in the hallway, Vasili said, "Your telegram won't improve Madame Nijinsky's sleep, I dare say!" [20]

Grigoriev gave a start and looked around. He remembered these scornful words and the silent laughter of Nijinsky's ex-servant to his dying day.

7

THE UNEXPECTED TELEGRAM, INFORMING NIJINSKY so cruelly of the severance of relations with Diaghilev, hurt him very deeply. Diaghilev had tamed Nijinsky for a long time and he could now see that his efforts had not been in vain. Nijinsky was very sad, although he would not admit this to himself. He missed Diaghilev, the man who had so oppressed him with his omnipotence and with his repellent solicitude. Nijinsky found it more and more difficult to breathe outside that artificial atmosphere to which he had grown so accustomed, without realizing it. How could he fail to remember Diaghilev's perspicacious mind, his ability to comprehend an idea even when in embryo, to guide it and give it his support? Of course, no one yet knew that—with or without Diaghilev—Nijinsky had already expressed the final aspiration of his time and that he now balanced tragically and inevitably above the abyss. Is it so very important whether or not Diaghilev really said what the jealous Romola has attributed to him: "As high as Nijinsky stands now, as low I am going to thrust him"?[1] The self-assured Magician was only an instrument of Fate, only another marionette in her theater, like Petrouchka. No matter that the ungrateful Petrouchka escaped the Magician. Having found his Ballerina, he embarked on a dangerous path. He broke through the cage, only to encounter the bars of another, even more confining than the first.

Nijinsky hoped to take a short trip to Russia and show it to his wife. But a lot of things stood in the way.

Romola knew about Russia from her husband's stories. As it was, he was no rhetorician, and now they had to talk in that strange pidgin language they had devised for themselves—a mixture of French, Russian, and Polish. So the young woman imagined Russia as a somewhat enigmatic country, and that was the image that appeared on the pages of her book written in the early 1930s. Only many years after the death of her husband and to honor his memory, Romola Nijinsky visited the Soviet Union. But what could she find of his childhood and adolescence there? The school building on Theater Street, now called Rossi Street? The former Mariinsky Theater, now called the Kirov Theater of Opera and Ballet? And there too only the walls had not changed. To that misfit of genius, Nijinsky, the life inside them would have seemed strange, unfamiliar, just as his biography written by his wife seems strange to the Russian reader.

More than ever before, Nijinsky now saw Russia as the promised land, into which entry was forbidden. What could he expect in St. Petersburg? His old place in the Imperial Ballet? It was possible that Teliakovsky might try to waive the interdict and take Nijinsky back, just to pique Diaghilev. But first of all, he would take him back only as a dancer under the ballet masters Legat and Fokine and, naturally, would not risk allowing him to choreograph. Second, Nijinsky would not have been able to survive on the official salary. Apart from his mother, it was now incumbent upon him to support a pampered wife who was accustomed to luxury. In addition, he was about to become a father: Romola was four months pregnant.

In the meantime, the rumor of Diaghilev's break with his premier danseur spread like wildfire, and many enterprising impresarios tried to hire Nijinsky. But he was not in a hurry, even though circumstances dictated that he should have been. The Nijinskys were staying in Budapest with Romola's mother and stepfather. Relations were strained. Emilia Markus had reckoned on a rather different kind of match. Moreover, as a celebrated and not so old actress she did not relish the prospect of becoming a grandmother in the next few months.

Nijinsky rejected offers of fabulous contracts and dismissed entrepreneurs who came to Budapest especially to see him. He was thinking of forming his own professional company and of its own dancing repertoire. He simply didn't realize that he lacked one thing—administrative talent. True, he knew that he was no good as a teacher or mentor. That's why he decided not to become ballet master and premier danseur of the Paris Opéra, although he rejected the offer of its director, Jacques Rouché, on the grounds that its ballet company was not very strong. When Serge Lifar, Diaghilev's last male star, took charge of this company in 1929, it was no better. But Lifar, a man of very different character and of a different era, transformed it into a first-class company.

Life in Budapest became intolerable, and they were forced to move to Vienna. Nijinsky saw that money was running out, so, while there, he accepted the offer of Alfred Butt, owner of the Palace Theatre, a huge music hall in London. It was a fatal move. In fact, only four years before, after the first Paris season, Nijinsky had been offered two thousand francs for one month's engagement in the London variety theaters, but he had refused. "These aren't theaters but cafés chantants," he had told a *St. Petersburg Gazette* reporter, "and I am surprised that our artists consent to dance in them."[2]

He had been making an obvious allusion to Anna Pavlova. And now, perhaps, he justified his own action by her example. But he made an even greater mistake in comparing himself to her. For all their resemblance in character, their individual destinies were entirely different.

Pavlova had created her own world, with its own rules, and she obeyed these and no other. Within this world everything served the dance, a single god, but of many visages. In the real meaning of the word, Pavlova transfigured the dance, whether it was classical, "free," or the most whimsical combination of both. She did not worry herself about the much acclaimed essential form of her "butterflies" or her "dragonflies," her "roses" or her "poppies." And she was right not to: at her very touch the essential form was born each time. Pavlova used music as befitted the moment, whether it was a cheap banality or a

287

masterpiece, and she justified it all by the very magic of her art. She was not afraid of being eclectic in the programs for her recitals because she could ennoble even the most tasteless trumpery. She knew very well that she could get away with dancing *The Dying Swan* or a classical variation on a bill with clowns doing music hall numbers and dogs doing tricks. She could make her own rules, because her dancing shone out brilliantly from whatever trash surrounded it.

Nijinsky's art was not so delightfully egocentric and, therefore, could not function independently. As a dancer he was unable to distort the length of a piece of music or to change a detail of costume just for the sake of heightening the effect of his dancing. On the contrary, he would refuse to show off his virtuosity in any way if he thought this might harm the totality of the artistic image. Diaghilev and his associates had taught him to be exacting, to develop a severe, even a prejudiced taste. And however dearly he paid for his experiments in new artistic expression, he, as a choreographer, had to be satisfied only with such experiments. Nothing like that was expected on the stage of a variety theater. A ballet based on the music of Bach remained beyond the bounds of possibility. Even the three ballets that Nijinsky had already made required a different kind of stage, a different audience, a different company. In the variety theater he would have to be content with excerpts from the classics or variations on Fokine's faded novelties.

There were other differences between Pavlova and Nijinsky. The "muse of the Russian ballet" was practical. She knew how to talk theater directors into giving her good terms; she knew how to surround herself with people who could guarantee her both financial benefit and the peace to create. Apart from that, however "aerial" and fragile she might look, Pavlova had great powers of endurance and great strength of character, which enabled her to overcome the most terrible periods of fatigue.

Nijinsky possessed muscles of steel, yet he tired easily, and, furthermore, it did not take much for him to doubt himself. During the years of his fame, his unsociable nature reached abnormal proportions. As for being practical—well, he simply was not, and by force of circumstances he had become the most impractical person in the whole world. A dancer who until recently had to think only of his

Anna Pavlova in *The Dying Swan*. Created especially for her by Fokine, this dance was Pavlova's most popular solo. She included it on her programs almost everywhere she appeared.

current role, a choreographer who had had first-class materials at his disposal, now turned up as an administrator who had to procure everything himself and who was responsible for everything too. He made each independent action with great difficulty, quite disproportionate to the result. And it would be his job to arrange the repertoire for future tours, to make contacts among composers, to seek out artists, and many other tedious trifles so important for the running of a theater machine.

First and foremost, he had to assemble a company. Bronislava helped in this. Loyal to her brother, she met with him in Paris and from there went to Russia in order to look for dancers. One dancer had

Nijinsky and his company in *Les Sylphides*, 1914.

already been found, her husband, whom she had persuaded to break with Diaghilev.

Nijinsky searched out Bakst in his Paris studio on the Boulevard Malesherbes. But Leon Samoilovich said that while nothing could influence his personal friendship with Vaslav, still he did not wish to spoil his relationship with Seriozha, and so both now and in the future he was compelled to decline collaboration with Nijinsky.

That was a blow.

But then fortune smiled on Nijinsky. He reached an agreement with Boris Anisfeld and, most important, gained the support of Maurice Ravel. The latter might well have nursed a grievance. Although Nijinsky had created a wonderful Daphnis, he had undermined the success of Ravel's ballet by his *L'Après-Midi*. However, affront and revenge were foreign to Ravel's nature. The rather dandyish composer, who enjoyed life so much, affirmed his full support and readiness to help. He began to select music, acquired the publisher's permission to use this or that piece, and orchestrated a new version of *Les Sylphides*.

Nijinsky and his new company began work with a rehearsal of *Les Sylphides*, although perhaps it is an exaggeration to describe the ten Russian and Polish female dancers, whom Bronislava and her husband had found after much difficultly, as a company. No male dancers could be found: Vaslav Nijinsky and Alexander Kochetovsky comprised the male section.

The timid little flock of girls was quite lost in the badly equipped accommodation. Their leader remembered despondently how, in the old days, crowds of drilled dancers would await him in the spacious halls under Grigoriev's command. After checking out the very uneven talents of his dancers, Nijinsky selected two soloists and arranged the remaining dancers into two groups, which he himself had to admit were mere caricatures of the clusters of sylphides who framed the action of Fokine's *Chopiniana*. He and Bronislava moved to the center; the soloists lay down in front of them with their backs to the audience; the "corps de ballet" formed semicircles on either side. Nijinsky explained that Monsieur Ravel had chosen a Chopin étude for the overture and he then demonstrated the introductory nocturne, which all participants were to dance. He tried not to depart from Fokine and, like him, ended the ballet with the same general dance. But he did introduce his own mazurka, an étude danced by one soloist, a mazurka for Bronislava, an étude for the second soloist, and another mazurka for Bronislava and himself instead of the memorable "Pavlova waltz." He excluded this waltz, a pearl of Fokine's artistic imagination, because Bronislava looked more effective while leaping than while being lifted into the air by her partner.

The work proceeded slowly. The very uneven training of the dancers made itself felt. Nijinsky tried not to get irritated and consoled himself with the fact that the "company" was not being used beyond the first program. He demonstrated for Kochetovsky his Siamese Dance to Sinding's music (which would be billed as *Danse Orientale*), and he chose *Le Spectre de la Rose* as the third number (in which Bronislava had learned Karsavina's part).

On 23 February Nijinsky saw a new playbill at the entrance to the Palace Theatre. It was advertising the performances for the coming week. He saw his own name, "Nijinski" (as usual the ending was misspelled), in fat letters at the bottom. His engagement for the coming week was already being announced. On 2 March someone brought him a copy of the *Times* and pointed out among the ads that the Palace Theatre that day would witness the "first appearance of Nijinski, the celebrated première danseuse, in *Les Sylphides* and *Le Spectre de la Rose*." Over recent months Nijinsky had grown unaccustomed to laughing. But now he burst out laughing, imagining how Diaghilev would ironically have removed the monocle from his eye after reading that his former premier danseur was now billed as a première danseuse.

An ominous mix-up. Nothing would go right. Ravel was the only one who was happy; he had orchestrated Chopin with great delight. (His orchestral score, together with Anisfeld's decors, got lost in one of London's warehouses during the war.) To Nijinsky everything else seemed pitiful and unnecessary.

With every day his irritability grew worse, although he still managed to conceal it from his wife and his sister, as he did his insomnia and his continual headaches. He nearly vented his spleen on Maurice Volny, manager of the Palace, who informed him that the orchestra would play between his "numbers" and that the house lights would not be lowered during acts or scene changes. Volny said something about the audience being used to it like that. Nijinsky said angrily that he was not obliged to do what the audience wanted, and he managed to get both rules waived.

He realized that the audience would be varied, and he put his hopes on that portion of it that was familiar with the Diaghilev seasons. He was not deceived. Many connoisseurs were visiting the famous variety theater for the first time. But perhaps it would have been better if they had not. Although Nijinsky was in excellent form, the Youth in *Les Sylphides* and the Spirit of the Rose lost their charm (which, in Nijinsky's dancing, meant much more than his phenomenal leap). During intermissions Nijinsky hardly managed to close the door of his dressing room before someone opened it inquiring about the most trivial things and hindering his concentration.

Regular visitors to the Palace moaned about the darkness; they didn't like it so quiet and they didn't like the long scene changes.

The next day there was a scandal backstage, an ugly scene, and Nijinsky was the cause of it.

Volny had decided that he did not really have to pay attention to Nijinsky, even if he was a famous dancer, and, without warning, restored the musical intermissions. Just as *Les Sylphides* ended, Hermann Finck gave a signal and the orchestra started to play the "peasant waltz" from *The Sleeping Beauty:* the permanent conductor of the Palace had remembered that Pavlova had approved of Tchaikovsky. Even before the waltz was half-way through, the assistant manager had located Volny, and, catching his breath, announced that Nijinsky had gone crazy. Volny rushed to Nijinsky's dressing room. Pushing the crowd aside, he stopped in the doorway.

Nijinsky had been about to put on the costume of the Spirit of the Rose when he had heard the orchestra giving full swing to the Tchaikovsky waltz. It had suddenly occurred to him that after Tchaikovsky they would play Weber, also some kind of waltz. Everything had seemed interminably vulgar and disgusting. He had become furious. And now he was no longer aware that he was rolling on the floor, sobbing and groaning in convulsions.

Volny looked at the frightened faces of the actors and the Palace employees crowding the dressing room; he saw the empty purple and violet Bakst tights dangling from the hands of the dresser; he noticed the armful of artificial rose petals lying on the table; and he took measures. He grabbed the water carafe from the table, splashed some water on Nijinsky, and roared, "Lève-toi!" The dancer quieted down, stood up, and, in distraction, screened his face with his hands. Volny commanded, "Habille-toi!" Nijinsky obediently turned to the dresser. In the ensuing silence could be heard the sounds of a serene melody: the orchestra had begun the "pink waltz" from *The Nutcracker.*

Five minutes later, a girl dressed in a crinoline and a cape ran onto the stage, she sank into a chair, closed her eyes. A young man in the costume of a fantastic flower burst through the window, flew through the air, and leaned over the sleeping girl. Hypnotized by their own discipline, Bronislava and Vaslav Nijinsky danced *Le Spectre de la Rose.*

But the next day Nijinsky had become very weak. Taking himself in hand, he rehearsed the third program: *Le Carnaval* (adapted to suit the abilities of the company), a pas de deux from *The Sleeping Beauty* entitled *L'Oiseau et le Prince,* and the *Danse Grecque* composed for the female corps de ballet. The second program was running at the moment. This contained a *Polovtsian Dance* (distantly related to the Fokine masterpiece) instead of *Danse Orientale.* The third program was scheduled for the evening of 16 March.

But that evening, not long before the beginning of the performance, the telephone rang in Alfred Butt's office. He was informed that Nijinsky was unable to dance that day. Butt hung up and then immediately took down the receiver again: from somewhere or other he had to find a replacement, and soon, for the world's leading dancer.

Nijinsky did not turn up the next day, or the day after that. His fans compensated themselves for his unexpected absence by looking at the portraits of the dancer exhibited at the Fine Art Society. In the soft pastels of Valentine Gross, Harlequin calmly embraced Columbine as he mysteriously squinted through the slits of his mask; and the Spirit of the Rose flew on high, twirling his finger-petals above his head. In John Singer Sargent's sketch, Armida's White Slave smiled with capricious arrogance. Jacques-Emile Blanche had caught the exquisite pose of Nijinsky in his Siamese Dance. Glyn Philpot's oil depicted the Faun advancing in the reflections of the footlights from the curtain to the orchestra pit, greeting the applause.

That was the last time that London applauded Nijinsky. After his two-month illness (which terminated his contract with the Palace Theatre) the dancer ended up poorer than he had been. The company brought from Russia requested enough money to cover travel expenses, and Nijnsky settled up with all the dancers.

His doctors insisted that he take an extended break, which was easy enough to do since Nijinsky had neither the strength nor the money to organize another company. The Nijinskys traveled to Semmering, a small Austrian resort. While they were there Nijinsky received an invitation from the American Embassy in Madrid to appear at a gala performance. Nijinsky attended, but without Romola. On a stage erected in the middle of gardens, he danced in the presence of the king and queen of Spain. He danced without a partner; he was responsible only for himself; and once again he established contact with his audience.

(*left*) Nijinsky and Karsavina in *Le Spectre de la Rose*. Pastel by Valentine Gross.

(*below*) Nijinsky in *Le Pavillon d'Armide*. Charcoal sketch by John Singer Sargent.

On the way back he stopped over in Paris at the height of the Diaghilev season. The playbills advertised *Joseph et Potiphar,* the Richard Strauss ballet that Nijinsky had been supposed to produce and dance in under the title *La Légende de Joseph.* He bought himself a ticket for an orchestra seat.

Unrecognized by the audience and shunning familiar faces, the former premier danseur had very mixed feelings. It seemed that Diaghilev had made a comeback and had "made a clean sweep," as they used to say at school. *L'Après-Midi, Jeux, Le Sacre du Printemps*—they had all been dropped with deliberate consistency. The action of *Joseph et Potiphar* unfolded in the sumptuous but languid decors of José-Maria Sert and in the costumes of Bakst, who had seen the biblical theme through the eyes of Veronese. It also relied on Fokine's typically jazzy staging as well as on his dazzling, orgiastic dances. Marie Kuznetsova-Benois, the St. Petersburg opera singer, flaunted her ample (but "non-balletic") charms as she attempted to reproduce one of Ida Rubinstein's femmes fatales in her role as Potiphar's Wife. The part of Joseph was performed by a young man with large, deep eyes: Leonide Massine. Nijinsky liked him and could sense definite talent beneath the timid behavior and still constrained movements. Nijinsky knew that Diaghilev would make a real dancer of this lad, perhaps even a ballet master. Jealousy was foreign to Nijinsky, but, all the same, he felt a vague melancholy. Most likely this arose because he missed the backstage atmosphere of the première; he missed the people who took part in the première, people who had never been close to him but who were, nevertheless, part of the same family. He missed the man in charge of all these people, the imperious and unhappy Diaghilev.

During the intermissions Nijinsky heard his name spoken several times by strangers in the audience. He remembered the paradoxical statement by one man that while Fokine had himself replaced Nijinsky in the role of Petrouchka, he obviously did not understand it at all! People also talked of Nijinsky's failure in London. But they did agree that without Nijinsky the Ballets Russes were just not the same.

While he was in Vienna at the beginning of July, Nijinsky read an article by Jacques Rivière (an ardent champion of his *Le Sacre*) published in the *Nouvelle Revue Française.* Rivière devoted his article to his impressions of the season, and the focus of attention was Nijin-sky, who was "more than the inspirer of the company, he was its conscience." Rivière explained: "He did not allow people to be satisfied with what they had achieved, he stopped people from cashing in on their success, from keeping to the beaten track and from indulging the public. He obliged one to search and, I venture to say, obliged one to make mistakes. Last year certain members of the company (which ones? I don't know) were inclined to 'rubber-stamp the Ballets Russes,' but Nijinsky was absolutely against this. The bridle was re-moved, Fokine came back and everything went like clockwork." [3]

Flattering, but not justified. Nijinsky suddenly recognized the truth, something that had been hidden from him for almost a year, even though he sought truth more and more often and with ever greater torment. The truth was as follows: one way or another he would have had to leave Diaghilev. The easiest way had been to get married and to create a family, even though it meant he would have a nomadic life like his father and mother had had. At the same time he was obliged to Diaghilev for his universal fame, for many of his ideas on art, and for his very attitude toward art. One thing he was sure of: Diaghilev would make out all right without Nijinsky. So Diaghilev had retreated. Well, so be it! It had to be so. Diaghilev had retreated; he had stepped back to prepare for takeoff, to flaunt his extraordinary discoveries, to astound by his new flight of fancy. And Nijinsky hoped that the time would come when Diaghilev would un-derstand and when they would again work together. Not right now, of course. That was impossible. He and his wife were preparing for an important event.

On 19 June 1914 a daughter, Kyra, was born to Romola and Vaslav Nijinsky. The celebrated dancer had dreamed of a son and had wished to christen him Vladislav, as the heir to the glory of the Nijinsky dynasty, to their gift for dancing. Even so, Nijinsky had only to cast eyes on the baby girl to become fond of her. He found it easy to relate to children and could forget himself in their company. His love for his daughter was soon to save him in the imminent years of disaster.

On 28 June 1914 the Archduke Franz Ferdinand was assassinated in Sarajevo. A month later the world was enveloped by war. The war found the Nijinskys in Budapest just as they were preparing, once again, to travel to Russia. Nijinsky, a Russian citizen, was now in a hostile country, a prisoner in the house of his mother-in-law.

Emilia Markus was still alive in 1933 when her daughter published the book *Nijinsky*, and she may have read the indictment against her in the chapter entitled "Prisoners of War." Romola narrated in detail how her mother grew to hate Nijinsky more and more as the days passed, and how she found the most varied occasions, from her hysterics to her police denunciations, for attacking the Russian "spy."

Not once did Nijinsky take up the challenge. He escaped into his daughter's nursery. And when the wet nurse abandoned the child, he prepared the food himself and made toys with his own hands.

There was more than enough free time. The authorities forbade the dancer to work in the theatre, and he had to make do with his room, where there was no space for him to jump. Occasionally, he was able to meet with Romola's cousin, a brilliant pianist. She played for Nijinsky and through her he discovered Richard Strauss's symphonic poem *Till Eulenspiegel.* The image of the vagabond man—wolf, persecuted but always buoyant, captivated him immediately. In seeking to overcome his enforced idleness, Nijinsky had the idea of notating a dance, in accordance with his own system, of course. The work engrossed him and, very soon, the dance notation of a Bach saraband appeared on the carefully ruled paper. There were other endeavors, but this was the sole memento of the unrealized ballet. These experiments aroused the suspicion of police detectives, who imagined them to be a secret code. Romola only just succeeded in explaining to the police that her husband's notations were quite harmless.

Nijinsky never concerned himself with politics. He loved Russia, and in response to the suggestion that he take out Hungarian citizenship, he said: "I was born a Russian; I can give thanks to my country, which made me an artist, and I will remain Russian." [4] However, separated from his homeland, he observed the course of war dispassionately, as if it were a monstrous nightmare that had hurled itself upon mankind and was breaking it mercilessly. Whenever he managed to obtain Russian books, he read Tolstoy with particular fondness. The doctrine of nonresistance to evil by force appealed to him and helped him in moments of adversity. He imagined in his naïve way that all that was needed for heaven on earth was for people to desire common happiness for all.

The isolation, the impossibility of working, the hostile ambience —all this had a considerable influence on his psychological state, which, in any case, was not exactly stable. Periods of melancholy were followed by periods of nervous animation, and at such moments Nijinsky reminded Romola of a little boy. He acted out scenes from his future ballets before her. He would turn into a Russian peasant girl, swim along. like a swan, beckon others to take part in a roundelay. He would demonstrate how the gypsies danced, "trembling all over . . . , shaking his shoulders as if they were independent of the rest of his body." [5] And then he would suddenly do takeoffs on the ballerinas of the Mariinsky, his funniest impersonation being that of Kschessinska.

The Nijinskys had now been interned in Hungary for one year. In the fall of 1915 the rumor gained ground that Diaghilev was assembling his company for an American tour and that he was trying to establish contact with Nijinsky. But then the rumor stopped. On one of their regular visits to the police, they learned that they were being transferred to Carlsbad, Bohemia. As he said goodbye, the prefect apologized for the recent constraints, blaming them on the severity of instructions he had received. He then hinted that they would do well to stop in Vienna for a while because, as they might say, of Romola's illness.

It was January 1916 when Nijinsky arrived in Vienna with his family. As before, he was still a prisoner of war and was almost penniless.

But here everything was quite different from Budapest. Nijinsky's fans, friends, and relatives of his wife greeted the refugees and gave them every care and comfort. There was now no need to move on. Diaghilev had actually obtained Nijinsky's release by enlisting the support of the high and mighty, including King Alfonso XIII of Spain. Only Diaghilev could do that.

The hotel rooms, the stage of the old Theater an der Wien, which was at Nijinsky's disposal for practicing (Fanny Elssler had once danced there)—these things reminded him of his former way of life. And now he could foresee working with a familiar and beloved company, working in his old position as dancer and as choreographer.

Nijinsky had formulated ideas for three new ballets.

One of them, which had found its inspiration in the painting of Hokusai, did not yet have music. As always, the choreographer demonstrated rather than related the ballet as he shared its idea with his wife. Romola was very struck by the movements, which refuted the canons of Japanese ballet, opera, and operetta. Nijinsky took an elegant and solemn pose and held it over an extended time. A slight incline of the head, eyelashes opening slowly, the wrist turning with trembling fingers, and the pose was replaced by a new force, one just as majestic, as mysterious and tragic. Here was the creator of *L'Après-Midi* and *Le Sacre*. His instinct now awoke after the enforced hibernation, but his ideas for this ballet were never realized.

The second ballet, set to Liszt's *Mephisto Valse*, had been finished in Vienna, and it had only to be shown to the dancers. Nijinsky had returned to the theme of Petrouchka and the Magician, but he had conceived a scenario in a Romantic key. Like two bosom friends, Faust and Mephistopheles have turned up at a wayside tavern. Old men are playing cards and drinking at their tables, while the young folk dance to the sounds of the village band. Faust and the landlord's golden-haired daughter fall in love at first sight. Mephistopheles helps them on. He deflects the attention of the card players by instilling a frenzied excitement in them. He borrows a violin from one of the musicians and, as he flourishes the bow, the couples begin to whirl in a dance of tender passion. They are interrupted from time to time by the duet of Faust and his beloved, who one moment restrain, the next moment accelerate, the climax of the dance. At length, Mephistopheles throws open the door, and the starlit night swallows up the couples one by one. Faust is the last to bear his love away: he has been freed, he is free in friendship and love.

The *Mephisto Valse,* an idealized image of friendship, was conceived in accordance with the rules of nineteenth-century ballet, in which the genre and character scenes served simply to support the classical dance. But the dancer of Fokine's ballets, the protégé of Diaghilev who had passed the test of modern experimentation, now stylized the structural forms of the classical dance in the manner of medieval art. He put on his rehearsal costume and, in front of his wife, played out the various characters: he transformed himself

300

Richard Strauss, composer of *La Légende de Joseph* and *Till Eulenspiegels lustige Streiche* [Till Eulenspiegel's Merry Pranks].

now into the fat landlord, now into the lascivious and wealthy merchant or the clumsy country bumpkin (the two suitors of the landlord's beautiful daughter), now into the ironic and mysterious Mephistopheles, now into Faust, the poet who had found his earthly ideal. Romola watched the golden-haired heroine whose variation sparkled with batterie, glittered with the staccato vibrations of pointwork, and blazed forth in pirouettes that conveyed the fire of the feelings consuming her. Romola forgot that before her danced one man, not a whole company. But, as before, she remained the sole spectator.

The third new ballet was to be *Till Eulenspiegel*. When Richard Strauss, the composer, met Nijinsky in Vienna, he suggested that the music might need reworking. The choreographer assured the composer that he did not wish to change a single bar.

Nijinsky was summoned to the American Embassy and was told that he could set off for New York where the Diaghilev company was already assembled. His wife and daughter were to be left as security. But Nijinsky refused to go by himself, even though he was dying to get down to work. At length he received permission to take the whole family.

It was February when the Nijinskys left Vienna in a train packed with soldiers. They were put in a first-class carriage, but one that had seen better days and that now had broken windows and was unheated. They were forced to wait for a pass at the Tyrol–Swiss border. The hotel room with its tiled stove, the feather mattresses on the beds, the white snow through the window—all this reminded Nijinsky of Russia and of his childhood. He cheered up a bit, threw snowballs with his daughter, and gave her sleigh rides. When they did cross the border and put up in Bern, Kyra tasted for the first time such earthly blessings as cream and chocolate.

Two days later, in Lausanne, the Nijinskys were met by a representative of the Metropolitan Opera, who was supposed to accompany them to New York. Stravinsky also called on them while they were there. He lived with his family in a villa on the lake, with a lovely view of Mont Blanc. It was quite near, and he invited the Nijinskys to drop by.

The two famous participants in the Saisons Russes met on an amicable footing. They both reminisced about the past and made plans for the future. But a dark shadow soon clouded their relationship.

At first Stravinsky asked Nijinsky to send a telegram to Otto Kahn, chairman of the board of directors for the Metropolitan, and to make it a condition of his touring engagements that Stravinsky be invited. Nijinsky at once wrote out the telegram. But he did not know that Romola prudently edited the text, replacing the demand by a polite request. There was no answer. The proud composer became reserved and rather stern.

Then Nijinsky, who was afraid that the voyage across the ocean and the traveling around America might have an adverse effect on his very young daughter, asked Stravinsky to take Kyra for a while. Stravinsky refused outright; he did not want such a responsibility. Two years later this incident was to find its extension in the scribblings

302

of Nijinsky's diary: "He is not my friend, but at the bottom of his heart he loves me, because he feels me. . . ." [6] And then, further on, in sentences that gallop along by fits and starts: "He is like an emperor and his children and wife are the soldiers. Stravinsky reminds me of Tsar Paul, but he will not be strangled because he is cleverer than the Tsar was."

When the Nijinskys left Lausanne, Stravinsky saw them off at the station. "I gave him my hand very coldly. I did not like him then, and therefore I wanted to show him this, but he did not feel it because he kissed me. I had a nasty feeling." [7] Nijinsky dotted his *i*'s—the breach between the two men, which had reached such fantastic proportions in his diseased brain, could no longer be repaired.

Even without these two episodes, the dissimilarity in character and lifestyle of the two men would have made itself known. At first glance such episodes might seem trivial but, essentially, they have great import.

The Nijinskys reached France safely, spent twenty-four hours in Paris, and the next evening went on board the steamship *Rochambeau*.

On 7 April 1916 a crowd of reporters met the *Rochambeau* in the Port of New York. They surrounded Nijinsky on deck, clicked their cameras, shouted their questions. It was almost as if those two years that had turned his life inside-out had never been. On the jetty down below waited the directors of the Metropolitan Opera, members of the Ballet Russe and, in front of them, Diaghilev with a bouquet of roses. Like a true grand seigneur, Nijinsky's once-time friend and patron wished to make peace, whatever the cost to himself. Diaghilev bowed his head to the hand of Romola Nijinsky and presented her with the bouquet, and then, according to the Russian custom, he kissed Nijinsky three times.

The most fantastic dreams seemed to be coming true.

But, whether moved by rational calculation or by jealousy, Romola made a fatal blunder. She did not terminate her litigation against Diaghilev that had begun before the war, but won a suit for half a million francs, which, supposedly, were due Nijinsky. A Pyrrhic victory, twice over: first, because Diaghilev did not pay anything anyway, even though he lost the case; second, in "winning" Nijinsky once more,

Diaghilev and members of his company, on tour in America, 1916. Adolf Bolm, Sergei Grigoriev, and Leonide Massine are at left. Lydia Lopokhova stands at Diaghilev's left. The sign on the railing shows the impresario's name in French transliteration: Diaghileff.

Romola at once laid the foundation for his and her own future adversities. Two years earlier, Nijinsky had been burdened by his position as Diaghilev's prisoner. Now that he had returned to his post as premier danseur and choreographer, he assumed that he would be keeping his privileges despite the fact that he had cast off his shackles. He expected attention to be given to his plans; he expected that very special atmosphere that had surrounded his rehearsals and performances. Diaghilev knew how to normalize relations between Nijinsky and the company. Surely, this was a fresh start. But Diaghilev renounced his obligations as friend and mentor, although he could not help seeing that Nijinsky's presence would enhance what had so far been only a moderate success on the American tour.

The tour had now lasted three months since its première on 17 January. For its opening at New York's Century Theater the following items had been billed: *The Firebird, La Princesse Enchantée* (the pas de deux of the Bluebird and Princess Florine), *Midnight Sun* (Massine's first ballet, to music from Rimsky-Korsakov's *Snegourochka*, designed by Mikhail Larionov), and *Schéhérazade*. Subsequent programs had included *Cléopâtre, Petrouchka, Le Carnaval, Les Sylphides, Narcisse, and L'Après-Midi d'un Faune.* Those who had already seen the Diaghilev company in Europe had lauded its "total synthesis of the arts" in advance, but they had experienced a slight disappointment. Without the original performers, the ballets—the music, the decor, the choreography—had seemed to leave a lot to be desired. Xenia Makletsova had displayed a brilliant technique (not so very essential for Fokine's exotic ballets), but the young Moscow dancer could not compete with the artistry and charm of Karsavina. Lydia Lopokhova had been delightful in *Le Carnaval* and *Petrouchka,* but even she lacked the mysterious enchantment of Karsavina in *The Firebird.* Bolm had excelled in his usual roles, but he was no match for Nijinsky in *Petrouchka,* just as Gavrilov could not replace Nijinsky in *Les Sylphides* or *Le Spectre de la Rose,* nor could Massine in *L'Après-Midi d'un Faune.*

After a two-week engagement at the Century, the company had toured sixteen U.S. cities. Returning to New York, the company had begun a new season at the Metropolitan Opera on 3 April. Nijinsky's debut was billed for 12 April, five days after his ship docked.

He arrived at rehearsal despondent, tormented by his old "fear of people," which had been intensified thanks to his years of enforced isolation. He had experienced something like it nine years before when he had attended a session of the Mariinsky company for the first time. Except that he had been made to feel more welcome there. But now Grigoriev introduced him to the dancers with a courteous detachment as if he were a foreign artist on tour. Their eyes were upon him, but Nijinsky could not cope with his own personality. He knew that they would interpret his timidity as arrogance, as the absurd complacency of a "world celebrity." He withdrew into himself and began to shun even those people with whom he had once worked.

Neither then nor later did Diaghilev attend rehearsals. He bade Grigoriev allow Nijinsky as many rehearsals as he wished, including rehearsals with orchestra, but he himself sat out the time in the Ritz, where Massine was also staying. He did not even come to the première.

The dancers approved of Diaghilev's action. But they could not know that it was not Nijinsky but his wife who was playing such a shortsighted game with their boss, now displaying such extraordinary patience. "Nijinsky is here and is making a lot of fuss—won't appear without tons of money, saying in the papers horrid things about the ballet. You know just how they always turn around on those who make their names for them"—such was the complaint of Lydia Sokolova, a new soloist in the company, in one of her letters home.[8] Nijinsky submitted to Romola just as meekly as he had to Diaghilev. He was silent, and only at the tensest moments did he bite his nails.

Nijinsky had one weapon, his art. As in the old days, his control was superb. Some observers even thought that Nijinsky was better than ever before. After Nijinsky's first appearance, Americans realized that until then they had seen not the authentic Spirit of the Rose or Petrouchka, but mere copies. The critic Carl Van Vechten, who remembered Nijinsky's European triumphs, declared that the dancer "had surpassed himself," that his movements contained "the unbroken quality of music, the balance of great painting, the meaning of fine literature, and the emotion inherent in all these arts." As an actor, Van Vechten went on, Nijinsky "makes of himself what he will. He can look tall or short, magnificent or ugly, fascinating or repulsive. . . . It is under the electric light in front of the painted canvas that he becomes a personality, and that personality is governed only by the scenario of the ballet." [9]

Romola was gladdened by such laudatory reviews, but she was vexed to see that Nijinsky remained indifferent to them. In any case, she was seriously alarmed by her husband's nervous excitement. Still, she continued to incite his suspicions by her talk of "Diaghilev's intrigues." She had no doubts whatsoever that Diaghilev "hates Vaslav frenziedly and persecutes him mercilessly," that only her vigilance was saving Nijinsky from vulgar gossip and machinations. But it was she who, in all innocence, occasioned such gossip.

As it was, Romola never really understood the role that she herself played in the Nijinsky tragedy. Life had bestowed upon husband and wife very different natures; their psychological attitudes were very dissimilar. In their tastes, their opinions, their artistic criteria these two young people had nothing in common. Artistic criteria, indeed, formed the most serious area of difference. If it had not been for this, then the energy and persistence of this lively young woman, her very normality, might perhaps have brought forth a salutary response in the character of this shy, ailing artist, in his unbalanced, diseased, mental state, in his delicate and sensitive soul. But Romola had grown up in an atmosphere of theatricality and self-indulgence. In the Emilia Markus household, talent, that is, real talent, was regarded as a divine favor that gave one the right to enjoy many other favors: luxury and comfort of lifestyle, high society connections, vanity, selfishness, caprice. Romola encountered the other side of the coin when she brought an unwanted son-in-law to her mother's house. And she grew to hate her mother with all the force of her pampered and obstinate nature. However, the way of life to which she had been accustomed since childhood remained her criterion. She was guided by it and wished to "reshape" her husband accordingly.

But Nijinsky, who felt he had been a prisoner all his life, did not realize that such imprisonment was more worthy. He did not realize that, in separating him from Diaghilev, Romola was separating him from genuine art, from free experimentation, from trial and error. Any clash of interests in the company always, inevitably, came up against the very aims and endeavors of the company, which, in essence, were always artistic. The more enviable, therefore, was Diaghilev's attitude to art. For all his egoism, Diaghilev did not "cash in" on art, but created it, although, of course, he was not indifferent to fame and glory. Romola, however, while entirely devoted to Nijinsky (indeed, she had forgone many things in choosing to be with him), was a stranger to the muse of artistic creativity. She had no idea how painful the financial litigation against Diaghilev was for Nijinsky. She had no idea that her worries about her family's income might lead to something of the utmost horror for Nijinsky, that is, that he would have to dance everywhere and with anyone. Diaghilev, meanwhile, was making new plans and was implementing them.

Nijinsky became increasingly dependent on Romola. He became more and more unsociable and regarded the dancers and staff of the company with ever greater distrust.

Toward the end of the three-week season, Otto Kahn proposed a new American tour for the fall, on the understanding, of course, that Nijinsky would participate. To this, Nijinsky advanced a counter condition: he would go as long as he was guaranteed total personal control of the company without Diaghilev and even without Grigoriev. As if the London flop had not been enough for him.

Since he had to provide for the company, Diaghilev agreed, although he understood perfectly well why the honest Grigoriev was so worried by this turn of events. Diaghilev realized, no less than Grigoriev did, the risk entailed in entrusting the company to Nijinsky and his wife, two very inexperienced people. But he was forced to take the risk. He could not foresee permanent contracts in Europe, and the end of the war was not in sight. Thank heavens that a summer engagement in Spain was in the offing. At the beginning of May, Diaghilev traveled there together with a small section of the company that included Grigoriev, Tchernicheva, and Massine.

Romola Nijinsky felt herself master of the situation. Her husband was now artistic director of a real professional company, even though it was not quite so brilliant as in the days of the first Saisons Russes. The important thing was that Nijinsky himself was at the height of his powers, that his talent flourished, and that, subordinate to no one, he was free to create in peace.

For the moment Romola enjoyed the life of an aristocratic young lady, the kind of life to which she was accustomed, the more so since invitations now came from all and sundry: weekends at millionaires' country houses, rides in her own automobile, dining to the sound of jazz at fashionable restaurants, meeting celebrities of all kinds, from singers to film stars. Romola was young, pretty, coquettish, and she sincerely believed that by appearing everywhere and making everyone's acquaintance she was popularizing her husband's name still more. Obediently, he followed her about, although he was often anxious for their daughter, cast into the arms of the latest maid.

All this gadding about hindered Nijinsky from concentrating on plans for the next season. Snatching free moments as best he could, he set to work on *Till Eulenspiegel.* The program for the tour still included the *Mephisto Valse,* but Nijinsky had rather lost interest in it: the utopia had not come to pass and, in retrospect, he found it irritating, naïve, and sentimental. Right now he found Till, the militant buffoon always changing his mask, to be more sympathetic: Till, the embodiment of laughter; Till, who was cruel even when he did good deeds. Mentally he listened to the music, adjusting himself to its sounds. He murmured, "People must be made to laugh, they must be made to laugh." But he did not notice how horribly irreconcilable the meaning of this sentence was with the dreary intonations of its reiteration.

He began to direct, to egg on Robert Edmond Jones with the same phrase: "pour faire rire, pour faire rire." The young designer of *Till,* who answered to the name of Bobby, was desperately afraid of the famous maestro, who was actually two years his junior.

Jones always remembered a summer afternoon in Emilie Hapgood's drawing room (Emilie Hapgood was president of the New York Stage Society) where he awaited his first meeting in great excitement. The drapes were drawn, but the shade offered little protection against the heat. The servant informed her mistress of the arrival of Mr. and Mrs. Nijinsky. A pretty, elegant lady came in, followed by a short, thickset young man. Jones saw in silent amazement that this man, this genius who had filled him with alarm, was also nervous. "His eyes are troubled. He looks eager, anxious, excessively intelligent. He seems tired, bored, excited, all at once. I observe that he has a disturbing habit of picking at the flesh on the side of his thumbs until they bleed." [10] That is how Jones recalled that distant day many years later, in 1945.

Jones just could not match the legends surrounding the name of Nijinsky with the simple, sympathetic person in front of him. As they chatted, fighting their way through the debris of their halting French, Jones found in Nijinsky an "extraordinary nervous energy . . . an almost frightening awareness, a curious mingling of eagerness and apprehension." He also sensed that *"oppressive* atmosphere" in which he perceived "a mental engine, too high-powered, racing . . . to its final breakdown." [11]

Tuned to the supersensitive waves of his artistic intuition, Nijinsky produced his last, but probably most memorable, ballet. In the music of Richard Strauss he found both a fairy-tale whimsicality and a sensation of contemporary reality.

The name of the hero in *Eulenspiegel* contains the words for "owl" and "mirror" and implies "mirror of wisdom." The symbolism of these words engendered the image of the hero: his sharpness of wit, his boldness, his sarcastic and invincible spirit embody the essential qualities of the common people. It seemed that Nijinsky, separated from his motherland, could still sense the anger and ferment of the Russian people. In his sharpness of perception he was both a prophet and a victim.

From Jones he desired a "modern" conception of the Middle Ages and a contemporary technique, just as he did from the music. They both agreed that the curtain for the ballet should be reminiscent of a sheet of parchment from an illuminated book emblazoned with the image of the owl perched above the looking glass. Behind the curtain everything was to resemble the colors of illumination to a legend in the manner of a medieval artist. Only the graphic design itself would be distorted and displaced. The marketplace in the Flanders town of Brunswick—where a rhythmic confusion of spires, towers, sharp-pointed roofs, chimneys, attic windows all thrown together any which way would whirl around the Gothic cathedral—would be as remote from literal analogies as Till's behavior was from established conventions.

The costumes were to be equally fabulous and exotic. The pointed headdresses of the three Châtelaines would transcend all norms and would reach the rooftops, and the trains of their dresses would trail across the entire stage, vying in their brightness with flowers in bloom. The Professors would wear shovel hats whose brims would extend several feet, and their robes would swell and subside as they walked

Nijinsky studying the score of *Till.*

along so solemnly. The Apple Woman with her huge basket full of apples would herself seem like a ripe reddish-green apple. The fat Baker would remind one of a pinkish cottage loaf. And the Confectioner would wear a long garment with red and white stripes, looking like one of his own candies. Urchins would scurry about among the noble ladies, the priests and scholars, the merchants and soldiers, one moment finding Till, the next moment losing him, chuckling at his pranks as they followed him about. For them, colors had to be coarse and dark, and their clothes were to be sewn together so that they just covered the body; in some cases they were to be split up the side revealing bare flesh. There would also be Inquisitors in black cowls and soutanes marked by a white cross on the back. The Inquisitors would set about persecuting Till, the rogue and scoundrel in his green tights and short blouse; Till, who would seem so very nimble among all these exaggerated and cumbersome characters.

Till Eulenspiegel had now been thought through and was ready down to the last detail. The choreographer waited impatiently for the beginning of rehearsals. But the managers of the American tour did not particularly hurry themselves, so as to cut down on their outlay for the dancers' salaries. Only at the end of September—three weeks before the commencement of the season—did Nijinsky meet his new company. It proved to be a rather motley crowd, and Nijinsky now saw how Grigoriev's experience would have come in handy. Grigoriev would have established order and discipline at once. Among the dancers who had taken part in the previous season were Lydia Sokolova and Flora Revalles (a French singer who had played the parts of Zobeide and Cleopatra). Two young dancers arrived from Russia—Olga Spessivtseva, a soloist at the Mariinsky, and the Muscovite Marguerite Frohman—and the Kostrovsky couple, husband and wife. Dmitri Kostrovsky was a strange, quiet man who suffered attacks of epilepsy and who preached the Tolstoyan philosophy. He and another dancer, Nikolai Zverev, were destined to play a decisive role in the fate of Nijinsky.

From the very start, everything went wrong. Nikolai Kremnev, the dancer and common-law husband of Lydia Sokolova, had been given Grigoriev's job. The sober Englishwoman was the first to realize the futility of this change. "Although I was in love with Kola, I saw

The three Châtelaines in *Till*.

his shortcomings all too clearly," she wrote almost fifty years later. "He had absolutely no sense of proportion and no tact. Without pausing to think, he blundered impetuously into every situation, and when diplomacy was called for he lost his temper." [12]

Nijinsky, at whose word Diaghilev had terminated the tour so as to give him maximum time for rehearsing, Nijinsky, who had absolutely no idea how to run the intricate mechanism of a theatrical enterprise, was once again in the position of a man whose plans are being wrecked like a house of cards. It had happened once before in London, but it was even worse now, because here in America everything was on such a grand scale and, moreover, he was starting up a new and, for him, much cherished ballet.

It was Nijinsky's job to work out the sequence of engagements with the theater managers; he had to make up the repertoire, to discuss technical problems with stagehands and lighting men. He had to sort out the orchestra business and to familiarize the dancers with their parts. He had to appear on stage five times a week, dancing two ballets on three evenings, and one ballet on two. That is why his meeting with Olga Spessivtseva scarcely left an impression on him, although another time her individuality would have aroused a response in him as forceful as the one Anna Pavlova had. They came together in *Le Spectre de la Rose*. As he embraced the frail waist of the young dancer, as he spun her around and led her forward, Nijinsky did not know, and would never know, that Spessivtseva would one day repeat his terrible fate—a retreat into madness.

The nervous tension soon became very evident, especially at the rehearsals for *Till*, which had to be done again and again and again. At the slightest hitch, Nijinsky flew off the handle. He could not conceal his despair from the dancers. He either walked out of rehearsals half way through or repeated parts that were ready time after time, even though a great deal still had to be done. The première was not far off.

There were cases of sabotage in the company that took the form of a general strike, resulting in the loss of two more days. Then Pierre Monteux, who had so nobly withstood the scandal of *Le Sacre du Printemps*, refused to conduct *Till* because he realized that the ballet would not be ready in time. He was hurriedly replaced by Anselm Goetzl, a very different kind of conductor.

Such was the nightmare through which Nijinsky led *Till* to the day of the première. And every moment the words "People must be made to laugh, they must be made to laugh" echoed insanely in his brain.

The company suddenly understood the value of the ballet at the last rehearsals. Until then the choreographer had delineated the actions of his hero with rigid accuracy, but now he turned into a dancer. He began to rehearse with all the power and strength at his command, and he transported his fellow dancers into the strange world of *Till*.

Two years later Nijinsky would insert the following sentence into

315

Nijinsky correcting the makeup of the
Wife of the Rich Citizen (Boniecka) for *Till*.

his discourse on God and the Antichrist in his diary: "Dostoevsky was a great writer who described his life under the guise of different personalities." [13] Nijinsky's contant empathy with Prince Myshkin and, in turn, with Dostoevsky also came out in *Till,* albeit in an eccentric manner. The ballet absorbed both Nijinsky's metempsychoses on stage and the very real agitations of his brief conscious life.

These two aspects of human existence came together in the scenes of the medieval marketplace, where conceit rubs shoulders with mercenary tenacity, where poverty is for the moment but a shadow needed to bring out the brilliance of vainglory. But the pages of the old book turn; things happen; the distribution of power changes; and each page is a novella about the exploits and excesses of Till.

Till dances in the midst of static personages, now breaking their angular movements, now deflecting their roundness and strength. He dances in the midst of the market place, so reminiscent of Dürer's drawings or Rabelais' descriptions. He is omnipresent but elusive. He wears a loose, short blouse fastened above his waist by a thick belt, tights, and his hair is disheveled. Is this the look of a commoner from the Middle Ages? Undoubtedly so. But it is also the look of a dancer from many epochs. One can trace elements of this same costume in the many photographs of Nijinsky—as a student of the Imperial Theater School, as the Youth in *Chopiniana,* as the hero of *Le Spectre de la Rose* and *L'Après-Midi d'un Faune,* as the Sportsman in *Jeux.* And Till's dance cannot be accommodated by any rules or conventions: it is free; it is natural in its curious mixture of styles and manners; it is the consummate behavior of the street urchin.

And here he is. The urchin jumps from the upper wings, is suspended in his leap above the crowd, lands firmly on one leg, and, his oriental eyes aglow, gives himself up to beatific contemplation. But off he goes again, playing his wanton tricks, slyly drawing circles around the ladies, weaving from one side of the stage to the other, playfully executing his breakneck pirouettes. Suddenly he grows still and listens to the music. His flight now takes on an unexpected fluency and seems to shine forth with the flutter of his batterie. The Apple Woman has attracted Till's attention: just as a kitten will idly catch a piece of paper on a string, so he catches the ends of her kerchief in which she bears her apples on her head. He is a silent, a soft and

Nijinsky as Till.

stealthy cat. One moment—and the apples are scattered all over the ground. Till grabs one and loses himself in the crowd. But here he is again. This time he is flapping a long veil, playing with it. As they watch Till's new trick, the owners of the marketplace slowly turn around. They are like dolls propped up by their social privileges. How has Till managed to tie up the owner of the castle and the judge, the abbot and the beggar, the merchant and the peasant in his veil? Well,

Till Eulenspiegel, 1916.

Nijinsky as Till, playing three of his "merry pranks."

he has, and that's that. He waits for the people to come out of the back streets and then rips open the fabric with a huge pair of scissors. The dolls are scattered and roll all over the ground, provoking the laughter of the people.

But the audience in the auditorium—would they laugh too?

"They must be made to laugh." Till commences to put on various disguises.

He appears in a monk's soutane. He blesses the bystanders, promises the beggars alms from heaven, and . . . throws off his cowl, turns his pockets inside out and crawls out of his soutane like an eel. Till has now become stronger. Till is handsome and bold. He is agile, like a beast of prey who has awakened in the spring.

He throws something like a cloak over his shoulder, and puts on a little cap decorated with feathers. This is melancholy, lovesick Till, just like Count Albrecht chasing the phantom of Giselle. But the cards are mixed up! His proud lady rejects his dancing no matter how passionately he crisscrosses the stage with the diagonals of his soaring leaps, no matter how ecstatically he whirls in the air, only to break off and fall on his knees before his vision of beauty. The Beautiful Lady . . . the Ballerina . . . a doll! What are Petrouchka's impassioned declarations of love to her? Her chosen one is the Moor. Till casts off his fine feathers. Once more he is a tramp, an outcast who is ready to amuse the bystanders.

He takes a good look at the Professors. Why not tease these adherents of hackneyed truths? The piece of material that had been a cloak now turns into a magistrate's gown. On his head he wears something like a shovel hat. It is a professor come from afar. His pompous colleagues listen to his "theses" with all due decorum, "theses" that he communicates by a series of whimsical gestures and by rhythmic intervals of movements and poses. In their efforts to make sense of this incomprehensible language, they become totally confused. So Till chuckles, and then explains how he had duped them so easily.

Till declares war on hypocrisy, stupidity, and spitefulness. He dances on, oblivious of the danger. At night, the common people flock the square, but they move differently from the owners of the market. The movements of the crowd are synchronous, seeming to be directed toward some invisible goal. Till dances on and on and is gradually carried toward the center of this strange procession. Reiterating their heavy tread, the people encircle him, close up, and, without interrupting their measured step, hoist him up on their shoulders.

Immediately a ripple breaks across this smooth human current. The crowd splits up into separate parts. The square is covered by monks' soutanes and soldiers' uniforms repressing and dispersing the crowd. Till lies on the ground. Flourishing their invisible whips, the guardians of the law stand over him.

What can Till say in his defense? He wanted only to make people laugh. But he cannot make the judges laugh. What sanctimonious faces, what ridiculous personages! The whole marketplace accuses him, threatens him, and decides his punishment. Till laughs and dances even as he is led to the scaffold.

And then what? Like Petrouchka, also a character born from the popular imagination, Till rises from the dead so as to dance immortally, to make people laugh, to search—eternally and vainly—for his ideal.

"Wistfully, prophetically—to Strauss's epilogue—the rabble eyes a perennial miracle. In fine, a mimodrama—to return to that exceedingly elastic category—like no other in the Russian repertoire; yet it is impregnated with an everlasting symbolism that under medieval guise masks intensely contemporary ideas; that takes its text from Strauss's music and from the folk tale of Till and leaves Mr. Nijinsky thereon to preach the sermon; that fills the eye with pictorial illusions, the imagination with thick-coming fancies, the mind with thoughts that twinge. It is the handiwork of an intellect, invention, and fancy that shows Mr. Nijinsky more than the master dancer of his time; that offers a new and fruitful field to mimodrama; that confirms the distinction that marks the Russian Ballet as one of the driving artistic forces of our time." That is what H. T. Parker, critic of the *Boston Transcript,* would write after the première.[14]

Everything was true in this article. But it was all actually inspired guesswork—perspicacious, but still guesswork. *Till Eulenspiegel* was staged prematurely. A superhuman effort enabled Nijinsky somehow or other to carry this ill-prepared and very imperfect production through to the end. But even if the piece had been staged brilliantly, it would still have been before its time.

And earlier, yet one more misfortune had occurred. Only a few

Romola, Kyra, and Vaslav
Nijinsky, in New York,
1916.

days before the première, Nijinsky had been at the end of his strength.
Physically and emotionally he was worn out. At one of the last rehearsals he had jumped up on stage from the auditorium in order to
demonstrate a certain passage of movement to a rather slow-witted
dancer, but he had stumbled, dislocated his foot, and sunk into un-
consciousness, as if into a beatific slumber.

The doctor had ordered complete rest for at least six weeks. This
would have meant breaking the contract and would have been a disaster for the whole company. Nijinsky had promised that, if the season
could begin without him, he would appear on stage in two weeks. For
the moment he had lain in bed, besieged by visitors, overwhelmed by
flowers and condolences, "sad as a dying prince out of a drama by

Maeterlinck." That is how Jones remembered him after he had been summoned to the hotel and had found the maestro in bed surrounded by all the characters from *Till* wearing their makeup and dressed up in their fantastic costumes (designed by Jones). "The little room is crowded to suffocation." [15]

Soon Nijinsky had been brought to the theater. He had directed the rehearsals half-lying down, speaking in words that were far less adequate than his eloquent movements and gestures. Two weeks later he had begun to dance. The première of *Till Eulenspiegel* had taken place. It was ill prepared and, in places, was more like an improvisation. It was the only ballet in the Diaghilev company that Diaghilev never saw, and it was never really finished. The company went on tour, so there was no time to think of working on it during the continual traveling from city to city. Nijinsky's *Till Eulenspiegel*, which had witnessed, engendered, so many hopes and fears, passed into history.

All over America, from east coast to west, from city to city, there were endless repetitions of *Les Sylphides* and *Le Spectre de la Rose, Cléopâtre, Schéhérazade*, and *Le Carnaval*. These ballets, which recently had seemed the foundation for great future accomplishments, had now become his one and only treasure, and they vexed him just as an involuntary betrayal provokes the pangs of conscience.

Nijinsky hated these ballets because he did not wish to regret the past. But they were witnesses. Nijinsky took himself in hand. He tried to convince himself that he was happy having a wife and daughter. He planned his departure for Russia—where his mother and sister were waiting for him, where, perhaps, he would instruct children and compose new ballets. It was then that Nijinsky began to pay heed to the words of Kostrovsky. Very soon this quiet man with the unmoving stare of the epileptic acquired a peculiar hold over him.

As a "pupil of Tolstoy," Kostrovsky censured the sinfulness of theater life. He urged Nijinsky to seek isolation, to withdraw into himself, and he explained what great feats Vaslav Fomich could accomplish if he were to give up dancing and plow the soil. This fanatic believed in all sincerity that he was doing good. He spoke unconstrained by Romola's presence. The poor woman knew only the most colloquial Russian so she tried to improve her vocabulary by chatting with Olga

Spessivtseva's mother, a kind and gentle woman who regaled the dancers with tea from her samovar as they traveled on tour.

The meaning of Kostrovsky's conversations became very clear to Romola when Nijinsky announced that he had no wish to accompany her on her business or social visits. He reminded her of her duties as a mother, which, he maintained, she was neglecting. He began to dress more simply, more casually and, to top it all, became an avid vegetarian.

It was one more dash for freedom, but as always, it was of no consequence.

Romola was also annoyed by the tragicomic episode with Zverev. Zverev gave himself out to be a Tolstoyan just for "kicks." While maintaining Kostrovsky's argument that everyone was equal, Zverev persuaded Nijinsky to let him have the part of the Golden Slave in *Schéhérazade* and to take for himself another role. That evening Romola saw an extraordinary Eunuch on stage, languid yet ominous. She did not guess at first that this was Nijinsky. But later she heard the dancers' comments: malicious remarks about "Rasputin" (Zverev's nickname in the company), ironic ones about Nijinsky. Romola then took decisive action. She went off to New York certain that, left alone, her husband would be unable to cope with the business of the tour and would change his mind.

Nijinsky was left without the support of his foolhardy but solicitous wife. He was as helpless as a child. "The words *food, drink, salary, clothes,* etc. were simply not in his vocabulary"—such was the amazement of André Olivéroff, a dancer who made Nijinsky's acquaintance a year later.[16] Besides, Nijinsky loved his wife and he soon missed her.

The tour ended on 24 February 1917. Romola met her husband at the station in New York and rejoiced to see that he was dressed in his previous manner. At dinner it soon became clear that he had rejected vegetarianism too.

Just at that moment a telegram arrived. Diaghilev invited him to join the company that would be touring Spain and that would then depart for South America in the fall. Nijinsky telegraphed his acceptance.

8

Diaghilev had been informed of all that Nijinsky had been doing. No doubt he regretted entrusting the reins of control for the American tour to the dancer, and he certainly did not intend to do it again. But he wanted to take one further action. He felt that Nijinsky, in his present nervous state, could not be trusted with new productions. So he decided to give Nijinsky the chance to calm down by letting him appear in his already famous roles. He divided the company. One section was to create new ballets and to propagate the latest artistic trends, toward which Diaghilev oriented Massine; the other section was to keep the old repertoire active and so bring in some cash, since the experimental ballets were always a risk and a financial loss.

Diaghilev decided to do something very unusual for him—to make a sacrifice. He intended to overcome his own feeling of hostility and to win the good opinion of Nijinsky's wife. It was a sincere desire.

The Nijinskys spent the spring of 1917 in Madrid. They found out from the newspapers there about the fall of the Russian monarchy.

Nijinsky again felt homesick. He felt that Russia would now really appreciate Diaghilev and would invite him to replace Teliakovsky as director. He began to make plans while he practiced on the stage of the Theater Royal in Madrid. Peace reigned between Romola and Nijinsky, and she tried not to notice what she called his relapses of Tolstoyism: from time to time her husband would reproach her for her partiality for luxury; for furs, which caused animals to be killed; and for jewels, which caused people to risk their lives diving to the depths of the sea or descending into mines. Of himself Nijinsky now said that he had an aim: he wished to earn as much money as possible so that he could retire from his dancing career at thirty-five and give his time to choreography. He now often imagined having a school where he would teach children in accordance with the laws of a pure and sound education. For the moment he was beginning something that had long interested him—dance notation. He wrote in pencil in one of the two red, hardcover books that he bought: "No. 1. Rough Notebook. Choreography. 1 April 1917. Madrid." On the next page he then cited certain ideas that were close to his own views on art:

"'Art is one of the ways of uniting people.' L.N. Tolstoy.

"'The wisdom of art and the wisdom of science is to be found in their disinterested and useful service of people.' John Ruskin.

"'Science and art are as closely interconnected as the lungs and the heart so that if one organ becomes distorted, the other cannot function properly. . . .' L.N. Tolstoy's idea."

Further on he wrote hurriedly and roughly, not sparing the eraser: "All movements by the human body can be notated by means of a notational system based on a segmented circle." Nijinsky clarified this idea of the circle, an idée fixe, by affirming that every part of the body "makes a circular movement" where the "moving part is attached to another part" [1]—the arm to the shoulder, the leg to the hip, and so on. He intended to use a three-line system of notes and signs for dance and ballet notation and, later on, in his Swiss notebooks, he renewed his efforts in this area. Right now his plans were on a much broader footing. He projected a workshop where composers, artists, and choreographers of all nationalities would develop the noble ideas of art. He dreamed of a ballet theater that would be free for everyone. And with his innate naïveté he imagined that Diaghilev would assist him.

Diaghilev arrived from Paris and met with Nijinsky the same day. He did all he could to pacify Romola, and scored success. Romola yielded to his charm, she was taken in by his well-proven methods. Diaghilev—demonstratively—did not attempt to separate her from Nijinsky. On the contrary, he was doubly attentive to her and always invited them together to theaters, restaurants, vernissages, and private receptions.

Yes, Romola was satisfied. Diaghilev too. But neither noticed then how the object of their common solicitude was growing somber and despondent.

This solicitude was dictated by sympathy and pity, but it terrified Nijinsky more than hate or revenge. In any case, Nijinsky was sharply aware of the real meaning of Diaghilev's new attitude toward him. When Diaghilev had embraced him at their first meeting and had uttered the words "Vatsa, my dear, how are you?" (so meaningful and so memorable to Romola), Nijinsky had experienced a moment of hope. But that had now faded. Nijinsky kept explaining to himself that the past was irrevocable and that for Diaghilev he belonged to the past: he was a museum curio, preserved only to enhance the newness and audacity of contemporary experiments.

Nijinsky observed these experiments and he realized how distant Diaghilev was from his own utopian fantasies. But he recognized Massine's talent and gave him his due.

True, only Massine's *Parade*, when viewed against his *Contes Russes* and *Femmes de Bonne Humeur*, was as audacious and as provocative as *L'Après-Midi d'une Faune* had been vis-à-vis *Firebird* and *Le Pavillon d'Armide*. Actually, *L'Après-Midi*, and *Jeux* and *Le Sacre du Printemps* even more, still retained their novelty and excitement when compared with *Les Contes Russes* and *Les Femmes de Bonne Humeur*.

The stylized folklore of *Les Contes Russes* and the Liadov music from *Kikimora* and other pieces were certainly ingenious. But the trump card in this ballet was really Mikhail Larionov's decor, inspired, as it was, by the arts and crafts of the Russian peasants.

Les Femmes de Bonne Humeur (its music was from the Scarlatti sonatas orchestrated by Vincenzo Tommasini) invited a war-weary public into the world of Goldoni's images. Bakst gave people a good laugh through his humorous interpretation of eighteenth-century Italy, and the jerky, marionettelike movements of Massine's characters integrated pantomime and the dance in a most remarkable manner.

The skillful search for a new form. Surely, a productive search. Perhaps by comparison the ideas in *Jeux* and *Le Sacre* might seem old-fashioned, or the prophecies in *Till* misplaced?

It was strange. But in all these new ballets Diaghilev, just like Nijinsky in *Till*, wanted to amuse people. It was as if Diaghilev was repeating, through clenched teeth, "They must be made to laugh." And he tried to amuse his public in every possible way.

Parade was intended to provoke a caustic and a humorless laughter. Pablo Picasso set the tone (Picasso was Diaghilev's new "miracle"). At the bottom of the curtain Picasso painted circus actors sitting at a long table. A second painted curtain hung above them and a long ladder was leaning against it with its top rung. In addition, a winged horse was balancing on a spherical ball. Two impresarios, a Frenchman and an American, conducted business to the music of Erik Satie: Europe and America played lord and master at an auction of modern art, two monsters in eight-foot Cubist constructions made of wood and papier-mâché, a montage of skyscrapers, parts of the human body, bits of clothing. It was the merry-go-round of the pitiless world of business and the collapse of traditional values. The flourish of the walking stick, the contract open on the table, the smoked cigar, the megaphone suddenly aimed like a rifle—and all accompanied by a relentless, frenetic tap dance. And in between the hasty business conferences comes the divertissment: the acrobats set to work on their imaginary wire; two people come on as a dancing horse; there is a Chinese Conjuror, a little wunderkind—a little American Girl who can lift an automobile into the air, can type to the onomatopoeic sound of the orchestra, and can imitate Charlie Chaplin.

Yes, Diaghilev now served other gods, however much he feared them. Diaghilev and Nijinsky had gone their separate ways. It is interesting to note that maestro Enrico Cecchetti took the part of the old Marquis in *Les Femmes de Bonne Humeur* and danced it elegantly even though he had turned sixty-seven. Vaslav Nijinsky was twenty-eight and was master of the dance as he had never been before. He did not have to fear any rival. But he remained outside the new experiments of Diaghilev with their affectation and spiritual insolvency.

The best intentions failed, and it would be useless to try to find a malefactor or a guilty party in this episode. But people tried to find them long after the sad story of Nijinsky had ended. Both Nijinsky and Diaghilev died—but their defenders and their prosecutors went on crossing swords in their memoirs and their articles, hovering near the truth and sometimes colliding head on. But the truth is concealed in the irrevocability of time.

Those who heap the blame on Romola Nijinsky are wrong. It is true that this woman severed the golden chain that joined Nijinsky to the imperious hand of Diaghilev as if he were a falcon. But in so doing, she underestimated the strength of her hero. She stubbornly refused to recognize failure after failure, and, unconsciously, she hastened the onslaught of the tragedy. But her blindness was the blindness of love. And her love, after those first short months of happiness, endured painful ordeals; it survived the grievous trial of a long life.

Those who hold Diaghilev responsible for the terrible outcome of Nijinsky's destiny are wrong. There is much tempting evidence to assume Diaghilev's guilt, evidence both real and unreal. It is true that Diaghilev cruelly dropped Nijinsky from his company and that his action was dictated by the master's wounded vanity. But it is not true that thereafter he continued to wreak his vengeance upon Nijinsky. In fact, nobody was ever so close to Diaghilev, and so needed by him, as Nijinsky, even though Diaghilev sought substitutes. In any case, of all the "miracles" wrought by Diaghilev, Nijinsky was the first and the most fantastic one. Not in vain did Diaghilev try to make a comeback, to bring back Nijinsky. Still, Diaghilev, like Nijinsky as a matter of fact, was more sagacious than Romola, and, realizing that the past could not be resurrected, he ceased his endeavors. But did he suffer the less because of this? He was the magician who knows how to turn people into marionettes, but who has forgotten how to change them back again. His life was full of marionettes. He made them with great skill; he painted them and dressed them up. But he could not discern, he could not hear, the beating of the human heart that either responded only to a stranger's touch or simply froze like a block of ice. But Nijinsky's heart was alive; it was pure. Like a delicate and super-sensitive instrument, his heart responded to good and bad. It beat fast over the dissensions between good and evil; it lost its way in these feuds—and then found its terrible escape to freedom.

A few more steps remained. He groped his way and, at the point of suffocation, still tried to change the course of fate. In desperation he himself declared war on Diaghilev. At first he avoided him, and retired from the delusions of *Le Spectre de la Rose, Les Sylphides, Cléopâtre,* and *Schéhérazade* by seeking conversation with Kostrovsky and Zverev more and more. Then he marched into open battle. In Barcelona Diaghilev suddenly learned that the Nijinskys were departing, regardless of that evening's performance, and he was forced to enlist the aid of the police in order to detain them. Thereafter Nijinsky neither greeted Diaghilev nor spoke to him when they saw each other. He consented to take part in the South American tour only when he found out that Diaghilev would be staying in Europe. It was the consent of one doomed, of the criminal who always has the urge to return to the scene of his crime. Perhaps it was because he still feared that Diaghilev would accompany the company after all that he booked tickets on a separate ship. So Diaghilev never did say goodbye to Nijinsky, and he met him again only many years later when Nijinsky was no longer a dancer or a choreographer, but a creature standing beyond human friendship or hostility.

Once again Montevideo, Rio de Janeiro, Buenos Aires, the cities of his perfidy and of his happiness. On the map of Nijinsky's glory that spread across half the globe, one more stroke, the last one, had been laid.

Nijinsky was still at the zenith of his matchless art. He practiced and worked for hours at a stretch, embellishing a work, reviewing it, polishing it. He seized every moment of freedom from his theatrical duties, just as a drowning man snatches at a straw. And a miracle occurred every evening. *Le Spectre de la Rose, Les Sylphides,* and *Cléopâtre* brought friends and enemies backstage. Sergei Leonidovich Grigoriev, who knew the score of any Nijinsky role by heart and who could hardly tolerate his offstage capriciousness, could not take his eyes off the onstage Nijinsky. His dancing charmed all; it compelled great musicans to bow before him. Artur Rubinstein accompanied the Youth's (Nijinsky's) mazurka from *Les Sylphides* when they did a charity recital for the benefit of the Red Cross in Montevideo.

As the dancer transformed and deepened the meaning of the familiar images—in his elusive manner—he astounded people. He did not notice the Petrouchka decors and costumes becoming tarnished by travel or the inexperienced supers spoiling and confusing the ensemble arrangement of the fairground crowd. Petrouchka was even more doll-like, even more sorrowful, and he laid bare his martyred soul with a force that raised the ballet to dramatic tragedy. This was the Petrouchka that overwhelmed the poet Paul Claudel with his terrifying mystery (Claudel was then the French ambassador to Brazil). At a luncheon in the embassy, Claudel introduced Nijinsky to a young composer by the name of Darius Milhaud and suggested that they all put their heads together and think about a new ballet. They dreamed in vain.

Nijinsky was becoming very close to Kostrovsky, and sometimes would spend whole nights deep in conversation with him. Friends and colleagues began to notice something strange going on. The premier danseur was becoming more and more taciturn and irritable. Finally, Nijinsky stopped concealing the fact that he suspected Grigoriev and other emissaries of Diaghilev of attempting to kill him.

At one time, just before the beginning of *Narcisse*, he declared to Grigoriev that he had forgotten his part. And then, already made up and in his costume, he threw himself flat on the floor, right on stage, repeating that on no account would he descend into the trap because he was certain that Grigoriev would give the wrong signal and he would plunge to his death.

He almost ruined *L'Après-Midi d'un Faune*. Wearing his spotted tights and his wig of tightly woven golden threads with the protruding horns, he rushed about the stage, hitting the back of the drop curtain like a wild beast flinging itself against the bars of a cage. Grigoriev waited. But time went by, and the audience began to get restless. Grigoriev decided to take emergency action. He ordered everyone else off stage and then ordered the curtain to be raised. Beneath the gaze of scores of people, Nijinsky cringed, squatted down, shrank into himself—and then, with a mighty leap, disappeared backstage. Then, after the curtain had been lowered, the Faun slowly clambered up onto the hillock, lay down obediently, and submitted to the commands of the music.

Very soon people guessed that the stranger who was following Nijinsky everywhere was a detective hired to protect him from imaginary murderers.

It had been only recently that everything had favored Nijinsky's elevation to the heights of success and fame. Now everything was sliding downhill, as if someone was pushing him, chasing him. It was a diabolical trick of fate that caused a spark from a railroad engine to set fire to the decors for *Le Spectre de la Rose* and *Cléopâtre* as they were traveling through a tunnel between Rio and São Paolo. Such things happen all the time with touring companies. Grigoriev quickly overcame his initial alarm and knocked together some temporary decors. But Nijinsky imagined all this to be the machination of secret enemies.

He was tormented by a persecution mania, and he now preferred chance encounters to old acquaintances. In Buenos Aires the Diaghilev company met up with Anna Pavlova's touring company. Nijinsky did not especially relish meeting with Pavlova, but he did become intimate with one of her partners, André Olivéroff. The young Olivéroff adored both Pavlova and Nijinsky, the only male dancer who could match her. Understandably, he sought comparisons, and saw that Nijinsky, like Pavlova, "never seemed quite accountable in human terms, but whereas with Madame you always felt there was a strong cord of sanity that bound her to this world, in Nijinsky's case there was a mere thread and if you knew him you felt this thread was liable to snap at any moment. He seemed literally not to 'belong' here—there was something eerie, almost frightening about him." Olivéroff did not realize that he was recording the clinical symptoms of Nijinsky's imminent illness. He never forgot the slant of his "quizzical eyes, at times brooding, at times full of life," the ceaseless movement of his hands with their extraordinarily sensitive fingers, the manner of talking, breaking up sentences illogically, shouting out words or muttering to himself. Olivéroff remembered that two themes dominated conversations with Nijinsky: the war and the insidiousness of the Diaghilev clique.

"The War was a reiterating refrain, a *leit-motif* running through his ejaculatory speech. Again and again he would come back to it. He would pass his hand over his forehead and murmur, or exclaim furiously: 'Why . . . why is there this massacre, this murder . . . this sea of blood (he would repeat "sea of blood," then finding no adequate phrase, end up with an illuminating gesture of those articulate hands)—all over the place . . . everywhere, everywhere the sea of blood! Why . . . why . . .?' " [2]

His fear of persecution became evident in everything he did. Nijinsky twice invited Oliveroff to practice with him. And each time he spent a long time leading him around the theater, searching out the darkest corner, far away from the hateful "spies."

But as soon as the class began, Nijinsky turned into the professional and amazed his casual friend by his captious interest in the "least important details of his technique" and by his continuous lack of confidence in his own prowess. "He would turn a half-dozen flawless [pirouettes], then ask me nervously, 'How did I finish? Are you sure they were clean enough?' " [3]

The disease advanced slowly, by degrees. Many people saw even his intense outbursts as merely the caprices of a pampered celebrity. The more so since the disease, lying in wait for its victim, did not, as is usual for it, follow an even course. A period of gloomy distrust would be followed by a moment of sociability, albeit intense, nervous. With the lightheartedness of youth, Romola rejoiced at her husband's cheerful mood. She attempted to preserve this mood by making acquaintances among the Brazilian elite, even though they never guessed that a mundane life was, in fact, quite alien to the character of the "magic dancer." How could the composer Estrade Guerra know that Nijinsky, even at the height of his fame, was timid and shy? When he went backstage after *Le Spectre de la Rose,* he saw the dancer surrounded by fans and friends. Nijinsky greeted them "with touching modesty and simplicity, continuing from time to time to leap and gesticulate." [4] It seemed that the dance itself had flown backstage. Smiling, Romola explained to the astounded Brazilian that her husband had not gone mad but that it was impossible for him to calm down immediately after such turbulent movements; it was essential that his heart regain its even tempo.

But the tempo remained uneven: when despondent, Nijinsky would avoid all meetings; when elated, he would suddenly set off in search of entertainment. Like many other observers, Guerra was justified in recalling in later years: "Sometimes one felt there was something mystical about him, but that did not strike me as unusual. I assumed it was typical of the Slav character. He was certainly highly strung, but not abnormally so for an artist. Intelligent? Most decidedly so. One of his most endearing aspects was the rather childlike, natural side of his character, without the slightest pretension. He was certainly conscious of his worth and knew quite well what he was about, but he was totally without vanity. . . . When I heard subsequently that Nijinsky had gone insane, I was unable to believe it. Nothing in our meetings in Brazil could have led me to foresee that." [5]

During his moments of spiritual uplift, Nijinsky liked to talk about his daughter. The little girl was living in a children's sanatorium in Lausanne, and her father missed her. Even when the disease had conquered Nijinsky, Kyra remained for him a symbol of pure love—whereas Diaghilev, alas, symbolized insidiousness.

The South American tour was coming to an end. Ten years before, on 17 September 1907, Nijinsky had made his debut on the stage of the Mariinsky. Those ten years had witnessed a fantastic voyage. Behind the magician's screen, countries and cities had passed by like shadows; people had administered his strange fate. The roles that he had created passed by like constellations. His ballets blazed up, and then faded.

What did Nijinsky feel on 26 September 1917 when he came on stage in the final South American performance by the Diaghilev company—which for him was, in fact, his very last? In *Le Spectre de la Rose*, the Spirit, the embodiment of the flower's fragrance, swept the Girl off her feet and bore her away in her romantic dream. As the final chords of the Weber waltz sounded he soared into the air and flew away forever. The hero of *Petrouchka* challenged fate to a duel, and perished; then, to the piercing wail of the orchestra, he rose from the dead, high above the silent fairground. Nothing had changed: the usual encores, the usual bows. Only Grigoriev, whom Nijinsky imagined to be Diaghilev's "bravo," seemed unusually sad.

The Nijinskys went to say goodbye to the Diaghilev dancers as they set sail for Europe. Many of them guessed that Nijinsky was parting with the company for good. Many of them could make out his stocky figure standing in the sunlight amid the exotic, motley crowd. Maybe some dancers recalled the wharfs of Cherbourg, the liner *Avon*,

One of Nijinsky's "circle
drawings," of Kyra, 1917.

the tugboat that came alongside, and Nijinsky cheerfully running up
the gangway. Right now he had taken off his hat and was waving it to
his comrades as the breeze ruffled his hair. A motionless, almost artificial smile spread across his face, competing with the melancholy
in his slanting eyes. Romola would soon be destined to fathom the
secret of this smile. Not so long before, Bolm had given Romola a
warning when he noticed her interest in Nijinsky and had talked about
the "callousness of the pampered premier," because Bolm had been
shocked to see Nijinsky smile when he (Nijinsky) had received the
news of his father's death in 1912. And now that smile was exactly the
same as Nijinsky gazed at the receding ship. A few months later, in
Switzerland, Nijinsky would suddenly smile on being informed that
his brother Stanislav had died in a lunatic asylum. Romola would

335

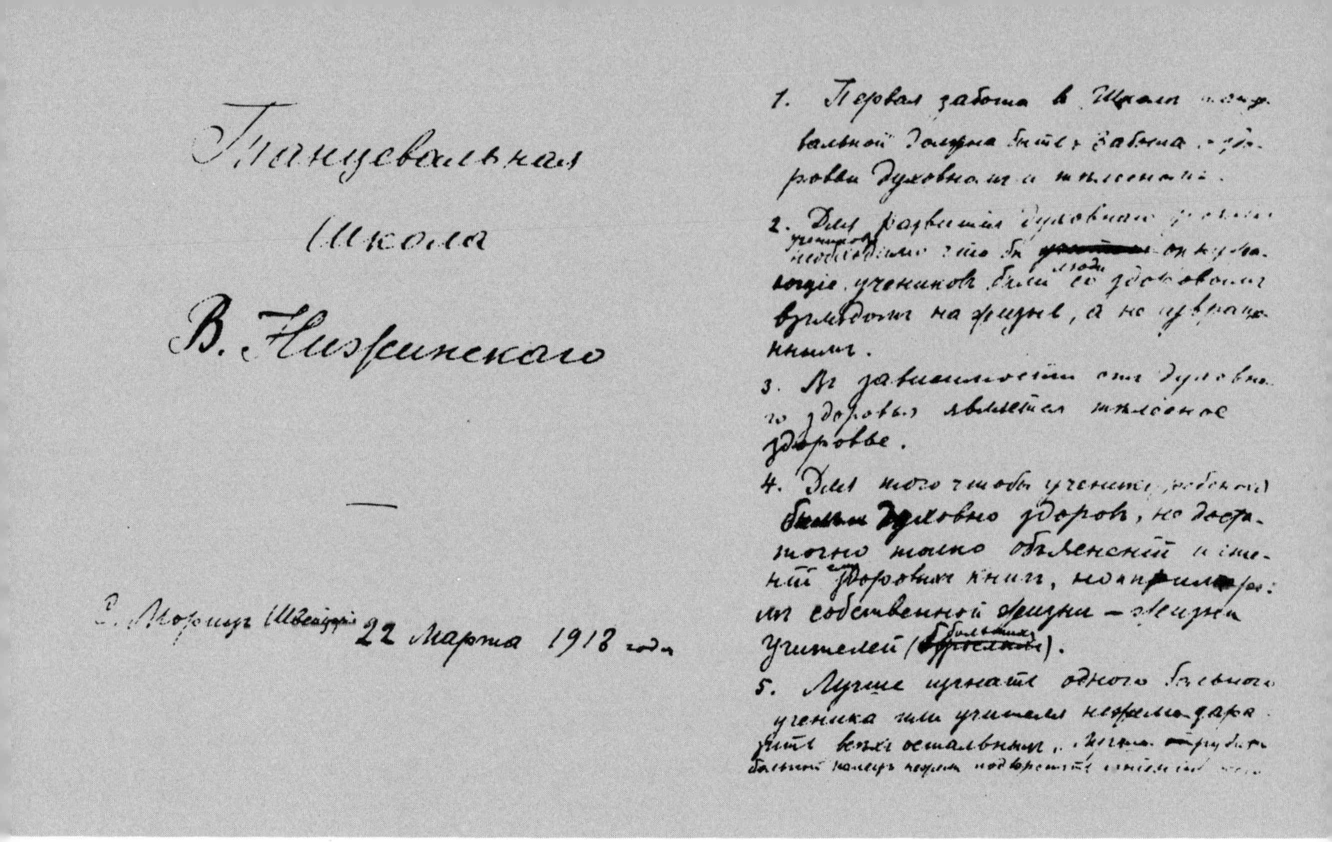

Танцевальная
Школа
В. Нижинскаго

—

г. Моритц (Швейцарія) 22 Марта 1918 года

1. Первая забота в Школѣ ...
...

Pages from Nijinsky's notebook, with rules for his School of Dance.

learn the terrifying truth: that was how her husband responded to grief.

But in those first months in the Swiss village of St. Moritz, Romola chose not to think about her husband's eccentricities. She imagined, both then and later on, that they had at last settled down to a happy life and that the letter of mourning was the only cloud on their horizon. Indeed, she had every right to imagine so. They had returned to Europe in December 1917 comparatively well off, thanks to Nijinsky's earnings of the past two years. They took their daughter, already four years old, and moved into a villa in the hills above St. Moritz.

No doubt Nijinsky also thought that it was wonderful to relax after his long peregrinations.

He loved the snow. For the first time he cast aside his precautions and became keen on winter sports, skiing and tobogganing. He gave time to his system of dance notation, sketched, read. He used to practice for two hours every morning on the wide enclosed terrace. He formed friendships, something he had dreamed of since childhood. Romola was touched by his readiness to "play with all the children in the village." Kyra took up a lot of his leisure time. His attachment to her was the fragile anchor that, stronger than anything, kept Nijinsky afloat on the surface of the troubled seas that had swallowed up so many hopes.

In fact, there were times when hope still promised something, when it still beckoned him on.

He pondered new ballets: *La Chanson de Bilitis* to music by Debussy, scenes from bohemian life in the style of Toulouse-Lautrec. He devised one ballet based on autobiographical motifs in which everything was supposed to move in circles. The hero, an artist of the Italian Renaissance, strove to learn true beauty and love. In the first part of the ballet he met a great master, a universal genius of his age. In the second part he abandoned his mentor after encountering a woman, his true love. It would seem that the finale was a radiant one. But what was the point of all this moving in circles, in closed lines amid the spiroid vortex of the decors?

On 22 March 1918 he carefully spelled out in his childish handwriting on the first page of his notebook "V. Nijinsky's School of Dance. S. Moritz. Switzerland." And he filled in the date. He had long cherished this hope, almost from the time of his final classes at the Imperial Theater School. Now he entrusted to paper his ideas on the training of dancers. It was as if he were writing his will.

In the fall, still in St. Moritz, the Nijinskys heard that the war was over. Only after that did they learn of the Russian Revolution. By the end of the year they had received news of Bronislava and "grandmother," as Nijinsky had come to call his mother since the birth of Kyra: both had moved from Petrograd to Kiev and both were well.

But by now Romola could not help but notice that something was wrong with her husband. The final stage of the disease was now very evident. Moments of perspicacity were followed by periods of depression often caused by terrible headaches.

Nijinsky met with Professor Pichler, the Hungarian mathematician, and amazed him by his interest in mathematics and by his understanding of its complex problems.

He invented a fountain pen, and the designs, which have come down to us, testify to the accuracy of his experiments.

As before, he was now very interested in painting, although his sketches began to take on an increasingly abstract character. They are frightening in their convolutions and intersections of lines and in the insane eyes that stare out of this spider's web of forms. Nijinsky explained the meaning of these drawings as "The Faces of Soldiers," "War Masks."

He spent long hours writing his diary, his "message to mankind."

Once again he refused to eat meat and, with a severity quite uncharacteristic of him, insisted that little Kyra follow his example. At such moments his "strange, metallic gaze" frightened his wife.

He also experienced periods of silence when he would stay away from the house for a long time. Romola would go out to look for him and would see him running along the slippery paths covered in snow. He did this, so he maintained, because his daily class did not give him enough movement. An absurd, and yet a logical answer: there were, indeed, no rehearsals or evening performances.

Once, when he was taking his wife and daughter for a sleigh ride, he accelerated downhill so furiously that the sleigh capsized. Romola returned home on foot and found her husband in the bedroom. He was lying on the bed fully clad and wearing a large cross on his chest on top of his sports sweater. He appeared to be asleep. But Romola suddenly noticed that tears were falling from beneath his closed lids.

Nijinsky wore a cross wherever he went. It was the symbol of the new shift in his consciousness and of a further step toward insanity. This insanity had now taken on a religious connotation. Maurice Sandoz, the Swiss writer, happened to meet Nijinsky at a skating championship at that time, and he recalled: "He had a sugar-loaf beaver bonnet, a sporting outfit of very dark, almost black, cloth, and on his chest he carried a bronze crucifix. . . . His face was pale, slightly yellow in tint, and his slit eyes made him look Mongolian. . . . In his hands . . . he held the rope of a toboggan on which was seated an exquisite little girl. . . . With a very soft, sing-song voice,

338

"War Mask." Drawing
by Nijinsky, 1919.

he asked me in a strong foreign accent: 'Can you tell me the name of that skater?'" Receiving the answer, Nijinsky explained that the skater interested him because he had given his heart to his sport. In response to his neighbor's remark that the skater was graceful even though there were greater virtuosi present, Nijinsky said, "Grace comes from God. . . . Everything else . . . can be acquired by study." To the question whether grace could not also be acquired by work, he answered, "The kind that can be learnt stops short; grace that is innate never ceases to grow." [6]

But Nijinsky's rejoinders seemed to contain an appreciation not of the skater but of his own individuality, an appreciation of intuition as the basis of creation. At the end of the conversation, Nijinsky invited Sandoz to his hotel the next day. He was scheduled to appear there in a solo recital.

On 19 January 1919 Sandoz saw Nijinsky's last tragic dance. Romola was apprehensive, but she thought that the illusion of a theatrical presentation, the encounter with an audience, would be beneficial to her husband. Nijinsky, who had always been so straightforward and simple-hearted, now learned to dissemble as the caprices of the disease urged him to. Shortly before the recital, Nijinsky con-

339

sented to join his wife at a five o'clock. He heard the guests discussing the events of the Russian Revolution and Chanel's new dresses with uniform lightheartedness, and he suddenly adopted a foppish pose. One of the ladies asked him playfully, "Well, and you, Nijinsky, what did you accomplish last year?" And she received a reply in the same tone: "You know, I don't have a company right now. So I don't have enough performances going. Still, I have been thinking: it would be interesting to check up on my stage abilities. So I have been playing the role of a madman for the past six weeks. And everyone believed it—the whole village, my family, even doctors."

Romola remembered for a long time thereafter how indescribably happy she was, if rather shocked, at learning of her husband's ruse. At this juncture he really did play and dissemble. And he should have suffered for hurting his wife. For all their differences in character, he loved the woman who, from the first days of their marriage, Nijinsky had called "Femmka" (from the French *femme* and the Russian endearment of the word *zhena,* that is, *zhenka* [little wife]).

But the attraction toward insanity was more powerful than his love of people or love of art. And, as he prepared himself for his last performance, Nijinsky ceased to resist.

Romola was surprised that the dances for the recital were not ready and had not been rehearsed. Nijinsky put her at ease by saying that he would be improvising and that he wished to show the public the torture and the pleasure of the creative act. In preparing his final "dash for freedom," he seemed to be striving to register the image of Nijinsky, dancer and choreographer, in the minds of the audience.

There were about two hundred, people resting and idling away the time in St. Moritz. It was a mixed public, representing many countries, although not Russia. Nijinsky greeted them at the entrance to the salon. He was dressed in a black costume, rather reminiscent of pyjamas, and in white shoes. He ran off and then reappeared ready to dance.

He was wearing a long white tunic made of soft, light silk, decorated with pieces of black embroidery. He also had on a short black and white blouse, even more flimsy than the tunic, with sleeves of uneven lengths. The dancer unfurled sheets of white and black velvet over the floor, putting them together to form a gigantic cross. And then, as the audience waited in tense expectation, he stood at the head of the cross, stretched out, flung open his arms—and was himself a cross.

He stood like that about a minute, which seemed like an eternity to Romola. At long length the pianist took the initiative and began to play Chopin's Prelude no. 20. Nijinsky did not move from his place, but responded to each chord with a gesture. He stretched out his hands, palms upward, in a gesture of defense. Then he opened his arms in a gesture of greeting, raised them in supplication, and then let them fall as if they had broken at the joints. Until the final cadence, he repeated this plastic ritual of defense, supplication, and renunciation for each phrase of the prelude.

The pianist began to play something faster, more impetuous. Those who remembered Nijinsky on stage suddenly recognized his aerial style. Nobody ever saw that effortless flight again. The waves of black and white silk floated through the air, the wide sleeves billowed out like wings, rising around his neck so strong and handsome and encircling his face with its mysterious, slanting eyes. That face had changed masks so many times—and it was now weary of them all.

Did he not have this in mind when he stopped, put his hand on his heart, and said, "The little horse is very tired"?

But, pausing for breath, he exclaimed immediately, "Now comes war!"

The pianist echoed his cry by striking up the chords of a march.

The mask of tranquility was exchanged for the mask of despair and terror, the final mask. The genius of Nijinsky now revealed a boundless force. It compelled the audience to see the field of a huge massacre not on the stage, not in the decors or the light projections, but there, right in front of them. A soldier of the Great War and of wars to come threw himself into attack. With doll-like movements strangely reminiscent of those of Petrouchka, he leaped across corpses, fell headlong as the shells exploded, raised himself again, and covered a furrow of the earth now drenched in the blood clinging to his feet. Once again—attack and retreat. He ran on, trying to dodge a tank. Wounded, he was dying, tearing at his clothes with his expressive hands, clothes that were now but rags. But once again he got up. . . .

Poor audience. They had come to be entertained, to be able to boast later on that they had been present at a very special and distinguished performance by Nijinsky. Special? It most certainly was! The nightmare occurring before their very eyes was about to flood the crowded hall; it was approaching the hushed spectators. More than thirty years later Maurice Sandoz recalled, "Another moment and the audience would have cried out 'Enough!' " [7]

The final convulsive leap left far behind the picturesque death throes of the Golden Slave in *Schéhérazade,* of Petrouchka, collapsed beneath the Moor's scimitar, of Till, swinging on the scaffold. The soldier who had never been to war but whose martyrlike consciousness epitomized the agony of war now fell in battle.

That night Nijinsky wrote in his diary: "The public came to be amused, and thought I danced for their amusement. My dances were frightening. They were afraid of me, thinking I wanted to kill them. I did not. I loved everybody but nobody loved me and I became nervous and excited. . . . I danced badly; I fell when I should not have. . . . I wanted to go on dancing but God said to me: 'Enough.' I stopped." [8]

The "God" dwelling within Nijinsky became more exacting, more pitiless, and erected a wall between him and the world. Nijinsky would now sit for long periods staring into space, a smile fixed on his lips. Only the tips of his bent fingers moved nervously but weakly.

During his periods of nervous excitement he again began to sketch, committing his tormenting hallucinations to paper. And he continued to write, in his fever coming ever closer to the concluding page. Just as a drowning men sees his whole life flash before him, so Nijinsky's life raced past in his oblique, impetuous sentences dictated by "God."

"I want to cry but God orders me to go on writing. He does not want me to be idle. My wife is crying, crying. I also. I am afraid that the doctor will come and tell me that my wife is crying while I write. I will not go to her, because I am not to blame. My child sees and hears everything and I hope that she will understand me. I love Kyra. My little Kyra feels my love for her, but she thinks too that I am ill, for they have told her so. . . . Soon I will go to Paris and create a great impression—the whole world will be talking about it. I do not wish people to think that I am a great writer or that I am a great artist nor even that I am a great man. I am a simple man who has suffered a lot. I believe I suffered more than Christ. I love life and

342

want to live, to cry but cannot—I feel such a pain in my soul—a pain which frightens me. My soul is ill. My soul, not my mind. The doctors do not understand my illness. I know what I need to get well. My illness is too great to be cured quickly. I am incurable. My soul is ill, I am poor, a pauper, miserable. . . . I am a man, not a beast. I love everyone, I have faults, I am a man—not God. . . . I want to dance, to draw, to play the piano, to write verses, I want to love everybody. . . . I *do not* want war. . . . I have a home everywhere. I live everywhere. I do not want to have any property. I do not want to be rich. I want to love. I am love—not cruelty. I am not a bloodthirsty animal. I am man. I am man. . . . God seeks me and therefore we will find each other." [9]

This epilogue to his diary is signed and dated: "God and Nijinsky. Saint Moritz-Dorf. Villa Guardamunt. 27 February 1919."

The next day Nijinsky was just thirty.

Romola could stand it no more. She sent for her mother and her stepfather, who were destined to play the role of watchdogs a number of times, the kind of watchdogs, in fact, who lay in wait behind the screens of Petrouchka's theater. After a family conference it was decided that Vaslav must be persuaded to see Professor Bleuler, a famous Zurich psychiatrist. Nijinsky raised no objection. One morning in March the Nijinskys crossed the now deserted St. Moritz in a sleigh, heading for the station. It was thawing. Dirty snow splashed out from underneath the runners.

The professor gave his verdict: schizophrenia—in those days an incurable disease.

Romola Nijinsky came out of the doctor's consulting room into the reception room where her husband was waiting. He turned from the table where he had been idly leafing through various magazines and faced her. She said nothing. Nijinsky, pale and despondent, said, "Femmka, you are bringing me my death warrant."

So ended the first half of Nijinsky's life, his life as dancer and choreographer. The second half was yet to last thirty years, and it, too, would be full of events. But Nijinsky participated in them in the same way as Petrouchka might have, Petrouchka dragged along by the Magician of Fate through the melting snow of the deserted fairground. The smile froze on the face of this doll, and the body took on the deliberate movements of a machine: the impulse to freedom had won through—the soul was now divorced from mortal cares. There were times when this soul made itself known through piercing screams, through violence, through pitiful and useless protest. But that happened rarely.

The first time that a catatonic crisis of this kind happened was in Zurich, shortly after the visit to Professor Bleuler. According to Romola, Emilia Markus and her husband were to blame for this. While Romola was away and without her knowledge, they sent for an ambulance to fetch the unsuspecting Nijinsky from the hotel. Submissively, he allowed himself to be taken to the city lunatic asylum. But once he was in the asylum, in a ward containing thirty inmates, he began to resist and became violent. Romola found her husband and transferred him to a private sanatorium, where he spent six months. Moments of mental clarity came and went. The clinical symptoms of schizophrenia became more and more prominent. The illness advances by fits and starts, remains at one stage for a time, may even recede for a while, but, in general, it maintains its ceaseless movement forward. Slowly but surely, Nijinsky lost contact with reality and immersed himself in his own fantastic world. The forms of reality grew turbid and were enveloped by darkness.

For a long time Romola hoped that a miracle would happen. This eccentric and extravagant woman did herself perform miracles of patience, devotion, and courage.

After six months at the sanatorium she took her husband back to St. Moritz in the hope that customary surroundings would have a favorable effect on the invalid. Once again Nijinsky started off on his peregrinations, this time not to theaters but to the finest clinics in the world.

One other person also prayed for a miracle. Perhaps Diaghilev blamed himself for this tragedy even more than did those who lay the blame on him. Several times he attempted to restore consciousness to the sick man.

In 1922 Diaghilev requested that Nijinsky be brought to one of the current rehearsals. The one-time premier danseur arrived, accompanied by a hospital attendant, and obediently passed into the auditorium. But he stared ahead at a fixed point, almost as if his eyes were unseeing. Diaghilev gave the signal and the orchestra struck up the first bars of *Le Sacre du Printemps*. Nijinsky's face changed; his expression grew animated. Knitting his eyebrows, he seemed to be trying to recall something. He started to get up from his seat, only to flop down again. The momentary spark in his eyes was extinguished.

Serge Lifar has described the second attempt to help Nijinsky. It happened in 1924: "It was impossible to look at him without an obscure feeling of dread, for he went on gazing intently over their heads, while a senseless half-smile played on his lips, the terrifying, unearthly half-smile of a human creature, *oblivious to all things*. There we stood with hanging heads, both newcomers and long-established members of the ballet, once his familiars, when his fame had resounded through the world, while sad thoughts and bitter memories passed through our minds and were reflected in every motion of our dancing. Every *pas* we danced was slow, solemn and unwilling, as though fear-

Nijinsky, 1922.

(*left*) Karsavina, Diaghilev, and Nijinsky, before a performance of *Petrouchka,* in Paris, 1928. Detail of a famous photograph (see page 184).

(*below*) Vaslav and Romola Nijinsky, 1939.

ful we might offend; while he, the King of Dancers, looked on as one who would *never dance again.*" [10]

Diaghilev's third attempt—immortalized by a famous photograph—occurred in December 1928 at a performance of *Petrouchka* at the Paris Opéra.

During his periods of calm, which lasted for months on end, the eternally silent Nijinsky would sometimes respond automatically to the call of his art. Romola rejoiced when the "music of *Petrouchka* or *Carnaval* lights up his face with joy" or when a "Fugue, a Prelude of Bach, a piece of Debussy's or Stravinsky's music is played to him, and if the music stops he goes on whistling correctly the bars that follow. . . . When one of his own parts is danced before him and a false step is made he corrects it; if a dancer slips, he jumps up to help. . . . Only once in a while he leaps up and makes a *tour en l'air* or pirouette as if he had just a few moments before finished the *Spectre de la Rose.*" [11]

In 1938 a new course of treatment involving insulin injections was tried out on Nijinsky. It worked. After his long years of withdrawal, Nijinsky began to answer questions rationally. His wife gradually helped him establish contact with the real world and took him to theaters and restaurants. Twenty years earlier Professor Bleuler had considered the invalid incurable, but he now declared that complete recovery could be expected, even though Nijinsky remained silent and timid and grew alarmed if conversation were thrust upon him. Once, however, in August 1939 he broke his silence after seeing the newspaper headlines and pronounced, "Act II begins." Fate could not have taunted him more spitefully by bringing him back to reality on the eve of World War II.

The war found the Nijinskys in Switzerland. Romola tried to get to America, but failed, and was then forced to depart for Hungary with her husband. They reached Budapest in July 1940 and were confronted by a run of bad luck that quite overshadowed their experiences of 1914–1915.

When Hungary declared war on Great Britain and America, Romola tried to leave but again failed. She then tried to get to America via the Soviet Union and China. But with the Soviet Union's entry into the war on 22 June 1941, this also proved to be impossible. Her relatives were as hostile as ever, and she was forced to find the wherewithal to live. Trying to defend himself against reality, Nijinsky returned to his condition of detached calm.

Romola published Nijinsky's diary in Hungarian. The money she got from this enabled her to rent a little house on Lake Balaton. But the Hungarian police were suspicious and forced the Nijinskys to return to Budapest. Those were hard times for them, for they had neither enough food nor enough fuel. After the victory of Stalingrad, the police regime in Hungary adopted more stringent measures. In March 1944 the Germans occupied Hungary and began the systematic liquidation of anyone who showed the slightest resistance. They annihilated both "inferior" people such as Jews and gypsies and also the insane. Bombardments made the nightmare even more horrible. Romola and her husband escaped to the border town of Sopron and took shelter in a hotel.

In August 1944 the Soviet armies entered Hungary. But Sopron remained a long time in Nazi hands. Bombs destroyed the hotel where the Nijinskys were living. But Romola managed to install her husband in the local hospital, where a Polish attendant took him under his wing. During air attacks he took Nijinsky down to the bomb shelter. Instinctively, Nijinsky would cringe whenever he heard the sounds of airplanes up above. Romola sold her last clothes to obtain food.

One spring evening in 1945 the Polish hospital attendant brought his patient to the house where Romola had taken refuge together with other homeless people. He announced that the Germans were retreating and that liquidation of lunatics was scheduled for the next morning.

For several days the Nijinskys took refuge in a hideout up in the hills—one that was meant to accommodate eight hundred people but where thousands were living.

Silence suddenly reigned. It was a frightening silence after the ceaseless crash of shells and explosions. Romola decided to return to the town, and she took Nijinsky back to their bombed-out house. Three soldiers armed with Tommy guns immediately came in after them.

"Who are these people?" one of them asked abruptly in Russian.

Nijinsky, who had been standing to one side, unconcerned, suddenly raised his head; his eyes flashed, and, instead of responding in

French to a question asked in Russian (as had long been his wont), he said distinctly in Russian, "Take it easy."

When the officers of the Soviet command heard the name of the famous dancer and learned his tragic story from Romola, they extended their sympathy to the Nijinskys and took care of them.

Romola Nijinsky decided not to settle in the Soviet Union. Vaslav was fifty-six and even if his reason returned, he would still have been unable to dance or stage ballets. Russia had long been the Soviet Union. He himself had become a legend and few would have recognized Armida's young page, Cleopatra's slave, the hero of *Giselle* and *Les Sylphides* in this exhausted and sick old man. Furthermore, Bronislava Nijinska was living in America, Kyra in Italy—she had married Igor Markevitch, the conductor, in 1936 and had had a son by him. Even so. . . .

Even so, soon after peace had been declared, Romola took her husband to a recital in Vienna at which Galina Ulanova was appearing. And a miracle occurred, perhaps too late, perhaps only for a second, but it was the miracle that the late Diaghilev so desired. As the first chords of Chopin's waltz sounded, a sylphide soared into the air on the arms of her partner; she lightly touched the ground and once again rose into the air. She did not resemble Pavlova, Nijinsky's partner in *Chopiniana*. This dancer was of another era and embodied a different ideal. Passion, tragic emotion, the ardent call to "other worlds" were not expressed in Ulanova's dancing. It radiated light and it expressed disquiet. But its clarity was strangely serene. Her dancing suddenly touched the soul of the wanderer who all his life had striven to return home. It touched him as the snowflakes swirling above the statues in the Summer Garden had done, as the transparent air of the White Nights, as the wing of the seagull touching the water of the Neva just before sunrise.

Romola Nijinsky noticed that Vaslav responded to each movement of the Russian dancer with an almost imperceptible nod of his head.

But then life resumed its "normal" course. For another five years Romola Nijinsky continued to lead her husband everywhere, sincerely attempting to cure him—and also playing on the romance of his biography just a little bit. From time to time various individuals would

relate their meetings with Nijinsky to ballet correspondents. Photographs of an old man, always in the same pose, would suddenly appear on the pages of magazines surrounded by portraits of ballerinas dressed as Giselle and Odette or dancers wearing the long-established tights: Nijinsky sat, staring at something only he was aware of, something invisible, staring with his slanting eyes, and holding the tips of his fingers together, fingers that were no longer pliant and supple.

Born into a nomadic way of life, Nijinsky died on the road. He suffered the onslaught of a kidney disease in one of London's hotels. Romola transferred her husband to a clinic, and he died in her arms on 8 April 1950. But his wandering had still not ceased. On 16 June 1953 his ashes were taken to Paris and were buried in the Montmartre Cemetery.

However, during the last thirty years of Nijinsky's life it was his body that had wandered about the world, not his soul, the soul of "God's clown," as he called himself in his diary. His constant moving in circles ended with his final dance. The long-awaited escape to freedom was made good by the only possible path, for him.

How many times had he tried to free himself from incarceration in institutions, whether enforced or voluntary? How many scars now covered his soul after that scar inflicted by a Cossack whip many years before? The bars of the cage broken, he took a step toward freedom, only to be confronted by a new cage whose bars were even stronger.

First circle: the prisoner of the ballet school who escaped to become the prisoner of the state theater system. Second circle: the dancer who was expelled from the state theater and who again fell captive, this time to the tender imperiousness of Diaghilev. Third circle: the break with Diaghilev and the captivity of marriage. The tragic white clown, Petrouchka and Till, Nijinsky chose the fate of his favorite hero. Like Lev Nikolaevich Myshkin, he created his own world, his own reality, accessible only to him. The same could be said of Nijinsky as is said of Pushkin's poor knight:

> Returning to his distant castle,
> He lived alone in prison,
> Ever silent, ever sad,
> He died bereft of reason.[12]

Nijinsky, in the last years of his life.

After Nijinsky's second, physical, death, his fame as a dancer returned. His legendary leap immediately became the subject of memoirs. The poets of Romanticism had dreamed of such a flight. Nijinsky had manifested the essence of the dreams of his neo-Romantic contemporaries, dreams of the art of bygone eras. People remembered his many mysterious transformations on stage, and the two poles therein that both attracted and repelled: the serene, intrinsic beauty of the White Slave, the Golden Slave, and Harlequin; and the human qualities so cruelly mocked in the immortal Petrouchka but so vibrantly alive in the wild Faun.

For a long time Nijinsky the choreographer remained an enigma. Which is understandable. It often happens that the paintings of an artist are discovered after he has died unrecognized and in penury; or an author's manuscripts come to light, an author who before his death had vainly made the rounds of all the publishers; or the score of a composer penetrates the soul of generations whose fathers had rejected the bold harmonies of a new world of sound. The choreographer creates for the present. Once his works of art have left the stage, they can never be restored in their unique and perfect totality. The participants themselves forget the ridiculed attempts to look into the future of the art of dance. Memory, however, is capricious, whether it is the memory of contemporaries or the memory of successors. Memory watches over ideas; it nurtures them, it regenerates them, without realizing that it is correcting a former injustice. And forms that had once vexed and frightened people because they were so different from everything that had gone before suddenly become incontrovertible because they embody the absolute value of their time.

Such is the law of artistic memory. But there is also another law—the law of material, living material, whether it be the singer's voice, the musician's hands, the dancer's body. Often it refuses to embody the flight into the unknown. Moreover, the singer, the musician, the dancer may, in all sincerity, be unable to respond to this impulse. But time passes, material heeds its call, and the performer suddenly rejoices in the versatility with which he overcomes roles that were once considered difficult.

As independent, original works, Nijinsky's ballets have disappeared into history. It could not be otherwise. When they were born, the world was celebrating a funeral feast for the moribund conventions of beauty. It did not wish to feel the wind of change. Nijinsky ruffled that elegaic surface and that complacent serenity.

When the twentieth century really came into its own and won new concepts of beauty, *L'Après-Midi d'un Faune, Jeux, Le Sacre du Printemps,* and *Till Eulenspiegel* had sunk into oblivion, leaving behind only vestiges of the scandals they once caused. Or so it might seem. But, in fact, the aesthetic conceptions of the new era inspired art to remember and to reincarnate the forgotten past. It was then that the spirit of Nijinsky's search was resurrected in the ballet theater, and the choreographic forms that he had discovered were returned. What a genius had divined now became the possession of many artists. No longer did it provoke indignation, but proved to be the criterion for judging the reality of art.

Notes

CHAPTER ONE

1. Details of the exact date of Nijinsky's birth and of the legend of the chalice were communicated to the author by Bronislava Nijinska in letters of 11 December 1967 and 25 January 1968. Author's collection.
2. In Warsaw, Nijinsky could be christened by a Catholic priest. See the document *Gorod Varshava. No. 669. 1891 god. Prikhod Sv. Kresta. Svidetelstvo o rozhdenii, vydannoe na osnovanii metricheskikh knig.* Collection of the Central State Historical Archive, Leningrad, Fund 497, List 5, File 2223, Sheet 3.
3. "Krestianskaia svadba" in *Russkie vedomosti*, Moscow, 1889, no. 207, 29 July, p. 3.
4. "Souvenirs de Nijinsky" in *Je sais tout*, Paris, 1912, vol. 94, 15 November, p. 471.
5. The *balagan* (plural *balagany)* was a booth used at fairgrounds for theatrical performances, especially for more intimate productions such as Punch and Judy shows. Alexandre Benois remembered the *balagany* of St. Petersburg with particular fondness. See his *Reminiscences of the Russian Ballet* (London: Putnam, 1941), pp. 26–36.
6. The *konfederatka* (plural *konfederatki)* was a kind of Polish national or military headgear, a rectangular cap with no peak.
7. The demonstration and reprisals that Nijinsky witnessed were part of

the widespread civil unrest in Russia in 1905, often referred to as the First Russian Revolution.

8. N. Karamzin: *Pisma russkogo puteshestvennika*, vol. 2, (St. Petersburg, 1900), p. 39.

9. In sympathy with the revolutionary mood of 1905, members of the Imperial Ballet, including Fokine, decided to "mutiny" and, for example, to sign a petition demanding greater autonomy and even to attempt to prevent performances at the Mariinsky. Sergei Legat, who signed this petition, immediately regretted his move. His feeling of remorse, coupled with his discordant relations with his mistress Marie Petipa, drove him to commit suicide.

10. Gorsky devised the choreographic score for this dance in his explication for the ballet *Clorinda*. The score is preserved in the Museum of the State Academic Bolshoi Theater of the U.S.S.R., Gorsky Archive, File II–33.

11. The World of Art (*Mir iskusstva*) was a group of artists, literati, and aesthetes that played an important cultural role in Russian life in the late 1890s and 1900s. The organizer of the group was Sergei Diaghilev, and many important figures of the day, including Leon Bakst, Alexandre Benois, Mstislav Dobujinsky, and Konstantin Somov, contributed to its journal (1898–1904) and/or to its exhibitions (1899–1906). Although the members of the group (the *miriskusniki*) were based in St. Petersburg, they maintained close contact with Moscow, provincial, and foreign artists.

12. A. Bourman: *The Tragedy of Nijinsky* (New York: McGraw-Hill, 1936; reprinted by Greenwood Press, Westport, 1970).

13. Instead of the name Aspicia used by Petipa in his production of *The Daughter of Pharaoh*, Gorsky called the heroine Bint-Anta. In stressing the first part of this name, Legat was being sardonic. In Russian the word *bint* means "bandage."

14. Petipa had produced *Raymonda* in 1898. Legat borrowed and rehashed passages from the variation of the four cavaliers, that is, passages that Petipa had choreographed.

15. A reference to the dramatic poem *Mtsyri* (1840) by Mikhail Yurievich Lermontov (1814–1841). Set in the Caucasus, the poem describes the impassioned bid for freedom by Mtsyri, a rebellious young Georgian.

16. Romola Nijinsky (editor), *The Diary of Vaslav Nijinsky* (London: Panther, 1966), pp. 67, 66. All subsequent page references are to the Panther edition.

17. The words belong to Prince Myshkin. F. Dostoevsky: *The Idiot* (Frunze, 1964), p. 100.

18. Ibid.

19. Igor Glebov [pseudonym of B.V. Asafiev]: "O detskom teatre (iz vospominanii)" in *Zhizn iskusstva,* Petrograd, 1918, no. 11, 12 November, p. 4.

20. From the Russian text reproduced in Françoise Reiss, *La vie de Nijinsky* (Paris: Plon, 1957), opposite p. 128.

21. That is, by the polite form of the Russian pronoun for *you. Ty* is used to address members of the family, close friends, and persons of lower status; *vy* covers most other categories. Cf. the French *tu* and *vous.*

22. L.L.K.[ozlianinov]: "Teatr i muzyka" in *Novoe vremia,* St. Petersburg, 1907, no. 11170, 17 April, p. 5

23. Ibid.

24. G.: "Balet" in *Slovo,* St. Petersburg, 1905, no. 123, 12 April, p. 7.

25. N.: "Baletnyi spektakl uchashchikhsia" in *Petersburgskaia gazeta,* St. Petersburg, 1907, no. 105, 17 April, p. 4.

26. Document from the collection of the Central State Historical Archive, Leningrad, Fund 497, List 5, File 2223, Sheet 4.

CHAPTER TWO

1. Employment paper dated 25 May 1907. Collection of the Central State Historical Archive, Leningrad, Fund 497, List 5, File 2223, Sheet 4.

2. The Lebiazhii Canal divides the Summer Garden from the Field of Mars in St. Petersburg (Leningrad).

3. V. Svetlov: "Balet. Pervyi vykhod g-zhi Pavlovoi 2-i" in *Birzhevye vedomosti,* St. Petersburg, 1907, no. 10104, 18 September, p. 3. The reference to "Pavlova #2" is to Anna Pavlova. "Pavlova #1" was a dancer in the corps de ballet who was older than Anna and who had graduated before her.

4. Tamara Karsavina: *Theatre Street* (New York: Dutton, 1961), p. 182.

5. V. Svetlov: " 'Tshchetnaia predostorozhnost': 'Prints-sadovnik' " in *Birzhevye vedomosti,* St. Petersburg, 1907, no. 10174, 29 October, p. 4.

6. M., "Mariinskii teatr" in *Teatr i iskusstvo,* St. Petersburg, 1907, no. 44, 4 November, p. 176.

7. The preparations for a production of *Sylvia* involving Benois, the Legat brothers, Preobrajenska, Bakst, Korovin, et al. and supervised by Diaghilev ended abruptly after an altercation between Diaghilev and Volkonsky. See Benois, op. cit., pp. 210–18, and chapter 1, note 11 above.

8. R[ozenberg]: "Pavilion Armidy (U Aleksandra Benua)" in *Petersburgskaia gazeta*, St. Petersburg, 1907, no. 317, 18 November, p. 11.

9. From the poem *Poema bez geroia* (1940–1962), a triptych by Anna Andreevna Akhmatova, pseudonym of Anna Andreevna Gorenko (1889–1966).

10. V.A. Teliakovsky, director of the Imperial Theaters, wrote in his diary for 29 May 1908: "It transpires that our young dancer Nijinsky has grown fantastically rich. He's rented a big apartment and he's all dressed up in diamonds and precious stones. And he's very friendly with M[itia] Benkendorf and Prince P. Lvov. People say that's where he gets his money from. Nijinsky's present situation is inspiring a lot of rumors among the ballet artists." V.A. Teliakovsky Diaries, Notebook 23; document no. 225.643 in the collection of the Bakhrushin Central Theater Museum, Moscow.

11. "Teatralnoe ekho" in *Petersburgskaia gazeta*, St. Petersburg, 1908, no. 331, 1 December, p. 4.

12. A. Volynsky: "Tri Kleopatry ('Egipetskie nochi')" in *Birzhevye vedomosti*, St. Petersburg, 1913, no. 13766, 23 September, p. 6.

13. Levinson spoke of this on a number of occasions; see, in particular, his book *Staryi i novyi balet* (Petrograd, 1918), p. 48.

14. A. Volynsky: " 'Evnika': 'Shopeniana' " in *Birzhevye vedomosti*, 1912, no. 12826, 8 March, p. 4.

15. A. Volynsky: "Na zubok (L.N. Egorova)" in *Birzhevye vedomosti*, 1913, no. 13852, 12 November, p. 5.

16. Quoted from Mark Etkind, *Aleksandr Nikolaevich Benua* (Leningrad and Moscow, 1965), p. 167.

17. Sergei Lifar: *Diagilev i s Diagilevym* (Paris: Dom knigi, 1939), p. 173.

CHAPTER THREE

1. See chapter 1, note 8.
2. *The Diary of Vaslav Nijinsky*, p. 74.

3. Charles Chaplin: *My Autobiography* (New York: Simon & Schuster, 1964), p. 192.

4. V.A. Teliakovsky Diaries, Notebook 27, entry for 30 September 1909; document no. 225.743 in the collection of the Bakhrushin Central Theater Museum, Moscow.

5. Teatral: "Pryzhki i polety na stsene (U P.A. Gerdta)" in *Petersburgskaia gazeta*, 1909, no. 130, 14 May, p. 5.

6. "Teatralnoe ekho" in *Petersburgskaia gazeta*, 1909, no. 179, 3 July, p. 4.

7. Ne teatral: "Beseda s g. Nizhinskim" in *Petersburgskaia gazeta*, 1909, no. 274, 6 October, p. 5.

8. Tragos: "V balete" in *Obozrenie teatrov*, St. Petersburg, 1909, no. 917, 27 November, p. 8.

9. From unsigned text in *Petersburgskaia gazeta*, 1909, no. 280, 12 October, p. 4.

10. "Teatralnoe ekho" in *Petersburgskaia gazeta*, 1909, no. 325, 26 November, p. 7.

11. The adjective *nezhnyi* in Russian means "tender" or "delicate." Teliakovsky, therefore, corrupts Nijinsky's name into a neologism that might be translated as "Tendersky."

12. N. Leikin: "Iz kadrilnykh razgovorov" in *Petersburgskaia gazeta*, 1889, no. 26, 27 January, p. 3.

13. Ibid.

14. "Vcherashnee baletnoe torzhestvo" in *Petersburgskaia gazeta*, 1909, no. 329, 30 November, p. 4.

15. V. Svetlov: "Proshchalnyi benefis O.O. Preobrazhenskoi" in *Birzhevye vedomosti*, 1909, no. 11443, 1 December, p. 6.

16. Vidi [B.V. Shidlovsky]: "Teatralnyi kurier" in *Peterburgskii listok*, St. Petersburg, 1910, no. 31, 1 February, p. 4.

17. V. Svetlov: "Talisman" in *Birzhevye vedomosti*, 1910, no. 11544, 2 February, p. 6.

18. Diaghilev's famous Black Book is located in the Dance Collection of the New York Public Library at Lincoln Center, New York City.

19. The St. Petersburg journal *Satirikon* lasted from 1908 to 1914. That year it changed its name to *Novyi Satirikon* [New Satirikon] and continued publication until 1918. *Satirikon* started up in Paris again in 1931 (thirty-one issues only) when Benois, Dobujinsky, et al. contributed to it.

20. The Pavlova Hall had nothing to do with the ballerina Anna Pavlova. In this case Pavlova was the name of the owner of the hall, who leased it for concerts.

21. Sergei Auslender: "Bal 'Satirikon'" in *Apollon,* St. Petersburg, 1910, no. 6, March, Chronicle Section, pp. 35–36.

22. The reference is to the play *Neznakomka* [The Stranger] by Alexandr Alexandrovich Blok (1880–1921). *Neznakomka,* whose title may also be translated as "The Unknown Lady," was one of Blok's lyrical dramas written during 1906–1907. The play uses a recurrent theme in Blok's work, the Beautiful Lady. This apocalyptic image symbolizes a radiant, feminine presence that the poet hoped to attain, and she figures prominently in his early poetry. The play *Neznakomka* and its more famous poetical prototype of the same name (1906) reflect the poet's bitter realization that she is, precisely, a stranger and his resultant disillusionment in his ideal.

23. Karsavina, op. cit., p. 268.

24. Levinson, op. cit., p. 26.

25. Jean Cocteau: "Vaslav Nijinsky" in *Comoedia,* Paris, 1910, June.

26. Acmeism was a literary movement born as a reaction against Symbolism. Led by Nikolai Gumiliev, the Acmeists, who included Akhmatova, Mikhail Kuzmin, and Osip Mandelstam, grouped round the St. Petersburg journal *Apollon* [Apollo], 1909–1917. In contradistinction to the mystical and cosmic concerns of the Symbolists, the Acmeists sought to reflect the clarity and precision of the primitive, everyday world of nature and objects.

27. Alexandr Blok: "Predislovie [k sborniku "Liricheskie dramy']" in *Sobranie sochinenii v 8 tomakh,* vol. 4 (Moscow and Leningrad, 1961), pp. 433–34.

28. Ibid.

29. See note 22.

30. From Act 4, Scene 4, of Maurice Maeterlinck's play *Pelléas et Melisande* (1892).

31. Original source not traced.

32. "Teatralnoe ekho" in *Petersburgskaia gazeta,* 1910, no. 356, 28 December, p. 6.

33. Teatral: "Baletnaia zloba dnia. Uvolnenie v otstavku g. Nizhinskogo" in *Petersburgskaia gazeta,* 1911, no. 26, 27 January, p. 7. (Interview with Nijinsky.)

34. D.M.: "Teatralnyi kurier" in *Petersburgskii listok,* 1911, no. 23, 24 January, p. 4.

35. V. Svetlov: "Balet" in *Birzhevye vedomosti,* 1911, no. 12138, 24 January, pp. 4–5.

36. N.O-r: "Pervyi vykhod g. Nizhinskogo" in *Rech*, St. Petersburg, 1911, no. 24, 25 January, p. 6.

37. Teliakovsky Diary, entry for 24 January 1911.

38. Ibid.

39. Ibid, entry for 27 January 1911.

40. In his diary entry for 26 January 1911 Teliakovsky wrote about this episode and referred to the "principal scandalmonger" as being Ludmilla Schollar.

41. D.M.: "Teatralnyi kurier" in *Petersburgskii listok*, 1911, no. 26, 27 January, p. 14.

42. Teliakovsky Diary, entries for 3 and 7 February 1911.

43. Document from the collection of the Central State Historical Archive, Leningrad, Fund 497, List 5, File 2222, Sheet 21. The document is dated 5 February 1911.

44. Teatral: "Baletnaia zloba dnia," op. cit.

CHAPTER FOUR

1. Théophile Gautier: *Le Spectre de la Rose* (1837).

2. Jean Cocteau: "Vaslav Nijinsky," in *Comoedia Illustré*, Paris, 1911, no. 18, 15 June.

3. S.L. Grigoriev: *The Diaghilev Ballet, 1909–1929*, translated and edited by Vern Bowen (London: Constable, 1953), p. 51.

4. Michel Fokine: *Fokine: Memoirs of a Ballet Master*, translated by Vitale Fokine, edited by Anatole Chujoy (Boston and Toronto: Little, Brown, 1961), pp. 190–91.

5. Igor Stravinsky: *Khronika moei zhizni* (Leningrad, 1963), p. 72.

6. Françoise Reiss: *Nijinsky: A Biography*, translated by Helen and Stephen Haskell (London: Black, 1960), p. 88.

7. A reference to the long poem *Mednyi vsadnik* [The Bronze Horseman] (written 1833) by Alexandr Sergeevich Pushkin (1799–1837). In Pushkin's poem Falconet's famous statue of Peter the Great in St. Petersburg comes alive and, as a symbol of autocracy, chases one Evgenii—the "little man"—through the streets of the city after a flood has bereft Evgenii of his beloved.

8. As reported by Prince Peter Lieven in *The Birth of the Ballets Russes* (London: Allen & Unwin, 1956), p. 126.

9. Jean Cocteau: "Vaslav Nijinsky" in *Comoedia,* Paris, 1910, June.
10. I. Erenburg [Ehrenburg]: *Frantsuzskie tetradi* (Moscow, 1959), p. 186.
11. The People's House or People's Palace, also known as the House of Tsar Nicholas II, was a popular entertainment center and theater on the Petersburg Side in St. Petersburg. It was destroyed by fire in 1911.
12. M'as-tu-vu: "Nijinsky, le danseur" in *Mon Dimanche,* Paris, 1912, 14 July, p. 24.
13. Cyril W. Beaumont: *The Diaghilev Ballet in London* (London: Putnam, 1945), p. 31.
14. Grigoriev, op. cit., p. 59.
15. Ibid.
16. Romola Nijinsky: *Nijinsky* (New York: Simon & Schuster, 1934), p. 15.
17. Ibid., p. 16.

CHAPTER FIVE

1. Sergei Volkonsky: *Otkliki teatra* (Petrograd, 1914), p. 45.
2. Fokine, op. cit., p. 206.
3. Ibid., p. 204.
4. This comment from a French newspaper on the première of *L'Apres-Midi* quoted from the article "Sensatsionnyi balet" in *Rampa i zhizn,* Moscow, 1912, no. 22, 27 May, p. 11.
5. Ibid., p. 12.
6. Gaston Calmette: "Un faux pas" in *Le Figaro,* Paris, 1912, 30 May.
7. Ogiust Roden [Auguste Rodin]: "Vozrozhdenie tantsa" in *Studiia,* St. Petersburg, 1912, no. 32–33, 26 May, p. 8. Russian translation of Rodin's article "La Renaissance de la danse" that appeared in *Le Matin,* Paris, 1912, May.
8. Fokine, op. cit., p. 212.
9. N. Minsky: "Sensatsionnyi balet (Pismo iz Parizha)" in *Utro Rossii,* Moscow, 1912, no. 118, 24 May, p. 2.
10. A. Lunacharsky: "Parizhskie pisma. 27. 'Elena Spartanskaia.' Baletnaia buria" in *Teatr i iskusstvo,* St. Petersburg, 1912, no. 22, 27 May, p. 454.
11. Chronicle Section, *Rampa i zhizn,* 1912, no. 22, 1 July, p. 6.
12. Hector Cahusac: "Debussy et Nijinsky" in *Le Figaro,* 1913, no. 134, 14 May, p. 1.
13. *The Diary of Vaslav Nijinsky,* p. 148.

14. "Pisma I. Stravinskogo N. Rerikhu" [Letters from I. Stravinsky to N. Roerich] in *Sovetskaia muzyka*, Moscow, 1966, no. 8, August, p. 59. This comment comes from the letter of 12 July 1910.

15. The painter and stage designer Alexandra Alexandrovna Exter (1884–1949) painted a number of pictures dealing with the hunting theme in 1911–1912. The one that Diaghilev showed Nijinsky, *The Hunt* (1911), was formerly in the collection of the poet Benedikt Livshits in St. Petersburg. It is reproduced in his memoirs, *Polutoraglazyi strelets* (Leningrad, 1933), p. 23, and in the translation of them, John E. Bowlt (editor), *Benedikt Livshits: The One and a Half-Eyed Archer* (Newtonville: ORP, 1977), p. 40.

16. Karsavina, op. cit., p. 290.

17. "Teatralnoe ekho. Balet khudozhnika N.K. Rerikha" in *Petersburgskaia gazeta*, 1910, no. 235, 28 August, p. 4.

18. Ibid.

19. Velimir [Velemir or Viktor] Vladimirovich Khlebnikov (1885–1922) was one of the most original literary members of the Russian Futurist movement and made a particularly rich contribution to its linguistic discoveries. Khlebnikov was a proponent of *zaum* or transrational (alogical) language and wished to return the word to a more expressive condition, to which end he composed neologisms, added new prefixes and suffixes to roots, and made frequent recourse to archaisms. The lines quoted here are from an untitled, undated poem beginning *Tebe poem rodun!* of ca. 1912.

20. "Pisma I. Stravinskogo," p. 62. This letter is dated 1 December 1912.

21. Marie Rambert memoirs.

22. The dance of the Chosen Virgin has been reconstructed here on the basis of material supplied by Bronislava Nijinska in a letter to the author of 11 December 1967; details were also supplied by Maria Piltz in conversation with the author 28 March 1968.

23. Volkonsky, op. cit., p. 51.

24. Ibid., p. 48.

25. Ibid., p. 47.

26. John Galsworthy: *The White Monkey* (New York: Grosset & Dunlap, 1924), p. 138.

27. From a letter written by Stravinsky to the composer Maximilian Steinberg and dated 20 June 1913. The original letter is in the collection of the Leningrad State Institute of Theater, Music and Cinematography, Section for Source Study, Fund 28, List 1, Unit 489/1-30.

CHAPTER SIX

1. Klod Debiussi [Claude Debussy]: *Stati, retsenzii, besedy* (Moscow and Leningrad, 1964), p. 199.
2. From Akhmatova's *Poema bez geroia*. See chapter 2, note 9.
3. Levinson, op. cit., p. 84.
4. Debiussi, op. cit., p. 200.
5. V. Svetlov: "Russkii sezon v Parizhe (ot nashego korrespondenta). 'Sviashchennaia vesna.' Grandioznyi skandal na pervom predstavlenii baleta," in *Petersburgskaia gazeta*, 1913, no. 139, 23 May, p. 14.
6. From conversation between Maria Piltz and the author 28 March 1968.
7. Igor Stravinsky and Robert Craft: *Conversations with Igor Stravinsky* (London: Faber, 1959), p. 47.
8. Igor Stravinsky: "Chto ia khotel vyrazit v 'Vesne sviashchennoi'" in *Muzyka*, Moscow, 1913, no. 141, 3 August, p. 491.
9. Henry Postel du Mas: "Le Sacre du Printemps. Un entretien avec M. Stravinsky" in *Gil Blas*, Paris, 1913, 4 June.
10. I. Stravinsky: *Chronicle of My Life* (London: Gollancz, 1936), p. 74.
11. Fokine's article appeared originally in Russian under the title "Pechalnoe iskusstvo" in the New York newspaper *Novoye Russkoye Slovo*, 1 March 1931. An English translation appears in *Fokine: Memoirs of a Ballet Master*, pp. 249–56.
12. Henri Quittard: "Théâtre des Champs-Elysées: Le Sacre du Printemps, tableau de la Russie païenne, en deux actes, musique de M. Igor Stravinsky; chorégraphie de M. Nijinsky; décors et costumes de M. Roerich" in *Le Figaro*, 1913, no. 151, 31 May, p. 5.
13. Pierre Lalo: "Au théâtre des Champs-Elysées. Le ballet russe. Première représentation de 'Jeux.' Première représentation du Sacre du Printemps" in *Le Temps*, Paris, 1913, 3 June.
14. N. Minsky: "Prazdnik vesny (Pismo iz Parizha)" in *Utro Rossii*, 1913, no. 123, 30 May, p. 2.
15. N. Kostylev: "Nashe iskusstvo v Parizhe (k postanovke 'Igr' i 'Prazdnika vesny' v teatre 'Eliseiskikh polei')" in *Russkaia molva*, Moscow, 1913, no. 160, 24 May, p. 3.
16. The reference is to the famous novel *Master i Margerita* [The Master and Margharita] (1930s) by Mikhail Afanasievich Bulgakov (1891–1940). This line appears on page 363 of the Possev (Frankfurt) edition of 1969 and on page 281 of the English translation published by Signet (New York) in 1967.
17. See chapter 5, note 22.

18. From a conversation between Yuri Grigorovitch and Stravinsky on 13 October 1967.
19. Romola Nijinsky, op. cit., p. 223.
20. Grigoriev, op. cit., p. 91.

CHAPTER SEVEN

1. Romola Nijinsky, op. cit., p. 264.
2. Ne teatral: "Beseda s g. Nizhinskim" in *Peterburgskaia gazeta*, 1909, no. 274, 6 October, p. 5.
3. Jacques Rivière: *Nouvelle Revue Française*, Paris, 1914, 1 July.
4. Romola Nijinsky, op. cit., p. 293.
5. Ibid., p. 288.
6. *The Diary of Vaslav Nijinsky*, p. 50.
7. Ibid., p. 51.
8. Lydia Sokolova: *Dancing for Diaghilev* (New York: Macmillan, 1961), p. 78.
9. Carl Van Vechten: "Vaslav Nijinsky," in *Dance Index*, New York, 1942, vol. 1, no. 9-11, p. 172.
10. Robert Edmond Jones: "Nijinsky and Til Eulenspiegel," in *Dance Index*, 1945, vol. 4, no. 4, p. 45.
11. Ibid., p. 45.
12. Sokolova, op. cit., p.87.
13. *The Diary of Vaslav Nijinsky*, p. 30.
14. H.T. Parker: "The Strangeness of Til" in *Boston Transcript*, 1916. Quoted from Paul Magriel (editor), *Nijinsky: An Illustrated Monograph* (New York, 1946).
15. Jones, op. cit., p. 52.
16. André Olivéroff: *The Flight of the Swan* (New York: Dutton, 1935), p. 164.

CHAPTER EIGHT

1. Nizhinsky [Nijinsky]: "Khoreografiia," in his *Chernovaia tetrad* [Rough Notebook], No. 1. Collection of the Museum of the State Academic Bolshoi Theater of the U.S.S.R., Unit No. 9, Sheets 1 and 2.
2. Olivéroff, op. cit., pp. 161, 165–66.

3. Ibid., pp. 162–63.

4. Reiss, op. cit., p. 168.

5. Ibid., p. 169.

6. Maurice Sandoz: *The Crystal Salt Cellar* (London: Guilford, n.d.), pp. 66–67.

7. Ibid., p. 73.

8. *The Diary of Vaslav Nijinsky*, pp. 167–68.

9. Ibid., pp. 191–92.

10. Serge Lifar: *Serge Diaghilev: His Life, His Work, His Legend* (London: Putnam, 1940), p. 207.

11. Romola Nijinsky, op. cit., p. 430.

12. From Pushkin's poem *Zhil na svete rytsar bednyi* (1829). Aglaia Epanchina recites the poem to Prince Myshkin in Dostoevsky's *The Idiot*. See Dostoevsky, op. cit., p. 293.

Index

Boldface numbers indicate pages with illustrations; a
lower-case *c* after a page number refers to a caption.

373

DATE DUE

Demco, Inc. 38-293